IDEAS INTO POLITICS

JAMES JOLL

IDEAS

— INTO —

POLITICS

ASPECTS OF EUROPEAN HISTORY
1880-1950

EDITED BY R·J·BULLEN
H·POGGE VON STRANDMANN
AND A·B·POLONSKY

CROOM HELM
London & Sydney

BARNES & NOBLE BOOKS
Totowa, New Jersey

26870

©1984 R.J. Bullen, H. Pogge von Strandmann and A.B. Polonsky
Croom Helm Ltd, Provident House, Burrell Row,
Beckenham, Kent BR3 1AT
Croom Helm Australia Pty Ltd, First Floor,
139 Kings Street, Sydney, NSW 2001, Australia

British Library Cataloguing in Publication Data

Ideas into politics.
    1. Europe—History—1871-1918
    2. Europe—History—20th century
    I. Bullen, R.J. II. Von Strandmann, H. Pogge
    III. Polonsky, A.B.
    940.2'8   D359

    ISBN 0-7099-0696-X

First published in the USA 1984 by
Barnes & Noble Books,
81 Adams Drive,
Totowa, New Jersey, 07512

Library of Congress Cataloging in Publication Data
Main entry under title:

Ideas into politics.

    1. Political science—Europe—19th century—
Addresses, essays, lectures. 2. Political science—
Europe—History—20th century—Addresses, essays,
lectures. 3. Europe—Politics and government—
1871-1918—Addresses, essays, lectures. 4. Europe—
Politics and government—20th century—Addresses,
essays, lectures. 5. Europe—History—1871-1918
Addresses, essays, lectures. 6. Europe—History—
20th century—Addresses, essays, lectures.
7. Ideology—Addresses, essays, lectures.
I. Bullen, R.J. II. Pogge von Strandmann, H.
(Hartmut) III. Polonsky, A.B.

    JA84.E9I33 1984   320.5'094   84-2854
    ISBN 0-389-20484-6

Printed and bound in Great Britain

CONTENTS

IDEAS INTO POLITICS

JAMES JOLL

James Joll, who retired from the Stevenson Chair of International History at the London School of Economics in the summer of 1981, has been and indeed still is one of the most influential historians of his generation. He has had a distinguished career as a teacher of modern history in the Universities of Oxford and London and is well known as a writer and lecturer in Europe, America and the Far East.

Throughout his academic career James Joll has studied and written about European history since the French Revolution. Recently he has concentrated on the fateful century since 1870. In the preface to his masterly survey of Europe since 1870 he stated that he had observed four decades of European history 'from the comparative safety and detachment of an English middle-class life'. This characteristically modest statement tells only a small part of the truth about James Joll the historian. To his pupils and friends he has seemed the least insular of men. His great gift for languages, the wide sweep of his interests and his generous humanity have brought him to the very centre of the international community of scholars engaged in the study of modern history. He is himself a member of that community which he described as 'a European intellectual and artistic world that was truly international'. Through his sensibilities and his friendships he has been as much at home in the world of artists as in the community of scholars. This has profoundly shaped his outlook as a historian and his attitude towards the purpose of history. In 1964 he wrote that 'the aim of the historian, like that of the artist, is to enlarge our picture of the world, to give us a new way of looking at things'. Throughout his teaching career and in his books he has been faithful to these two fundamental aims.

James Joll was educated at Winchester College in the company of other pupils such as Hugh and Christopher Seton-Watson who have like himself become well-known historians of modern Europe. He then spent a year at the University of Bordeaux before going up to New College, Oxford to read Greats. In October 1939 he was drafted into the army and for the last two years of the war he served in the German and Austrian sections of S.O.E. Although he has not yet joined that company of historians who have written autobiographical essays it is not difficult to discern the impact of the events through which he lived and played his part on his outlook and interests as a historian. At Oxford he had studied the great achievements of European societies and of civilisations at their zenith while the European state system was slowly but surely set on the road to war. During the war he witnessed the destructive and savage force of irrational ideas and movements. After the war he spent a brief period with the Allied occupying forces in Germany and saw the plight of individuals caught up in events over which they had no control. James Joll's historical writings have displayed a triple interest, each perhaps related to those separate phases of his early manhood: an interest in the achievements of states and societies and of the evolution of state systems; a determination to uncover and explain the impact of ideas upon society; a marked preoccupation with the role of the individual in

1

history. To him these three aspects of European history were never separate categories but part of the larger whole of international history.

In 1947 he was appointed Fellow and Tutor in Politics at New College, Oxford. It was then that he began to develop his interest in the modern European states and the European states system. Initially his interests were concentrated on Germany and on German foreign policy between the two world wars. In 1947 he was the British editor in chief of the Documents on German Foreign Policy. His first book, Britain and Europe. Pitt to Churchill 1793-1940, was an attempt to explain the traditions of British foreign policy in the 19th and 20th centuries and to illustrate the ideas and assumptions of politicians about their own state and its relations with others. In that book he recognised the diminished influence of Great Britain in the post-war world and the fact that the ideas of 19th century Englishmen had in the 20th century become part of a larger western tradition, encompassing both Europe and the United States of America. In the late 1950s and early 1960s he turned increasingly to the study of ideas and to the examination of their impact on society. Out of these endeavours came two important books, The Anarchists and The Second International. In these books his aims were threefold: firstly to examine 'the moment in history when ideas, long discussed by intellectuals, begin to acquire political reality', that is to say the force and impact upon individuals, classes and eventually the state of new ideas about the way society could be organised and could be changed. Secondly he used these studies to reject the notion that history was a success story. Both books rescued ideas, men and movements which others had relegated 'to the dust heap of history'. It was significant and indeed important that both the anarchists and the socialist internationalists were failures. Both books set out to explain why the ideas, the men who espoused them and the movements they directed were so unsuccessful. Moreover in his detached and careful account of their internecine squabbles, indeed of the depths of wickedness to which some of them were prepared to stoop, he sought to throw 'light on the psychology of individuals'. There was therefore a direct link from this line of enquiry to that characteristic aspect of James Joll's writings, the role of the intellectual in politics, 'the difficulties and frustrations which confront the man of theory in the world of practice'. In 1960 he published his studies of Blum, Rathenau and Marinetti as Three Intellectuals in Politics. Several years later he returned to this theme in his book on Antonio Gramsci, the Italian Communist leader.

Throughout the period in which he was developing and expanding these interests he was a noted Oxford teacher and supervisor of research students. In 1951 he became sub-warden of the newly founded St Antony's College, a post he held until 1967. St Antony's was intended to provide a home for the growing number of postgraduates in Oxford specialising in modern history and politics. From the outset the College was an international centre of research and remains so today. It has played its part in forging links between the scholarly community throughout the world and James Joll has made a notable contribution to this development. His Oxford pupils now teach in Universities throughout the world.

In 1967 James Joll was appointed to the Stevenson Chair of International History at the LSE. Like St Antony's the LSE has always had strong international links and a consciousness of the part played by thinkers in changing society and the way men and women think about the societies in which they live. His inaugural lecture at the LSE: 1914, the Unspoken Assumptions, fused in a remarkable way the three interests of his professional career. He sought to ask questions about the European states system which plunged into war in 1914 and what ideas hidden and implicit had guided the individuals who took these decisions. The lecture was in part a response to the work of a new generation of German scholars working on pre-First World War German politics, whose important work James Joll had played a significant role in inspiring and had helped to introduce to the English speaking world and it was equally a challenge to scholars to broaden the scope of international history. He generously encouraged many of his research students to take up this challenge and for more than a decade much of the historical re-assessment of pre-First World War diplomacy, a significant body of books and articles, was conducted under his auspices. In 1973 James Joll produced his great survey of a century of European history, Europe since 1870: an International History. Again it bore the marks of the balanced emphasis on the state, on the impact of ideas and on the role of individuals in the making of modern history. In his retirement James Joll set himself the task, which as a busy teacher, superviser and lecturer was necessarily set aside, of extending the ideas suggested in his inaugural lecture into a book. In 1977 his contribution to historical scholarship was recognised by his election as a Fellow of the British Academy. His responsiveness to new areas of historical enquiry was reflected in the interest he took in film both as a historical source and as a new means of historical communication. He was chairman of Inter-University History Film Consortium and he was co-director of its film Fascism and its narrator. In this Festschrift his pupils have attempted to put together a collection of essays which bear upon the history of European states, on the history of international relations, on the history of Europeans ideas and upon those individuals who for better or worse have shaped the modern world. It is with admiration and affection that they present them to him.

THE 'ORTHODOX' MARXISTS: FIRST GENERATION OF A TRADITION

David W. Morgan

The historical study of Marxism has been oddly slow to spread beyond a small circle of cognoscenti. To be sure, there is shelf upon shelf of literature about particular Marxist thinkers and political leaders, and many more shelves are filled with studies of the political parties that have considered themselves Marxist. But Marxism, historically speaking, is an intellectual tradition or school; a body of thought whose exponents, no matter how diverse or mutually combative, have been aware of working within and developing (or correcting) a received tradition. As such it is not adequately understood through the thought of particular eminent representatives of the tradition; nor is it identical with - though related to - the formulas or behavioural patterns of soi-disant Marxist labour movements. It has its own history, and requires analysis specifically directed toward that history. This kind of study is only now beginning to gather momentum.

We need to understand better even the very first stage of Marxism, the stage often called 'orthodox' Marxism, when a coherent core belief was assembled and maintained for some time against a variety of challenges.[1] This stage lies roughly in the twenty-five years after Marx's death in 1883. Here the 'ism' came together, was defined and delimited intellectually against proposed variants and eclectic combinations and heresies, and developed politically in association with several important European labour movements. Nowadays there is a general tendency to regard the doctrines of orthodox Marxism as theoretically weak - to see the era as a trough in the history of Marxist thought, between the peaks of Marx's own achievement and the somewhat less towering eminences of a later generation: Lenin, perhaps, or Lukàcs, or Gramsci.[2] Plainly, the thinking of the Marxists of that generation speaks less to the political and theoretical imagination of today than that of Marx himself, or many later thinkers from the school. But it was a marvel in its day, an intellectual force in itself and (at least seemingly) a powerful asset to various national labour movements. As Lichtheim puts it, this was 'the "classical moment" in the history of Marxist Socialism considered as a body of doctrine: the moment when the inherent disharmonies of the system were held in balance and brought to rest.'[3] For Kolakowski, it was 'The Golden Age' of Marxism.[4] For better or worse, parts of that age's achievement are still with us.

This paper, however, is less concerned with evaluating orthodox Marxism than with delineating its place in the long history of the tradition, and suggesting explanations for a few of its salient features. We must start by specifying our subject more precisely. We begin with the start of Marxism itself - Marxism as distinguished from Marx's own thought, which he left undeveloped and tension-filled in some key respects at his death. (For this reason the orthodox Marxists are here called the first generation of Marxists, rather than the second generation, as is more usual. For this reason, too, it is wrong to apply strictures such as 'denatured Marxism' to their work: their doctrines constitute the original Marxism.)[5] The beginning of the 'ism' comes with attempts at a systematic understanding of Marx's thought that are new around 1880 but routine by the later 1880s;[6] indeed, the codification of Marx's ideas could hardly have proceeded very far, at least on the course it took, while the master was still alive to object, and he died only in 1883. A terminal point for the orthodox stage is less easy to set. The vitality of this mode of Marxism is surely at an end (with local exceptions) before 1914, when so many things ended; some years before, in fact. Soon after 1900 there were coming to be alternative Marx-understandings that rose to rival the orthodoxy - Lenin's and Luxemburg's, for instance - and by about 1910 orthodoxy no longer enjoyed the presumption of being the most adequate. When orthodoxy lost its dominance, a new phase had begun.

The giants of the school during this period are Friedrich Engels and Karl Kautsky. Engels is only partially captured under the heading of orthodox Marxism, even the late Engels of the Anti-Dühring (1878) and after, for the impulses and expectations of the 1840s were still alive in him; in some ways Engels' participation in the formulation of orthodox Marxism seems to have been based on a misunderstanding.[7] But his authority was essential to the emergence of a Marxist orthodoxy in his lifetime, and the doctrine that coalesced contained some highly characteristic elements of Engels' later thought. The much younger Kautsky, a collaborator of Engels for a time, was after 1895 his recognized successor, in a sort of apostolic way. For a long time he was accepted, even by socialists who disagreed with him on important issues, as being in a high degree representative of the best traditions of Marxism known to that era.

Others also played important roles. Eduard Bernstein helped create the doctrine in the 1880s and early 1890s, until he turned away to become the prince of 'revisionists'. G. V. Plekhanov had much better philosophical abilities than his German contemporaries, but less wide influence. The beliefs of forceful practical politicians like August Bebel and Victor Adler also played a role. And younger figures emerged who assimilated a large part of orthodoxy (in some instances carrying it on into the embattled 1920s); Rudolf Hilferding and Otto Bauer are perhaps the most distinguished of these. Even some of the socialists whom we think of as opposed to Kautsky worked within the orthodox tradition for much of their careers; a case in point is Rosa Luxemburg, who broke with Kautsky only in 1910 and then over political rather than theoretical issues.

The list of the founders is heavily Central European. Elsewhere in Europe Marxism was part of the high cultural scene - forming an episode in the intellectual career of figures as diverse as George Bernard Shaw, Georges Sorel, and Benedetto Croce - and often had a significant following in the labour movement. There were a few serious orthodox Marxist thinkers in other countries, such as Antonio Labriola in Italy. But the continuous tradition of systematic development of Marxism in interplay with the needs of the day had only weak representation outside its Central European home (with East European outriders) where the soil was fertile for it to flourish, intellectually and politically.

The peculiarities of the orthodox phase of Marxism raise many questions, and we can touch on only a few in this essay. One is its philosophical and methodological divergence from Marx's own ideas: we shall seek the source of this in the very process of systematizing and propagating a formal doctrine, an endeavour necessary to the creation of Marxism but one with extensive unintended effects on the ideas themselves. A second problem is orthodox Marxism's political passivity: here we will look to the peculiar forms of Marxism's encounter with the new mass socialist parties, an encounter which not only had profound practical consequences but also both shaped and reflected a particular understanding of the Marxist historical vision. The coming histories of orthodox Marxism will have to be written from a better understanding of issues such as these.

* * * * *

Notoriously, Marx left his doctrines in an ambiguous, unfinished state, with nothing from his own hand (at least during the last two decades of his life) to serve as guide to the whole of his work. In his later years Marx was infuriated with supposed followers who misunderstood his intentions, or who mixed up their Marxian ideas with borrowings from Lassalle, Dühring, and others. But so long as it was up to each new follower to work out for himself what the Marxian world-view entailed, what possibilities it contained and what it excluded, Marx's scattered and complex thought could never give rise to a school or movement. Those who thought that it should were obliged to turn to working out a systematized understanding of Marx's thought. They became the first Marxists by creating Marxism.

Engels began the process in 1878 with the publication of his Anti-Dühring, which aimed to close off the Dühring vogue among socialists (such as Bernstein), in part by defining the central elements of Marx's teaching more coherently and clearly than before. The general chapters from this work, refashioned into the pamphlet Socialism: Utopian and Scientific in 1880, are still perhaps the best introduction to orthodox Marxism (though by no means a good introduction to Marx). In 1881 Bernstein took over the emigré German socialist newspaper Sozialdemokrat, and in 1883 Kautsky founded the journal Neue Zeit, both with the intention of developing and propagating consistently Marxian principles. Kautsky's plain-language summary of The Economic Doctrines of Karl Marx, published in 1887, was another landmark. With the official enunciation of the Marxist historical perspective (as then understood) by the German Social Democratic Party in its Erfurt Program of 1891, the process was virtually complete.

In introducing system, however, the founders (including many others besides those named) had also injected foreign elements into the doctrine's method and substance. The interconnections of Marx's thought follow Hegelian logic; nothing can be isolated from its process of becoming, nothing can be considered apart from the relationships that make it what it is and at the same time are changing it into something different, while negation, transcendence, and other elements of the Hegelian dialectic shape the processes of change. Such a method was simply not available in the 1880s to the younger men who set out to reconstruct the essential meaning of Marx's complex writings; the sense for its workings was even much attenuated in Engels, who had never had such an intensely Hegelian phase as Marx himself. Instead the reconstruction infused a large measure of standard, late nineteenth-century positivistic method into the system. And it produced a doctrine that had drifted far from Marx's own ideas in its understanding of (for instance) what constitutes a causal explanation, or what is meant by necessity.

The drift is not hard to understand. The Left Hegelian moment had passed well before Kautsky's generation was learning an intellectual method; it seemed a quaint episode not worth trying to understand. No radicals were Hegelians any longer in the 1870s. If Marx's propositions were true, they must be true in terms the coming men of the last decades of the century had made their own. And so the Marxist thinkers of the first generation, while they knew their method should be dialectical and said that it was, developed a Marxism characterized by strict causal logic, predictive tendencies, and determinism - a mechanistic materialism.[8] This was the Marxism received by serious Marxists for a full generation; it was the Marxism perceived by the greater number of interested non-Marxists until the 1950s, and by some to this day; it is the Marxism underlying the school of dialectical materialism that remains official in Soviet Russia.

A second, related set of modifications introduced during the construction of Marxism has been more widely noticed: the fusing of Marx's thought with the scientific naturalism of the late nineteenth century, and in particular with the evolutionary biases the generation had received from the powerful impact of Darwin's work. Whereas the modifications of Marx's fundamental method came into the system unintentionally, the adoption into Marxism of the other class of alien perspectives like Darwinism was often conscious. It was done partly in order to reinforce the doctrine with more recent insights, and partly to appeal to the preoccupations of thoughtful men of the time. For the initial form of Marxism was developed not just out of the concerns of its authors, but also in an interplay with the suggestions, objections, and general receptivity of educated men of the left, and of the working-class movement. That is to say, the impulse was not just schematization, but also popularization.

Many writers have pointed up the scientistic and Darwinian elements in first-generation Marxism.[9] Probably its best-known dimension is the attempted extension of Marx's understanding of process - which focused explicitly on the human historical process - to include all phenomena, those of physical nature as well as those of human development. Engels, who was largely responsible for the extension, was confident that he had assimilated natural science to Marx's human sciences without damage to the latter. Few people in the West would agree with him today. Instead, the new doctrines tended to make human history subject to the scientific mode of understanding and quasi-scientific laws, which reinforced the tendency to a positivistic method in Marxism. The resulting universal science - which gave a new sense to the term 'scientific socialism' - acquired the name of 'dialectical materialism'; it has also been called 'Engelsism'.[10] With refinements, it lives on in the Soviet Union.

Engels was partially influenced by Darwin's famous success in bringing aspects of human development into the realm of natural science; for Engels' pupil Kautsky, Darwin was even more central. Kautsky was a social Darwinist before he became a Marxist, and his conversion to Marx did not entail a repudiation of Darwin.[11] This is not to say that natural selection or other specific conceptions of Darwin's work found a place in orthodox Marxism, but the conception of evolution by struggle, of long linear development proceeding irregularly (and sometimes displaying sudden leaps) was the intellectual model for historical progress that dominated orthodox Marxism, particularly in the hands of Kautsky.

Again, sources for this development in the intellectual climate of the time are not far to seek. Darwin was a culture hero of a generation of social radicals, the generation which included the Marxist 'epigoni' as well as their intended audience; varieties of social Darwinism had immediate appeal for them, formed as they were by confident optimism in peace, progress, and science.[12] Darwinism was for many in this generation the natural way of expressing the rationalism of progress, a kind of evolutionary materialism, which - since a sense for Marx's premisses was largely lost - did not seem out of keeping with faithful adherence to Marx. It surely aided the reception of Marxism, particularly among the less educated. Indeed, it may have been the side of orthodox Marxism that was most completely understood by the masses of the burgeoning labour movement.

The first Marxists, then, in creating a doctrine for the 1880s and 1890s, necessarily drew on the available intellectual materials of their day, without which they could not have achieved what they and their contemporaries would see as system, intelligibility, and cogency. The mix of materials owes a good deal to Engels, something to Kautsky and others; the materials themselves were largely given. With its positivistic naturalism, its scientism and evolutionism, the doctrine now seems at once too grandiose and too limited. But it made possible the two great achievements of Marxist orthodoxy: a widespread appreciation of the power of Marx's social and historical analysis, and the spread of the Marxist labour movement. It also made possible the later offshoots and deviations from orthodoxy, including Leninism. To be sure, Marx's writings would have endured even without orthodoxy, and in the high culture men such as Weber and Croce would have continued to learn from them while rejecting them, while others might have found their way to the richer parts of Marx's thought and carried on an esoteric tradition of Marxist belief - just as there was an academic Hegelianism in that period. Instead, Marxism appeared in the guise of what now seems to us 'Engelsism' and 'Kautskyanism': idiosyncratic and imperfect, but effectively launched on its career of broad historical significance.

* * * * * *

A different kind of broad formative influence on first-generation Marxism came from its ties to the labour movement. The relationship of those years - Marxism as the official doctrine of a mass democratic labour parties - is sometimes taken as archetypal, but was actually peculiar to that era; with few exceptions, it has not shown itself in major European countries since the First World War. And it was the source of much that now seems limited in orthodox Marxism.

The paradigmatic form of the relationship of orthodox Marxism to the labour movement occurred in Central Europe - where the doctrine itself was most vital as well, which was no coincidence. The model case was the massive German Social Democratic Party. This was a legal political party, fully democratic in its internal structure, operating in a prosperous industrial society marked by substantial civil liberties and political freedoms.[13] It had very broad popular support - 32 per cent of the vote in the 1903 elections - and the largest organized membership of any party in the world. But up to 1914 the party faced a constitutionally and socially entrenched ruling class whose authority was very little shaken, and it seemed to have no notion how to break through to real influence or power. It rejected the idea of party alliances that might, under some circumstances, have opened the way to the liberalization of Germany; but it equally shied away from developing a violent confrontation to overthrow the old order. It contributed little to national debates on matters of policy, with the exception of social policy. Ultimately, for all its size, it was an ineffectual presence within a blocked political order.

And yet this party was the leading embodiment of political Marxism in that era. Its national congress at Erfurt in 1891 had adopted the Marxist perspective on the necessary supersession of capitalism by socialism, in a form drafted by Kautsky and Bernstein under the watchful eye of Engels. The party, though internally diverse, thereafter identified itself with orthodox Marxism - while German Marxism identified itself, to a remarkable degree, with the party. For in capturing this imposing movement German Marxism found itself subsumed by it. Orthodox Marxism was official within the party, and for all practical purposes there was no Marxism in Germany outside the party. The identification was profound.

As official party doctrine, orthodox Marxism served to legitimate the party's notably sterile form of politics. The doctrine's outstanding feature in this respect was its passivity - its failure to encourage any form of effective political action in its followers. The party considered itself revolutionary, and focused its future expectations on revolutionary changes in society; no attempt - as for instance by Bernstein and his fellow revisionists - to change the party's revolutionary self-image had any success up to 1914. But it preached revolutionary goals without revolutionary activism. Revolution would come: it was guaranteed by the historical analysis of orthodox Marxism (which was considered to have predictive power). It would come as a species of 'natural event'.[14] When and how it would come - perhaps with a collapse of capitalism, perhaps with a spontaneous rising of the workers - was not knowable in advance, and there was nothing the party could do to further the coming of these events except spread socialist consciousness among the workers. The doctrine taught the party to think of itself, in Kautsky's famous words, as 'a revolutionary, but not a revolution-making party'.[15]

On the other hand, because the opposing class plainly still had the upper hand, the possibilities for positive action in the here and now were considered to be strictly limited. The party could seek to palliate the harshness of the existing order of things by encouraging measures of social reform, but not at the cost of blurring its class position or its demand for fundamental change. Its ideology thus encouraged the party to conceive of itself as a 'non-participating opposition', its present impotence offset by the expectation of 'inheritance' at a future time.[16] Conceptually, the party's considerable piecemeal reform activity (and trade union work) was made secondary to sustaining the growth and untarnished ideals of the party. In this remarkably inward-looking task, the greater part of the energies of this splendid Marxist party exhausted themselves.

It used to be customary to blame the inadequacies of this political posture squarely on Karl Kautsky, the principal guardian of orthodoxy among the German Social Democrats. Erich Matthias gave the name 'Kautskyanism' to the passive radicalism in the party's ideology, whose critical function, as he saw it, was 'integrative' - serving to hold together radical and reformist elements in the party by the empty manipulation of concepts.[17] Since then others have pointed out that while the features he sums up as 'Kautskyanism' may have been important in the party, Kautsky's own ideas and purposes do not fit the model at all well.[18] There is now some tendency to charge August Bebel instead, and more plausibly, in that Bebel was the party's dominant figure and not hesitant to pronounce on ideological matters in his own right.[19] (Perhaps we shall soon have 'Bebelism' to add to the 'isms' that cluster around this subject.) At any rate, Bebel and Kautsky, who were old friends and leaders of great authority, worked to keep the theory and practice of the party in step. To a considerable degree, the fusion was conscious.

There was a theoretical premiss involved, and a novel one. In Marx's thought the 'proletariat' that is to overturn the old order and bring in the new is an abstraction not identified with any actual labour movement of the day. Even after Marx abandoned his youthful ideas of a vanguard party, there is no evidence that he intended to commit the future of the proletarian cause unreservedly into the hands of actual labour movements; in the First International, for instance, he remained a detached associate ready to break away in the event of a serious difference. Orthodox Marxism, however, had to deal with mass socialist parties of a kind Marx never saw. In working out its relationship with these parties, Marxism gradually lost its reserve and arrived at one of its defining assumptions: that the socialist labour movement (led by the party) embodies the proletariat on which the hopes of future socialism rest.

This slight shift of theoretical perspective entailed - or perhaps reflected - a drastic loss of critical distance. Acknowledging an existing popular party as expressing the historical essence of a (perhaps still ideologically immature) proletariat, as Kautsky and many of his fellows did, had the effect of binding theory to a practice it could not direct. For the Marxist Social Democratic parties of this period were formed far more by the political and social-psychological needs of their followers than by their formal doctrines. Of course, given a determinist, linear, and fundamentally optimistic view of the history of the working class, there seemed to be no danger in being tied to such a party. The dangers are all too clear in retrospect. As the serious Marxist thinkers became responsibly and officially involved in their parties, the doctrine, quite unconsciously, was put to the task of framing what was going to happen anyhow in such a way that it appeared to fit into the larger ideological perspectives, and to be justified by them.

Of course, this could only happen if there was a considerable degree of harmony between the doctrinal perspective and the movement's outlook in the first place. In Central Europe, for at least fifteen years after about 1890, this was the case. In Germany, politically conscious workers enjoyed a fairly open arena of politics and opportunities for educational self-improvement, but faced at the same time a system exceptionally resistant to gradualist change, a provocatively arrogant ruling class, and middle classes of a generally unprogressive bent. In these circumstances, a movement whose strongest impulses were towards social and political emancipation in a modern democratic - not transcendent - sense naturally took on a defiant and verbally aggressive tone. Repulsed by the holders of power and status in the society, the movement responded by defining itself as separate and distinct.[20] Confronted with a powerful state disinclined to compromise, the movement turned to a vision of a future triumph, a 'promised land'.[21] Disinclined to violence because of the strength of its opponents, and because, after all, life for many workers in Imperial Germany was far from intolerable, the movement was receptive to a deterministic vision. Faced with multifarious obstacles to effective political activity, the movement turned to what it could do well - propaganda and organization among the increasingly receptive working class. In all these ways orthodox Marxism had much to offer to the party. From separate sources the two elements, party and ideology, were brought into parallel alignment; and then, by the hypothesis of the identity of the movement and the historical proletariat, they became inseparable. True criticism of the party became exceedingly difficult from within the orthodoxy, as it tended by implication to challenge one of orthodoxy's own premises. We do not, in fact, encounter such criticism until the years of orthodoxy's dissolution, shortly before the war.

This lost independence, the lost freedom to criticize was the costly result of orthodoxy's unthinking absorption into the Social Democratic Party. We should be careful about supposing that an independent and critical Marxism would have brought a significantly different future to Central Europe, at least before 1914: the parties, after all, were open to ideological direction only in a limited degree, and labour's chances to change the fate of nations were not great at that time and place, whatever the party policies were. But when crisis approached in the last years before 1914, Social Democratic Marxism had lost most of its ability to think independently. It thereby lost its capacity to influence the movement in dangerous times, before, during, and after the war; and it ultimately lost its credit with the broad popular movement. When again Marxism won a position of influence in Europe, it was in a radically different form.

* * * * * *

Orthodox Marxism was a natural growth of its day; time and events worked to let other forms supersede it. Its political collapse is the easier to trace. Already in the last decade before the First World War the confidence on which the whole synthesis rested - confidence in automatic inheritance - was waning in Central Europe, and active party factions were calling for either determinedly reformist or seriously revolutionary policies - either of which would have required a wrenching change of perspectives. Then German Social Democracy suffered two crushing blows to its image, its collaboration in Imperial Germany's war effort after 1914 and its unimaginative helplessness in the revolutionary months at the end of the war; it ceased to be anyone's model. In the same years the equally orthodox Russian Mensheviks suffered an even more devastating fate. (The Austrian Marxists soldiered on after 1918 in much the same manner as before - 'Austro-Marxism' is an adaptation of the old orthodoxy in outlook and politics - but in so much reduced a sphere that they had little influence.) After this collapse the most active and widespread form of political Marxism was that derived from Lenin and his successful revolution. Lenin had never identified the theoretically postulated 'proletariat' with an actual, spontaneously arising working-class movement, so his triumph - and the Social Democratic crash, which was largely an independent phenomenon -meant the preeminence of a doctrine of the revolutionary vanguard. The elements of this Leninist political conception have turned out to be well suited to the ambitions of modernizing élites in early industrial or pre-industrial settings, and have given political Marxism a new lease of life. Ironically, however, in its own homeland area, Eastern Europe, Leninism has retained a version of the other side of the old orthodoxy: its dialectical materialism.

In Western Europe dialectical materialism also passed, if by more subtle stages. Politics surely had a large role here, as well: the political plausibility and apparent success of German Social Democratic Marxism always contributed to its theoretical dominance, and the loss of its presumption of superiority opened many issues to reexamination. But a new generation was also rising, one that had not been formed in the same way as Kautsky's generation; and new kinds of issues presented themselves that were not readily susceptible to solution by the old methods. Orthodoxy was still strong enough around the turn of the century to resist the attempted inroads of neo-Kantianism, the first of the intellectual currents after mechanistic materialism and Darwinism to make an appeal to Marxist circles. Later orthodoxy's resistance weakened, as the passing vogue of Ernst Mach among party intellectuals illustrates. But it was not until after 1917-18 and the collapse of orthodoxy's credibility that the philosophical renewal of the doctrine gained momentum. In a world which posed very different problems and opportunities from those perceived before 1914, Lukàcs, Gramsci, Korsch and others, with assistance from scholars like Ryazanov, wrenched the Marx-understanding of a new generation out of the old deterministic mould and recaptured, in their different ways, a sense for the creative application of Marx's ideas to the needs of active men.

But this achievement in the history of Marxism, like Lenin's, entailed costs. Since the end of orthodoxy, Marxism in the West has not been a unified tradition, but rather competing intellectual tendencies with only loose common identification. Only at passing moments has it appeared to have the relevance to speak to men of the left generally, and not just to particular groups of intellectuals. And at no time has it seemed to have the capacity to merge its purposes with a popular movement that had any prospects of achieving what the doctrine promised: the transcendence of the capitalist social order and the creation of a better world.

Notes

1.   The terms 'orthodox' and 'orthodoxy' occur in this paper only in their specialized reference to this phase of Marxism; accordingly, they can be used from here on without quotation marks.

2.   Official Soviet-bloc historiography stands almost alone in its respect for the Marxist generation we are discussing. Official Marxism-Leninism does have a conspective view of the history of Marxism, but it depends on the principle of the apostolic succession of expounders of the true faith. For this reason (as well as for others to be mentioned later) Soviet-bloc scholars are unable to find much fault with Engels' later writing and criticize only limited aspects of Kautsky's thought up to the point - variously set from 1905 up to the very eve of the First World War - when Lenin was ready to assume the mantle of the faltering older master.

3.   George Lichtheim, Marxism: An Historical and Critical Study, 2nd ed. (New York, 1965), p. 233.

4.   This is the title of the relevant volume (II) of his Main Currents of Marxism (Oxford, 1978).

5.   The quoted words are from Erich Matthias, 'Kautsky and der Kautskyanismus' in Marxismusstudien 2 (1957), p. 154.

6.   For the emergence of the terms 'Marxist' and 'Marxism' see George Haupt, 'Marx and Marxism' in The History of Marxism, ed. Eric J. Hobsbawm, vol. I (Bloomington, Ind., 1982), pp. 265-89.

7.   Both Matthias, pp. 157-58, and Arthur Rosenberg, Democracy and Socialism (New York, 1939), pp. 296-303, argue (from quite different perspectives) that Engels was partly the victim of a false apprehension of what was happening around him. Maximilien Rubel sees Engels' role in the making of Marxism as 'a bad trick' played on him by 'destiny'; 'The Marx Legend, or Engels, Founder of Marxism', in Rubel on Karl Marx: Five Essays (Cambridge, 1981), p. 23.

8.   One study of Kautsky's 'dialectic' finds it lacking the idea of the unity of opposites, the principle that the negation of the negation means development to a higher stage, or the notion that quantity changes into quality; very little is left except the focus on conflict as the motor of change. See Hans Jurgen Waldschmidt, 'Lenin und Kautsky: Verschiedene Wege der Weiterentwicklung des Marxismus' (unpublished dissertation,

University of Würzburg, 1966), pp. 18-19. Another author has pointed out that not even the neo-Kantian revisionists of the turn of the century, many of whom were academically trained philosophers, were able to reconstruct the role of the dialectic in Marx's thought; Hans-Josef Steinberg, Sozialismus und deutsche Sozialdemokratie, 3rd ed. (Bonn-Bad Godesberg, 1972), p. 57.

9. Of the many authorities who comment on this matter, I am relying most heavily on Lichtheim.

10. The term is used by Norman Levine, The Tragic Deception: Marx contra Engels (Santa Barbara, Calif., 1975).

11. Kautsky was never shy about admitting the influence of Darwinian thought on his ideas; see his untitled autobiographical sketch in Die Volkswirtschaftslehre der Gegenwart in Selbstdarstellungen ed. Felix Meiner (Leipzig, 1924), pp. 120-22; also Gary P. Steenson, Karl Kautsky, 1854-1938: Marxism in the Classical Years (Pittsburgh, 1978), pp. 24-30. As Steinberg, pp. 49-51, points out, Kautsky ceased to advocate Darwinian ideas in the later 1880s, but the influence remained.

12. The term 'epigoni' is taken from Lelio Basso's introduction to Rosa Luxemburg, Lettere ai Kautsky (Rome, 1971), pp. 12-14, where he also presents an exemplary brief account of the formative influences on that generation.

13. The bureaucratic limitations on democratic behavior in the German Social Democratic Party made famous by Robert Michels in his Zur Soziologie des Parteiwesens in der modernen Demokratie (Leipzig, 1911) grew significant only after about 1905; they do not belong to the formative or classic years of orthodox Marxism's involvement with the party.

14. Dieter Groh, Negative Integration und revolutionärer Attentismus (Frankfurt, 1973), p. 57.

15. Kautsky, 'Ein sozialdemokratischer Katechismus,' Neue Zeit XII/1 (1893-94), p. 368.

16. Peter Nettl, 'The German Social Democratic Party 1890-1914 as a Political Model', Past and Present no. 30 (April 1965), p. 67.

17. Matthias, op. cit. Matthias took the word 'Kautskyanism' from a 1929 polemic by Karl Korsch; Korsch, however, had used the term mainly in a critique of Kautsky's philosophical weaknesses.

18. Steinberg, pp. 75-86, and Walter Holzheuer, Karl Kautskys Werk als Weltanschauung (Munich, 1972), pp. 101-4.

19. E.g. Dieter Groh, 'Revolutionsstrategie und Wirtschaftskonjunktur' in Sozialgeschichte heute: Festschrift für Hans Rosenberg zum 70. Geburtstag, ed. Hans-Ulrich Wehler (Göttingen, 1974), pp. 354-64.

20. See Matthias, pp. 175-78, and Rosenberg, pp. 314 and 320.

21. Helga Grebing, Geschichte der deutschen Arbeiterbewegung (Munich, 1966), p. 115.

BRITISH AND GERMAN REACTIONS TO THE RISE OF

AMERICAN POWER

Paul Kennedy

In the nineteenth-century world of ideas, teleology and prediction assumed a prominence which must appear brash and disturbing to our own age of dissolving certainties. The 'discovery' of the ground-rules of laissez-faire political economy, the rise of geological and then biological notions of change and evolution, the positivistic faith in science and rational enquiry, all provided impulses to that general endeavour by early-to-mid Victorian intellectuals to explain the past and to forecast the future. That these forecasts emphasised different things does not matter here; the Whigs' belief in constitutional progress, the Cobdenites' proclamation of free trade as the 'great panacea', the Utilitarians' rules to improve institutional efficiency and moral behaviour, the Comtist vision of a technocratic, humanistic society, and the Marxist prediction of a proletarian revolution followed by a communist order, all radiated the sense that mankind was being carried forward to a higher and different destiny. Announcing that 'destiny' to the less percipient, pointing to the 'laws' which made it inevitable, and charting the telos of this evolution was, to put it crudely, one of the chief intellectual characteristics of the day.

This habit of prediction was by no means confined to socio-economic and domestic-constitutional issues: Weltpolitik, as Heinz Gollwitzer has recently shown,[1] was also high on the agenda of political forecasting. While these writings were often formulated along traditional lines - for example, as prognostications about aristocratic versus democratic systems, seapower (Britain) versus landpower (France) - it is remarkable how many commentators fastened upon the future growth of the USA. The impact of the 'Atlantic Revolution' of the eighteenth century, the strategical invulnerability of the American republic to large-scale invasion, its westward expansion on the one hand, and its demographic and commercial growth on the other, fascinated various observers well before Alexis de Tocqueville's Democracy in America appeared in 1835. In that famous work he, like writers such as the Abbé de Pradt and Constantin Frantz, alerted readers to the fact that only two nations - the USA and Russia - were 'still in the act of growth . . . along a path to which no limit can be perceived . . . Their starting-point is different and their courses are not the same; yet each of them seems marked out by the will of Heaven to sway the destinies of half the globe.'[2]

It is true that such prognoses fell away somewhat in the middle decades of the nineteenth century, probably because of Russia's poor performance in the Crimean War, the self-inflicted disasters of the American Civil War, the shift of attention to the new Bismarckian Reich, and then the assertion of Europe's technological and political dominance over new African and Asian colonies. But by the closing years of the century, the rise of the American and Russian 'superpowers' was fascinating intellectuals once again. In his 1883 Expansion of England lectures, for example, Seeley called his listeners' attention to the way in which 'steam and electricity' were transforming those 'enormous political aggregations' into units which would eclipse the existing European powers in the way that the new nation-states of the sixteenth century had eclipsed Florence.[3] Well before Stalin's aphorism, history was already seen to be on the side of the big battalions.

The rise of Russian power, and the reactions of Britain and Germany to it, will not be discussed here. But before analysing the responses of those two countries to the American challenge, it is worth making an obvious remark: that this forecast of a transatlantic power swaying 'the destinies of half the globe' was, unlike many of the other predictions of that positivistic age, essentially fulfilled. Perhaps this is because the interpretation of national-power indices is easier than the assessment of future social and constitutional changes. After all, by 1871 American manufacturing production was already 45% of Europe's; by 1890 it had soared to 75% of Europe's total (and was thus larger than Britain's and Germany's combined); by 1910 it was 86% of Europe's and, at that rate of increase, would have equalled the manufacturing production of the entire European continent by 1925.[4] All that the First World War did, in this respect, was to accelerate this relative decline of Europe, whose combined manufacturing production by 1920 was less than 75% of America's total.[5] In 1945, when Europe had exhausted itself in a further bout of total war, the United States accounted for slightly over half of the world's manufacturing production.

Although the two world wars could not have been foreseen by the Victorians, it was nonetheless clear to many of them that these shifts in the economic distribution of power were bound to have long-term effects upon international politics and diplomacy; and were bound, therefore, to cause a response in nation-states such as Britain and Germany (and in most other countries as well). But was it also foreseen that this rising American power would, in the coming twentieth century, ally itself with Britain and go to war against Germany? With the benefit of hindsight, it is all too easy to assume that the 'English-speaking peoples' were always natural partners against a Teutonic threat.

In the nineteenth century, in fact, such an assumption would have struck many observers as highly dubious. Indeed, connoisseurs of Weltpolitik as varied as Lord Palmerston and Kaiser Wilhelm II anticipated that the countries which would be hurt most by United States expansionism would be Britain and the British Empire. Following the independence of Latin America, Britain was the only European power with significant territorial interests in the western hemisphere; was, in other words, the chief exception to the principles of the Monroe Doctrine. American patriots who recalled the wars of 1776-83 and 1812-14, continentalists who foretold that one day the USA would embrace Canada, Mexico and the Caribbean, and Fenians who wished to strike a blow at the oppressors of Irish liberties, provided frequent evidence of a deep-rooted anglophobia in sections of American public opinion. Nor was there any lack of incidents to keep Anglo-American formal relations cool: quarrels over the Oregon and Alaskan boundaries, and over the

Bering Sea fisheries, the Alabama incident and the North's general touchiness about British policy during the Civil War, the traditional disagreement over blockade rights and 'freedom of the seas', a jockeying for position with regard to a future Isthmian Canal, the Sackville-West affair and other pinpricks, offered more than enough cause for British ministers of the nineteenth century to regard the United States as a potential foe rather than a potential ally.[6]

What was more, London's frequent expectation was that, if such a conflict arose, the Americans would always strive to secure European allies, as had happened in the two previous Anglo-American wars, to the strategical embarrassment of the British armed forces. Thus, Wellington in the 1840s was grimly warning that 'a war with the United States will not be with that Power alone'; Clarendon in the late 1860s was checking the Queen's desire for policies which could 'lead us into war in Europe, [for] we should find ourselves immediately called upon to defend Canada from American invasion and our commerce from American privateers'; and as late as 1896, in the aftermath of the (quite coincidental) 'Venezuela message' from Washington and 'Kruger Telegram' from Berlin, Lord Salisbury and his chancellor of the exchequer Hicks Beach appear to have been contemplating further trouble from those two rising powers, which would in turn necessitate additional spending on the Royal Navy.[7] A British alliance with the United States against a European nation would not have seemed likely to such men.

Nineteenth-century Germany, on the other hand, appeared to have no reason to apprehend the growth of American power. In the first place, until the founding of the Second Reich, one can hardly talk about German-American relations, as opposed to the relations which individual German states (Prussia, Hamburg, etc.) had with the USA, or the hopes which particular German groups (like the Liberals in 1848) entertained of American support. Even after 1871, of course, there were no German territories in the western hemisphere to cause bad blood in Washington. Separated from each other by thousands of miles of sea, and with neither of them possessing a substantial navy which might be regarded as a threat, Germany and the United States could stay on distant but amicable terms. In consequence, their growing trade, the family ties which still bound millions of German-Americans to their original homeland, and the rhetoric about cultural and historical traditions (e.g. the feats of von Steuben in the War of Independence) formed the 'stuff' of this relationship, rather than strategical and diplomatic issues.[8]

* * * * * *

Yet in the space of slightly more than a decade - between, say, the early 1880s and the late 1890s - German-American relations deteriorated so swiftly that each power felt it necessary to prepare contingency war-plans against the other; and, on the German side, the USA in particular was identified as one of the greatest (if more distant) obstacles to the achievement of a successful Weltpolitik. While there existed a number of separate reasons for this growing antagonism, they interacted with each other to intensify the trend. At the economic level, the spectacular improvement in rail and oceanic communications which permitted the

17

vast agricultural surpluses of the mid-West to flood across the Atlantic caused German peasants and Junkers to fear for their own survival; caused them also to press for ever-higher protective tariffs; and to employ a whole array of devices to ban the importation of 'unfair', 'unhealthy' American pork. Mingling with these commercial fears were the ideological resentments of German Conservatives at a country whose republican, materialistic, bustling way of life appeared the very antithesis to Prussian notions of monarchical authority, social deference and philosophical idealism.[9]

Yet if it was argued that Germany and the United States were culturally and ideologically dissimilar, were they not remarkably alike in their mutual strivings for world power? This, at least, was the conclusion of the intellectuals and pressure-groups of German imperialism, but this similarity did not make the latter any less anti-American as they watched these two, great rising nations going forward to claim a larger role in international politics than they had occupied in the outgoing nineteenth century. Anticipation of mutual rivalry was also in the minds of the German (and American) naval planners, who drew the same 'lesson' from the activities of their respective fleets in Samoa, the Philippines and Venezuela. If, by 1903, the General Board of the U.S. Navy was recommending that 'the most important war problem to be studied is based on the supposition that Germany is the enemy', then these thoughts pale in comparison with the calculations going on in Berlin about the feasibility of launching a continental invasion of the USA![10]

But behind these more specific naval clashes and colonial rivalries in the Pacific and Latin America, there lay the general atmosphere of political ideas about the future. Here especially German observers showed their ambivalence: on the one hand, the indices of the Reich's booming population, industrial production, export trade and naval vessels suggested - correctly - that it was swiftly overtaking the older European empires of France, the Netherlands, Portugal and in some respects even Great Britain; in a world of 'dying' and 'living' nations (to use Salisbury's phrase), Germany was unquestionably among the latter. On the other hand, in such a fast-changing era, would Germany grow quickly enough to be able to break out from its merely European power-base in time to join the 'Three World Empires' of Britain, Russia and the USA in deciding the global politics of the twentieth century? Above all, was not the even faster growth of American population, industry, exports and naval power threatening to cut off Germany's chances of entering the select club of the really great states? In that Darwinian scene so intensively studied by Wilhelmine professors and publicists around the turn of the century, the Reich was portrayed as facing many potential foes; but France, the traditional enemy, was now slipping behind in the global struggle for survival; even the still-dangerous but over-extended British Empire was feeling the pace; and the Tsarist colossus, whatever its immediate military strength, had economic feet of clay. In the longer term, then, it might be the USA which posed the most serious threat, precisely because it exhibited the same features of growth and destiny as German intellectuals ascribed to their own fatherland. Curiously, this image of die amerikanische Gefahr existed alongside dismissive German opinions about the Americans' lack of martial values, their miscegenation, and so on, without (as also in Hitler's case) this logical contradiction ever being resolved. The United States was, quite simply, a potential threat. It was scarcely surprising, therefore, that it was the German government, urged on by its 'national-economist' professors, which made repeated attempts to mobilise other European states into some form of customs union - a 'United States of Europe' - which alone could resist the industrial and agricultural and maritime expansionism of the 'Yankees'.[11]

* * * * * *

Even more remarkable than these growing German-American suspicions was the rapprochement which took place in Anglo-American relations around the turn of the century. The pace of this particular 'diplomatic revolution' was quite staggering: in 1895 Cleveland had been threatening war over the Venezuelan boundary dispute; but by 1903 that problem, and the even weightier issues of the Isthmian Canal and Alaskan/Canadian border had all been settled, and a new climate of friendliness existed among the élites and newspapers on each side.[12] Here, too, an interaction of reasons rather than one overriding cause appears to have been responsible.

At the economic level, the American impact on Great Britain was mixed but, on the whole, favourable. The fears expressed around 1900 about an American manufacturing 'invasion', and the dislike of the exceedingly high United States tariffs which helped to produce a chronic imbalance in visible trade,[13] were outweighed by other factors. The first was the large and increasing use by Britain of American foodstuffs and raw materials, which created a mutual dependency, since Southern cotton plantations and mid-Western farmers relied upon access to this open market as much as British consumers relied upon the massive annual imports of such produce. Lacking the Junkers' political muscle to impose tariffs, British farmers either succumbed to this flood of transatlantic grain or diversified into other fields. The second, equally important factor was the bonds created by high finance, where the City of London's banking, insurance and investment services fuelled American commercial-industrial growth and thus added handsomely to Britain's invisible earnings. With American investments of around $2.5 billion in 1900, and $4.5 billion in 1914, the British had engaged (in Bradford Perkins' words) in an 'invasion' of their own.[14] The nervous reaction of Wall Street to Cleveland's belligerent message in 1895 was an early indication that an Anglo-American war would be mutually ruinous. What all this suggests is that the economies of the two countries were becoming essentially complementary, whereas those of Germany and the USA were more antagonistic.

It is in the fields of ideology and culture, however, that the change in British views of the United States can be most easily detected. Here again, scholars who have investigated this trend point to a multiplicity of causes.[15] One suggestion has been that, as the steamship and railway made foreign travel much easier, Britons and Americans discovered how much they had in common, compared with other peoples. Certainly there was a massive emphasis upon the shared language, literature, laws and political practices of the two great branches of the Anglo-Saxon world - an emphasis given personal reinforcement by the rash of marriages between members of the British and American social élites (Chamberlain, Harcourt, Churchill, Curzon, the Duke of Marlborough, etc.) The late nineteenth-century popularity of ideas of 'race' was also important, offering pseudo-scientific support to the claim - made by imperialists on both sides of the Atlantic - that the English-speaking peoples, due to their superior characteristics, were jointly predestined to rule the world. Noteworthy, too, was the shift in British Conservative thinking about the United States: while still disturbed at the blatant power of money and the 'lobby system' in American politics, it was now being conceded by Tories that a written constitution, states' rights, and the powers of the Senate offered admirable barriers to 'radical' change which the rise of Labour and social-reform Liberalism threatened to force upon a more fluid British political structure.[16]

There was, to be sure, something 'mythological' in this growing assertion of an Anglo-American 'special relationship';[17] it obviously ignored Irish-Americans, German-Americans and other ethnic groups, and often overlooked the fact that even leading 'WASP' politicians were less emotionally attached to this relationship than their British counterparts - an imbalance which was to be observed as late as the Macmillan-Kennedy era. Nonetheless, the very fact that politicians such as Chamberlain, Balfour, Grey and Churchill all endeavoured to secure and then to preserve American friendship was of great significance - and contrasts markedly with the suspicions displayed by Bismarck, Kaiser Wilhelm II and many other Germans.

The difficulty for the historian of the Anglo-American rapprochement is in trying to establish just how far these cultural and ideological factors influenced the various British concessions to the USA over the Alaskan border, the Isthmian Canal, and so on. After all, in addition to economic motives, there also existed compelling strategical reasons for this early example of British 'appeasement' policy.[18] The Canadian frontier was always admitted to be indefensible in the long run and, while the Royal Navy could give a good account of itself in American waters, this would only be at the cost of maritime security in the Mediterranean and Far East. Since an Anglo-American conflict would be economically disastrous and strategically futile, would it not be prudent to make small-scale concessions in the western hemisphere - not merely to eliminate points of friction there, but also as part of a larger strategy of winning over the United States to a joint defence of the liberal-commercial system in China and elsewhere?[19] This, certainly, was a widely-held political attitude after 1898 and seemed to be swiftly replacing Salisbury's more sceptical, traditional views of the USA in world affairs.

Yet, despite these very pragmatic reasons for appeasing the United States, the fact remains that political ideas, and especially notions of a shared political culture, played an important role. It is nearly always easier to concede to a friend than to a perceived foe, and in this particular case the British habit of describing Anglo-American differences as 'family quarrels' made the act of reconciliation with the USA far less difficult than was the case with other nations. Conversely, this cultural-ideological factor allowed British commentators to justify American expansionism as 'good', whereas that by another power (Russia, or Germany) could be labelled 'bad'. For example, in one of the most remarked-upon articles of the time about 'The Anglo-German Rivalry', Philip Kerr expressed the essential distinction in the British imperialists' views of Germany and the USA:

> During the years of her supremacy has [England] lifted a finger against the United States, which have now a population twice her own and resources immeasurably greater? No, for the ideals of the United States, like her own, are essentially unaggressive and threaten their neighbours no harm. But Germanism, in its want of liberalism, its pride, its aggressive nationalism, is dangerous, and she feels instinctively that if it is allowed to become all powerful it will destroy her freedom, and with it the foundations of liberty on which the Empire rests.[20]

* * * * * *

By 1906 or so, it has been argued, a certain recession was occurring in the Anglo-American rapprochement. The crises in China and the Pacific, which had pushed the two powers together, had faded. The Foreign Office under Grey became increasingly involved in European issues, in which the USA displayed little interest. Conversely, German-American relations seemed to be much less tense than during their angry confrontations over Samoa and Venezuela a few years earlier. Even the German nationalists' cries about 'the American danger' were overshadowed and subdued by their much more immediate worries concerning the Bosnian, Agadir and Balkans crises. As the European scene darkened, and horrified American visitors such as House denounced the 'militarism run stark mad', Britain and Germany seemed to be increasingly regarded by United States opinion as powers equally tainted by the follies of the Old World. The lack of any significant American role in the July 1914 crisis, and Woodrow Wilson's appeal to his countrymen a fortnight later to be 'neutral in fact as well as in name', all suggested that the earlier trends towards Anglo-American friendship and German-American enmity had merely been ephemeral.

Yet such conclusions would be false. There were to be many specific stepping-stones (the U-boat campaign, the Zimmermann Telegram) on the way to the American entry into war in 1917, and it would be false to say that intervention had always been inevitable. Nevertheless, the changes in political attitudes which had occurred during the previous two decades did have an effect. The impressions of Britain and Germany which existed in the minds of those Americans directing policy - Wilson, House, Lansing, Page - were now fixed. If Germany won the war, Wilson privately informed House in late August 1914, 'it would change the course of civilisation and make the United States a military nation'. By contrast, Britain - the land of his hero W. E. Gladstone and the home of

21

liberalism - was no threat to the American way of life; even its decidedly illiberal blockading methods did not, therefore, alter this favourable image.[21] But the Germans - or, rather, the Huns, the ruthless violators of Belgium - were a menace to civilisation well before they began unrestricted sinkings of merchant ships and secret plots with Mexico. If at all possible, Washington would remain benevolently neutral to the Allies; but it would not require the East Coast 'business lobby' or even the General Board of the U. S. Navy to convince the President and his advisers that, if Britain and France were seriously weakened, they would need to be assisted against the Central Powers. In sum, by 1914 'the American image of Germany' and its converse, 'the American image of Britain', had been seriously and irreversibly influenced by those so-called background factors of political culture, language and ideology as well as by the more obvious strategical and diplomatic events of the preceding two decades.[22]

The consequences of this shift in political attitudes within the triangular relationship of Britain, Germany and the USA for the half-century following 1890 can scarcely be exaggerated. The Anglo-American antagonism, although often ignored by historians of European diplomacy, was one of the constant features of nineteenth-century power politics; in this century, it was replaced by the equally important Anglo-American alliance, which has been activated twice in order to check a German bid for European (and overseas) mastery. Such a combination certainly did not mean the end of all Anglo-American differences, and even at the height of Churchill's 'Grand Alliance' of 1941-45 the two powers were quarrelling over strategy, trade restrictions, colonies, oil concessions, and so on; becoming the 'junior partner to Uncle Sam' was not an easy process, even for pro-American Britons.[23] Nevertheless, the shared belief in common political aims - so distinct from those of Fascism or Communism - kept London and Washington together when other issues threatened to drive them apart.

Germany's relations with Britain and the United States also underwent a dramatic change between the nineteenth and twentieth centuries, and once again political ideology and perception played a role. I have argued elsewhere that, given the long-term economic and strategical shifts in Germany's favour after the 1870s, an alteration in the Anglo-German relationship was virtually certain - but it was the emphasis upon differing political cultures which gave that antagonism such a sharp tone.[24] The same can be said, by extension, about the German-American relationship. That those two nations would be jostling each other for world influence in the twentieth century was fairly easy to predict. But that such rivalry would be attended by ideological polemics - and, in particular, by the denigration of the United States as a corrupt, racially-mixed Unkultur by Germans from Tirpitz to Ludendorff to Hitler[25] - provided an added yet vital edge to this lack of harmony. At the very least, the German underestimation and dislike of the United States ensured that the latter would never enter a European conflict on Berlin's side. At the most, it gave force to the arguments of those Americans who urged, before 1917 and again before 1941, that Britain needed the support of the New World in order to preserve the liberal order in the Old. No doubt the élites of all three of these states manoeuvred with concrete national advantages in mind; but they did not act simply as calculating machines, freed from ideology and prejudice. It seems fitting, therefore, to end this survey with the comment of a distinguished nineteenth-century German-American, who in 1898 perceived the force of ideas in politics much better than many of his Realpolitik-obsessed contemporaries:[26]

> Neither do I think that the exchange of complimentary phrases which has become customary, about kinship, common origin, common love of liberty, common language, common literature, about blood being thicker than water and so on, is merely worthless stage claptrap and flummery. There is enough truth and sincerity in it to create and keep alive a real sentiment; and while those are mistaken who think international relations may be wholly governed by mere sentiment, those are equally mistaken who think that sentiment is no force at all in international relations.

Notes

1. H. Gollwitzer, Geschichte des weltpolitischen Denkens, vol. 1 (Göttingen, 1972), p. 325ff.
2. Alexis de Tocqueville, Democracy in America, ed. P. Bradley, vol. 1 (New York, 1945), p. 452. For a useful survey of this forecast, see P. Dukes, The Emergence of the Superpowers: A Short Comparative History of the USA and the USSR (London 1970).
3. J. Seeley, The Expansion of England (London, 1884), pp. 299-301.
4. L. L. Farrar, Arrogance and Anxiety: the Ambivalence of German Power 1848-1914 (Iowa City, Iowa, 1981), p. 18, fn.12;p.39, fn.18.
5. Calculated from D. H. Aldcroft, From Versailles to Wall Street, 1919-1929 (London, 1977), p.98.
6. C. S. Campbell, From Revolution to Rapprochement: the United States and Great Britain 1783-1900 (New York, 1974), covers these various quarrels.
7. For the quotations from Wellington and Clarendon, see K. Bourne, The Foreign Policy of Victorian England 1830-1902 (Oxford, 1970), pp.263-64, 396; and, for strategical details, idem, Britain and the Balance of Power in North America, 1815-1908 (London, 1967). For Salisbury's attitude, see Bourne, Balance of Power, p. 339; and J. A. S. Grenville, Lord Salisbury and Foreign Policy: the Close of the Nineteenth Century (London, 1964), chapter iii.
8. G. Moltmann, Atlantische Blockpolitik im 19. Jahrhundert (Düsseldorf, 1973), passim; H. Gatzke, Germany and the United States: A "Special Relationship"? (Cambridge, Mass., 1980), chapter 2.
9. The best survey of German-American relations in this period is still A. Vagts' enormous Deutschland und die Vereinigten Staaten in der Weltpolitik, 2 vols. (London/New York, 1935).
10. Ibid.; H. Herwig, Politics of Frustration: The United States in German Naval Planning 1889-1941 (Boston, 1976), part i.

11. F. Fischer, War of Illusions (London, 1975), p. 30ff.
12. The literature upon this topic is vast: for a good recent survey, see B. Perkins, The Great Rapprochement (London, 1969), passim.
13. In 1903 U.S. exports to Britain totalled £127 million; imports from Britain a mere £19 million, according to the visible trade statistics.
14. Perkins, op. cit., p. 125: and see especially the importance of the British deficit in visible trade with the USA, and surplus in invisibles, as analysed in S. B. Saul, Studies in British Overseas Trade 1870-1914 (Liverpool, 1960), chapter III.
15. Perkins, op. cit., passim; R. H. Heindel, The American Impact on Great Britain 1898-1914 (New York, 1968 reprint), passim.
16. H. A. Tulloch, 'Changing British Attitudes towards the United States in the 1880s', Historical Journal, vol. 20, 4 (1977), pp.825-840. For the surge in ideas about the 'racial unity' of Britons and Americans, see especially S. Anderson, Race and Rapprochement (East Brunswick, N. J.,1981).
17. M. Beloff, 'The Special Relationship: An Anglo-American Myth', in M. Gilbert (ed.), A Century of Conflict 1850-1950: Essays for A.J.P. Taylor (London, 1966), pp.148-171.
18. Bourne, Britain and the Balance of Power in North America, passim.
19. See again, Grenville, Lord Salisbury and Foreign Policy: Perkins, The Great Rapprochement, chapter 3.
20. Cited in P. M. Kennedy, The Rise of the Anglo-German Antagonism 1860-1914 (London/Boston, 1980), p. 399.
21. J. W. Coogan, The End of Neutrality: The United States, Britain, and Maritime Rights 1899-1915 (Ithaca, N.Y., 1981), chapter 9.
22. Ibid.; and see also the excellent article by Hans W. Gatzke, 'The United States and Germany on the Eve of World War I', in I. Geiss and B.-J. Wendt (eds.), Deutschland in der Weltpolitik des 19. und 20. Jahrhunderts (Düsseldorf, 1973), pp.271-286.
23. On which, see W. R. Louis, Imperialism at Bay (Oxford/New York, 1978); C. Thorne, Allies of a Kind (London, 1978); 'Waiting for Uncle Sam', The Times Literary Supplement, 6 November 1981, p. 1297.
24. Kennedy, The Rise of the Anglo-German Antagonism, p. 464ff.
25. Gatzke, Germany and the United States, p. 48. For useful details of Imperial Germany's arrogant underestimation of the USA, anticipating Hitler's rather similar attitudes, see R. R. Doerries, 'Imperial Berlin and Washington: New Light on Germany's Foreign Policy and America's Entry into World War I', Central European History, xi (1978), pp.23-49.
26. Carl Schurz, in Atlantic Monthly (October 1898), p. 435.

WHEN DEATH WAS YOUNG. . . : GERMANY, MODERNISM,

AND THE GREAT WAR

Modris Eksteins

'A poet will come,' wrote the German Colin Ross from the field of battle in 1916, 'who will write the history of this world war, after a few decades, perhaps after a few centuries.'[1] By the time Ross wrote, the struggle, intended by all sides as a brief cloudburst invoked to clear the air, had bogged down in a gruesome war of attrition and endurance; and many a soldier's, even civilian's, perspective on the war - its origins, especially its purpose, and also its possible length - had begun to fragment. For many, in all belligerent countries, 'meaning' for the whole had become a miasma of imprecise abstraction, a question of subjective interpretation, or simply a matter of reflex response. By the third year of the war, the view of Ross - that the war was a subject for poets rather than historians - was symptomatic of a much wider cast of mind. History had become, for many apart from Stephen Dedalus, a nightmare, a configuration of irrational forces and unconscious urges whose meaning the traditional historian had no chance of elucidating. For H.G. Wells' Mr. Britling the only meaning by 1916 lay in religion - 'Our sons have shown us God.'[2] For Dada the only saneness was to recognize that life was insane. The war had surpassed the bounds of traditional social and intellectual discourse and had become an existential riddle.

It is significant that despite the veritable mountains of literature which have built up on the subject of the First World War a good many of the more satisfying efforts to deal with the meaning of the war have come from the pens of poets, novelists, and even literary critics, and that by comparison professional historians have produced specialized and limited accounts, most of which pale in evocative and explanatory power before those of the littérateurs.[3] The spate of official and unofficial histories which issued forth initially in the twenties was largely ignored by the public. By contrast, in 1929 Erich Maria Remarque's All Quiet on the Western Front became, virtually overnight, the best-selling book of all previous time. Imaginative, not historical, literature it was that sparked an intense reconsideration of the meaning of the war at the end of the twenties. The historical imagination, like so much of the nineteenth-century intellectual edifice, had been sorely challenged by the events of the war; and it was consistent with the subsequent self-doubt of the discipline that H.A.L. Fisher's 1934 lament, in the preface to his History of Europe, should have become perhaps the most frequently quoted theoretical statement by a historian of our century: 'Men wiser and more learned than I have discerned in history a plot, a rhythm, a predetermined pattern. These harmonies are concealed from me. I can see only one emergency following upon another as wave follows upon wave . . . .'[4]

Whether the poems, novels, and other imaginative efforts provoked by the war stand as 'great' art is of course a debatable matter. W.B. Yeats in his 1936 edition of the Oxford Book of Modern Verse omitted the war poets on grounds that passive suffering could not be the stuff of great poetry which had to have a moral vision. Ten years after the war, amidst the glut of war novels which appeared during the 'war boom' of 1929-30, the Morning Post bemoaned in an editorial that 'the great novel of the Great War, which will show all things in a true perspective, has yet to be written'.[5] The chimera of the great war novel, explaining all, was a constant in the intellectual climate of the twenties and even the thirties. Mottram's Spanish Farm trilogy, Tomlinson's All Our Yesterdays, Aldington's Death of a Hero, and, in a different vein but with similar intent, Remarque's All Quiet and Renn's Krieg, to cite but a few of many possible examples, were motivated by this challenge and quest. 'The witness of a hundred thousand Nobodies [Tartempions],' wrote André Thérive in Le Temps in December 1929, 'isn't worth the semi-fiction conceived by a great man.'[6] This attitude, that 'art' might be truer to life than 'history', was hardly a new notion but never before had it been so widespread, in fact so dominant. Its acceptance not only reveals a great deal about the impact of the war on perceptions of reality and about the cultural and intellectual mood of the twenties, it underlines the general breakdown of a belief in objective reality and the turn to a 'culture of narcissism' which have become the central features of western existence and of 'modernism' in our century.

Doubts about the validity of history, about the ability of the historian to produce objective accounts of the past, of course existed prior to the First World War. Historians participated in the mounting wave of skepticism in the second half of the nineteenth century which questioned the drift of western industrial civilization and which posited as a reaction and alternative to materialism and standardization a renewed emphasis on spirituality and 'inner experience'. A century before James Joyce identified history with nightmare, Arthur Schopenhauer defined history as 'the long, difficult and confused dream of mankind', and derided all pretensions to objectivity and universality. He did not receive much attention during his lifetime but in the second half of the century his reputation and influence became firmly established. In 1870, an admirer of Schopenhauer, the historian Jacob Burckhardt, wrote: '. . . if anything lasting is to be created it can only be through an overwhelmingly powerful effort of real poetry.' In 1874, Theodor Mommsen, the historian of Rome, who earlier in his career had had positivistic inclinations, suggested in his rectorial address to the University of Berlin that 'the writer of history is perhaps closer to the artist than to the scholar.'[7] Nietzsche's tirades against objectivity - 'Nothing is definable unless it has no history' - became increasingly popular after his death in 1900; and widely read cultural critics like Julius Langbehn and Houston Stewart Chamberlain called for the complete aestheticization of life: history existed only as spirit and not as any objective reality; its truths could only be approached by intuition, not by a critical method; history was art, not science. German thinkers, as these examples are meant to suggest, were in the vanguard of the reorientation - or dismantling - of nineteenth-century historical thought, in the revolt against empiricism and positivism, and in the reaction to a social, political, and cultural order identified with western liberalism and materialism and with a long-standing Anglo-French political and cultural hegemony in the world.[8]

While in the realm of the visual arts Paris was certainly the venue for experimentation at the turn of the century, it was from areas of Europe and America which had experienced particularly sudden and striking social and economic change in the forty years before the outbreak of war that most of the impetus for artistic and intellectual innovation came. Asked to name the great French artists of his time, Jean Cocteau replied: Picasso, Stravinsky, and Modigliani.[9] Exile, the frontier, and the journey - notions evoking exoticism, sensuality, alienation, and especially movement, centrifugal of course - became the common motifs of avant-garde activity; and all these notions were a response to the hegemonic metropolitan power of London and Paris. Central to the self-image of the avant-garde was the idea of spirit at war, and central to an emergent modernism was a rejection of what were perceived to be the prevailing standards of the nineteenth century, a century which, in terms of the self-assertion of social classes, was very much the century of the bourgeoisie and a century whose dominant social code, as a result, was anchored primarily in concepts of efficiency, utility, and rationalism - in other words in externality.

Yet, while social negativism, a rejection of the bourgeois preoccupation with an external world of form - with taste, demeanour, etiquette, and respectability - was an essential tool of nineteenth-century modernism, its mood and substance were an emphatic vitalism, a quest for spiritual liberation, and hence ultimately optimism about the potential of man. The upshot of modernism may, in the long run, have been nihilism, as many critics have pointed out - one critic calls modernism 'aesthetic thanatophilia'[10] - but this was scarcely the original intention. Although virulently opposed to what were considered the stultifying and suffocating preoccupations of bourgeois society, neo-idealism, Lebensphilosophie, abstractionism, and even decadentism were in essence an extension, against a backdrop of high industrialization, of basic humanist principles which aimed at liberating man's potential for experience, beauty, and life. Initially modernism was a culture of hope, a secular religiosity.

In national terms Germany at the turn of the century embodied these tendencies of vitality, growth, and revolt most systematically. Since achieving political unity in 1871 she had experienced dramatic industrialization and urbanization and by 1914 had surpassed Britain in many areas of industrial and commercial activity. Her population was still expanding at a rate exceeding that of her western neighbours, and the prospect was that soon it would double that of France. Her constitution and political system were an attempt to produce a synthesis of monarchy and democracy, centralism and federalism - a 'democratic Caesarism' - which even many non-Germans regarded as a bold political adventure offering an alternative both to rule by the masses and to obscurantist authoritarianism. Her universities were admired centres of learning, and she encouraged research more actively than any other country. She had the largest socialist party in the world, looked to for leadership by the entire international labour movement. Her youth, women's rights, and even homosexual emancipation movements were large and active. These mushroomed in the general context of a Lebensreformbewegung which, as the name suggests, aimed at a reorientation of not only basic habits of living but also fundamental values in life. Berlin, Munich, and Dresden were vibrant cultural centres. Picasso said in 1897 that if he had a son who wished to be an artist he would send him to Munich to study and not to Paris.[11] Strindberg, Ibsen, and Munch got a warmer reception in Germany than in their own countries. In the decorative arts and in architecture Germany was more open to experiment than either France or Britain. In modern dance it was in Germany that Isadora Duncan and Emile Jaques-Dalcroze founded their first schools. The Germans called Duncan 'the divine Isadora'; and when in 1912 Diaghilev and Nijinsky were preparing their revolutionary production of Le Sacre du printemps, it was to Jaques-Dalcroze's school of eurhythmics in Hellerau outside Dresden that they went for assistance. At the turn of the century the country which had produced Marx, Wagner, and Nietzsche was also forced to confront the implications and repercussions of these unsettling imaginations most directly and immediately.

Germany's whole ethos prior to 1914 was one, then, of flux and dynamism involving a search for new forms, forms conceived not in terms of laws and finitude but in terms of symbol, metaphor, and myth. 'German creativity is fundamentally different from Latin creativity,' wrote the artist Ernst Ludwig Kirchner. 'The Latin takes his forms from the object as it exists in nature. The German creates his form from fantasy, from an inner vision peculiar to himself. The forms of visible nature serve him as symbols only . . . and he seeks beauty not in appearance but in something beyond.'[12] Even the idea of Wissenschaft, with its notion of creating (schaffen) knowledge, was a dynamic concept involving change motivated by intellect and will. Germany, more extensively than any other country, represented nationally the aspirations of 'avant-gardism' - the desire to break out of the 'encirclement' by Anglo-French power, the imposition of a world order by a pax Britannica and French civilisation, an order codified politically as 'bourgeois liberalism'.

Recent historiography on imperial Germany, with its general predilection for the Primat der Innenpolitik, has tended to regard the domestic impulses for war in a strongly conspiratorial framework: war as the outgrowth of the manipulatory politics of conservative élites; war, in other words, as counter-revolution. The belief that war would consolidate national energies and overcome internal social and political differences was of course well represented, to a greater or lesser degree, in all the official establishments which presided over the outbreak of war. Nevertheless, this interpretation of the advent of the war underestimates, certainly in the case of Germany, the popular energies, the revolutionary impulses which regarded the war as an avenue for a breakthrough to positive achievement. The idea of a Befreiungs- or Freiheitskampf was not imposed on Germans by a conservative counter-revolutionary establishment. The street scenes of August 1914 were not orchestrated manifestations.

While in some quarters of Germany there was a feeling that Kultur was under attack from superficiality, caprice, and ephemera and that steps had to be taken to consolidate it, and while there was a good measure of anxiety in all classes, a mood which naturally concerned governments and leaders, there was nevertheless overall a strong sense of confidence, optimism, and mission: <u>Denn am deutschen Wesen soll die Welt genesen</u>. The feeling was widespread that the reform wave was something larger and more meaningful than any of its specific - and in some cases unacceptable - parts and that it constituted the heart and soul of the nation. Friedrich Gundolf and Friedrich Wolters of the <u>Georgekreis</u> addressed this idea when they insisted in 1912 that there was nothing immoral or abnormal in homoeroticism. 'Rather we have always believed that something essentially formative for German culture as a whole is to be found in these relations.' The vision was of a culture committed to 'heroized love'.[13] The sexual imagery so prevalent in German <u>fin-de-siècle</u> discourse begs exploration. Bethmann Hollweg's later association of the idea of a softer, less aggressive German policy during the July crisis of 1914 with the notion of <u>Selbstentmannung</u>, self-castration, is highly revealing. A change of course would, in Bethmann's view, have betrayed Germany's entire cultural and political identity and self-esteem.[14]

There is, however, another important side to the picture. The middle-class victory was, on the surface at any rate, as complete in Germany as it was elsewhere in western Europe. The bourgeoisie not only controlled the industrial economy of the country but had made major inroads into such traditional bastions of aristocratic power as the army. Already by 1873, for example, 62 per cent of infantry lieutenants in the Prussian army came from the bourgeoisie. By 1913 70 per cent of all Prussian officers came from this class.[15] And of course the middle classes in Germany were just as committed to the bourgeois ethic of discipline and hard work necessary to promote efficiency and gain as they were, for instance, in Britain. The cult of <u>Technik</u> in imperial Germany would allow Eugen Diesel to remark that the invention of the dynamo was of equal world-historical importance to the outcome of the Franco-Prussian war.[16] Correspondingly, there was hardly universal appreciation in the middle strata for the plays of Wedekind, the art of Marc and Macke, or the <u>Leibeskultur</u> and rarified idealism of urban youth. The working classes, needless to say, were also hardly attuned to the pretensions of bourgeois bohemians. But, interestingly, none of this negated the general identification by most Germans with the ideas of newness, regeneration, and change. Imperial Germany thus had a culture which was divorced from many of the fundamental social and economic realities of the Reich.

Daniel Bell has pointed out, however, that this same striking paradox lies at the heart of modern western society as a whole: while our social and economic concerns are dictated still by a preoccupation with efficiency, our cultural inclinations lead us towards prodigality and absolute experience, a quest which, by definition, seeks to relegate the notion of efficiency to the realm of repression and neurosis.[17] Germany already prior to the first world war embodied this paradox openly; more energetically than, for instance, the Austria-Hungary of Carl Schorske's recent analysis.[18] Germany's capitalism, as Fritz Stern s important works have shown, was 'spiritually devalued'.[19] Germany is thus, one ventures to postulate, the modernist nation par excellence. Furthermore, as the Herzvolk of Europe, as a nation without natural - geographical or spiritual - boundaries, Germany and her modernism were bound to have international repercussions. 'To be the spiritual battlefield of European antagonisms - that's what it means to be German,' wrote Thomas Mann. More than thirty years earlier Nietzsche had forecast the European response to German effervescence: 'What is new is invariably evil, wanting as it does to break through the old limits and subvert the old pieties, while only what is old is good.'[20]

Germany has usually been described as a 'belated nation', because political unity, industry, colonies, and urbanization - the external social and economic trappings of modernity - all came late in relative terms. Such a description is certainly valid. And yet, paradoxically, from our present vantage point, Germany was also the most modern nation of the pre-1914 world - one which felt acutely the conflict between modernism in its spiritual and aesthetic sense and modernity in its social and economic form and which, while bowing to the necessity of the latter, preferred the former. That conflict which bedevils western culture as a whole today was clear in German-speaking Europe prior to 1914. Nevertheless, there is still an important difference. While our mood about the possibility of resolving the conflict is generally negative, that of Germany prior to 1914 was positive. A synthesis was possible. Will was the key. The turning point in the development of modernism is the First World War: those four years transformed the revolution of hope into the revolution of destruction, turned fantasy into nightmare, will into wilfulness, and modernism from a mood dominant in Germany to one prevalent in much of the western world. When William Faulkner wrote in 1931 in the wake of the 'war boom' that 'America has been conquered not by the German soldiers that died in French and Flemish trenches, but by the German soldiers that died in German books',[21] he was of course referring in the first instance to the sympathy Americans felt for the hapless Frontsoldat portrayed in recent German war novels, but the wider significance of Faulkner's statement was that the German syndrome had spread to America.

If Germany was the principal modernist nation of the fin-de-siècle world, then Great Britain was the major conservative power, conservative in that she felt not only her preeminence in the world but her entire way of life threatened by the instability Germany was seen to represent. Her involvement in the war turned it from a limited continental power struggle into a veritable war of civilizations. That Britain showed on the whole comparatively little interest in the manifestations of modern culture does not require extensive documentation. Despite Ford Madox Ford's later impression that the years 1910-14 were 'like an opening world', Britain in 1914 was still on balance thoroughly skeptical of modernism in all of its forms. Ford complained that 'the complete absence of any art' seemed to be 'a national characteristic' of the British.[22] The Spanish-American George Santayana spoke for many a pre-war British sensibility and its response to political and cultural developments abroad when he wrote: 'The spirit in which parties and nations beyond the pale of English liberty confront one another is not motherly nor brotherly nor Christian. Their valorousness and morality consist in their indomitable egotism. The liberty that they want is absolute liberty, a desire which is quite primitive.'[23]

From the start of the war the Germans regarded it as above all a spiritual conflict, one which did not require precise war aims even and which as a result could readily be regarded by virtually the entire population as essentially a struggle to assert the right to a spiritual freedom. The war was for the sake of 'honesty and sincerity', said Magnus Hirschfeld, the leader of the homosexual movement in Germany, and against the Smokingkultur of Britain and France.[24] The focus of explanation for Germans was directed inward and toward the future: the war was a 'spiritual necessity' (eine innere Notwendigkeit). The British and the French, in turn, regarded the war as a struggle to preserve social values and civilization, precisely those values and ideals which the pre-war avant-garde had so bitterly attacked: notions of justice, dignity, civility, restraint, and 'progress' governed by a respect for law. The focus was social and historical. For them the war was a practical necessity, a sentiment captured by the British slogan 'business as usual'. As one British soldier put it in a letter to his parents on 1 October 1914:
'We are just at the beginning of the struggle I'm afraid, and every hour we should remind ourselves that it is our great privilege to save the traditions of all centuries behind us. It's a grand opportunity, and we must spare no effort to use it, for if we fail we shall curse ourselves in bitterness every year that we live, and our children will despise our memory.'[25]

The war, as it dragged on, was to put those sentiments and values, on both sides, fully to the test, and, to the surprise of some observers at the time, the values appeared, at least on the surface, to stand the test supremely well. Central to those values, after the gloss of heroism had quickly worn off, and the key to the four-year effort, especially in the enervating war on the western front, was the idea of 'duty', devoir, Pflicht. For the British and French, duty and devoir remained – with some variations, particularly among the French – essentially social concepts revolving around family, comrades, regiment, and country. In the letters and diaries of front soldiers it is in fact surprising how little attention is devoted to the self, to discussions of personal emotions such as courage, fear, hope, or anger. The social content of duty retained significance, it seems, even if it could often not be verbalized and had to remain a matter of reflex response – what Wilfred Owen called 'the silentness of duty'. For German soldiers, however, Pflicht involved a powerful spiritual component linked usually with a personal sense of honour (Ehre) and will (Wille). The regimental motto of the 24th Brandenburgers was 'Do more than your duty.' 'Things go beyond mere strength here', wrote one young soldier from the front. 'Here the impossible is made possible.'[26] Parallel war slogans also reveal these distinctions: beside 'For King and Country' one can set 'Gott mit uns'.[27]

If, however, duty continued to motivate most French and British soldiers to the very end, the element of fantasy – the destruction of objective meaning and the consequent internalization of experience – became increasingly noticeable among the keener imaginations already during the war, and then among ex-servicemen as a whole and much of the general public as well after the war. Some soldiers began to find, as Percy Jones noted on seeing Ypres in late 1915, 'something horribly fascinating about such appalling devastation'. For David Jones the 'wasteland' of the trenches became 'a place of enchantment'. And Herbert Read provides ample evidence that for him the war was a 'journey to the interior'. Despite his hatred of the army as an institution, by May 1918 he was considering staying on once the war was over: 'I like its manliness, the courage it demands, the fellowship it gives.'[28] In other words, the war, despite its destruction or, indeed, owing to its pervasive horror, had become an evocative force, a stimulus not to social creativity as much as to personal imagination and inwardness. The perception of the war among British and French soldiers began thus to move distinctly closer to the German view. The same was true of the public at home. '. . . we can turn to seek comfort,' wrote Robert Bridges, the poet laureate, in 1915, 'only in the quiet confidence of our souls; and we look instinctively to the seers and poets of mankind . . . .' For Paul Bourget the war by 1918 had destroyed all epiphenomena; all that remained was 'man himself', without adornment, without meaning.[29]

Ironically, French and British soldiers became during the war the 'frontier' personalities identified with the avant-garde and with German Kultur before the war; they were men who had experienced the very limits of existence, who had seen 'no man's land', who had witnessed horror, mutilation, agony, and who because of the very experience which made them 'heroes' lived on the edge of respectability and morality. Given the failure of the post-war era to produce the apocalyptic resolution promised by wartime propaganda, the whole social purpose of the war - the content of duty and devoir - began, in most cases in retrospect, to ring hollow. Since the tangible results of the war could never justify the cost, especially the emotional toll, disillusionment was inevitable, and soldiers in the post-war world withdrew from social activity and commitment into themselves. Only a minority bothered even to join veterans' associations. Relatively few were able to articulate their alienation, but the statistics speak loudly: of those unemployed between the ages of 30 and 34 in Britain at the end of the twenties, 80 per cent were ex-servicemen. The incidence of mental illness among veterans was also staggering.[30] 'The worst thing about the war generation of introspects,' said T.E. Lawrence, 'is that they can't keep off their blooming selves.' Aldington talked about the 'self-prisons' in which former soldiers had become trapped, and Graves wrote about his 'cage-mates'.[31]

Yet while former soldiers suffered from a high incidence of neurasthenia and sexual impotence, they realized that the war, in the words of José Germain, was 'the quivering axis of all human history'.[32] If the war as a whole had no objective meaning, then inevitably all human history was telescoped into each individual's experience; every individual was the sum total of history. Rather than being a social experience, a matter of external documentable reality, history was individual nightmare, or even, as Dada insisted, madness. One is reminded of Nietzsche's statement in 1889, on the very edge of his complete mental collapse, that he was 'every name in history'.[33]

The burden of having been in the eye of the storm and yet, in the end, of having resolved nothing, was excruciating. The result often was the rejection of social and political reality but at the same time the rejection even of the perceptual self - only dream and neurosis remained, a world of illusions characterized by a pervasive negativism. Fantasy became the mainspring of action, and melancholy became the general mood. Nous vivons une triste époque. . . Tout est foutu - Quoi? Tout un monde. . . Il fait beau, allons au cimetière. . . Carroll Carstairs ended his book A Generation Missing with the words: 'It's a weary world and the raspberry jam sent me from Paris is all finished now. . .'[34]

What was true of the soldiers was true with somewhat less immediacy and poignancy of civilians. The wailing of the saxophone, the frenetic dance steps of the Charleston, the obsession with flight, with moving pictures, and with 'stars' evidenced on a popular level these same tendencies, a drift towards irrationalism, dictators, and darkness. Of course bourgeois Europe tried to 'recast' itself, but it was capable of doing so only superficially. The modern temper had been forged; the avant-garde had won. It tried to fight new battles, but these turned out to be the same old battles, or in fact no battles at all because the infamous bourgeoisie now often bowed with polite, if silent, respect. The 'adversary culture' had become the dominant culture, irony and anxiety the mode and the mood, hallucination and neurosis the state of mind. 'The war is breaking us but is also reshaping us,' Marc Boasson had noted in July 1915. Fifteen years later Egon Friedell asserted emphatically: 'History does not exist.'[35]

Germany's recent past continues to hold an enormous fascination for western minds. Her poets, philosophers, and musicians make us marvel; her statesmen, politicians, and warriors make us wince. The west has in this century approached Germany with a lofty sense of moral and political superiority: Germany, so the thinking runs, should have become a liberal democracy because that is the political system all good people should want. Germany, however, did not follow a straight path in this direction, and therefore there must be something intrinsically evil in the German character. Yet, the Bismarckian Reich, and Weimar, and the Third Reich continue to cast their spell. What went wrong, we continue to ask, oblivious usually of our own conundrums, our own conflicts between Geist und Macht, spirit and law, our own 'disjunction of realms'. Pre-modern, quasi-feudal, anti-modern we call Germany, even barbaric in our fits of pique. It is time that we analysed our fascination. We might discover that we have sensed all along that Germany in the modern era has been more modern than we have had the courage to admit.

Notes

1. Colin Ross, Wir draussen (Berlin, 1916), p.11. I owe the first part of the title of my essay to a line in Robert Graves' 'Recalling War', reprinted in I.M. Parsons (ed.), Men Who March Away (London, 1965), pp. 171-2.
2. H.G. Wells, Mr. Britling Sees It Through (New York, 1916), p. 442.
3. Only recently in the suggestive work of Robert Wohl, The

Generation of 1914 (Cambridge, Mass., 1979) and Eric J. Leed, No Man's Land (Cambridge, 1979) have some truly notable advances been made by historians in discussing the impact of the war on sense and sensibility. This paper is much in debt to these two authors, as well as to Paul Fussell -- whom I class as a literary critic -- and his intriguing The Great War and Modern Memory (New York, 1975). Appropriately, James Joll's inaugural lecture at the London School of Economics in 1968, 1914:The Unspoken Assumptions (London, 1968) has had great resonance in the past decade and a half. Roland N. Stromberg's Redemption by War: The Intellectuals and 1914 (Lawrence, Ks., 1982) also deserves mention as an important recent contribution.

4.   H.A.L. Fisher, A History of Europe, 3 vols. (London, 1935), I, vii.
5.   'War Novels', The Morning Post, 8 April 1930.
6.   André Thérive, 'Les Livres', Le Temps, 27 December 1929.
7.   Arthur Schopenhauer, Ein Lesebuch, ed. Arthur and Angelika Hübscher (Wiesbaden, 1980), p. 168. Burckhardt's letter to Preen, 31 December 1870, in The Letters of Jacob Burckhardt, ed. and trans. Alexander Dru (London, 1955), p. 145. Theodor Mommsen, Reden und Aufsätze (1905; rpt. Hildesheim, 1976), p. 91.
8.   For a fuller treatment of this subject see my essay 'Of Birds and Cages: History and Historians in the Nineteenth Century', in J.E. Chamberlin and Sander L. Gilman (eds.), Degeneracy (New York: Columbia University Press, forthcoming).
9.   Jean Cocteau, Professional Secrets: An Autobiography, ed. Robert Phelps, trans. Richard Howard (New York, 1970), pp. 70-1.
10.   Matei Calinescu, Faces of Modernity (Bloomington, Ind., 1977), p.124.
11.   William Rubin (ed.), Pablo Picasso: A Retrospective (New York, 1980), p. 18.
12.   Quoted in John Russell, The Meaning of Modern Art (New York, 1981), p. 83.
13.   James D. Steakley, The Homosexual Emancipation Movement in Germany (New York, 1975), p. 49. See also George L. Mosse, 'Nationalism and Respectability: Normal and Abnormal Sexuality in the Nineteenth Century', Journal of Contemporary History, 17/2 (1982), pp. 221-46.
14.   Theobald von Bethmann Hollweg, Betrachtungen zum Weltkriege, 1. Teil: Vor dem Kriege (Berlin, 1919), pp. 142-3. Words like Selbstbehauptung, Genugtuung, and Integrität occur again and again in the memoir. See also Fritz Stern, 'Bethmann Hollweg and the War', in The Responsibility of Power, ed. Leonard Krieger and Fritz Stern (New York, 1967), p. 267.
15.   Karl Demeter, The German Officer-Corps in Society and State 1650-1945, trans. A. Malcolm (London, 1965), pp. 28-9.
16.   Eugen Diesel, in his introduction to Werner von Siemens, Lebenserinnerungen (1892; rpt. Leipzig, 1943), p. 3.
17.   Daniel Bell, The Cultural Contradictions of Capitalism (New York, 1976).
18.   Carl E. Schorske, Fin-de-siècle Vienna (New York, 1980).
19.   Fritz Stern, 'Capitalism and the Cultural Historian', in From Parnassus: Essays in Honor of Jacques Barzun, ed. Dora B. Weiner and

William R. Keylor (New York, 1976), pp. 209-24; 'Money, Morals, and the Pillars of Bismarck's Society', Central European History, III/1-2 (1970), pp. 49-72; and Gold and Iron (New York, 1977).

20. Thomas Mann, Betrachtungen eines Unpolitischen (Berlin, 1919), p.172. Friedrich Nietzsche, Die fröhliche Wissenschaft, quoted in Ronald Hayman, Nietzsche (New York, 1980), p. 237.

21. William Faulkner, in The New Republic, 20 May 1931, pp. 23-4.

22. Ford Madox Ford, Thus to Revisit (1921; rpt. New York, 1966), pp.136-7.

23. George Santayana, English Liberty in America, Character and Opinion in The United States, in The Works of George Santayana, VIII (New York, 1937), p. 120.

24. Magnus Hirschfeld, Warum hassen uns die Völker? (Bonn, 1915), pp.11,18.

25. Second Lieutenant A.D. Gillespie, in John Laffin (ed.), Letters From the Front 1914-1918 (London, 1973), p. 12.

26. Letter of Walter Harich, 14 October 1914, in Philipp Witkop (ed.), Kriegsbriefe deutscher Studenten (Gotha, 1916), p. 70.

27. These generalizations of course demand a fuller treatment which I hope to provide in a forthcoming book on the war and modernism.

28. The First World War Papers of Percy H. Jones, Imperial War Museum, London. David Jones, In Parenthesis (New York, 1961), p. x. Letter of 9 May 1918, in Herbert Read, The Contrary Experience (New York, 1973), p. 128.

29. Robert Bridges (ed.), The Spirit of Man (London, 1916), n.p. [iii]. Paul Bourget, in his preface to Raymond Jubert, Verdun (Paris, 1918), p.31.

30. Leed, No Man's Land, chapts. 5 and 6.

31. Lawrence, quoted in Wohl, Generation of 1914, p. 120. Richard Aldington, 'The Eaten Heart', quoted in A.C. Ward, The Nineteen-Twenties (London, 1930), p. xii. Robert Graves, 'The Marmosite's Miscellany', Poems (1914-26) (London, 1927), p. 191.

32. José Germain, in his preface to Maurice d'Hartoy, La Génération du feu (Paris, 1923), p.xi.

33. In a letter to Jacob Burckhardt, in The Portable Nietzsche, ed. and trans. Walter Kaufmann (New York, 1954), pp. 685-6.

34. Carroll Carstairs, A Generation Missing (London, 1930), p. 208.

35. Letter of 2 July 1915 to his wife, Marc Boasson, Au Soir d'un monde (Paris, 1926), p. 12. Egon Friedell, A Cultural History of the Modern Age, trans. C.F. Atkinson (New York, 1954), III, 467.

FOREIGN OFFICE VIEWS, GERMANY AND THE GREAT WAR

Zara Steiner

The British Foreign Office was staffed before and after the Great War by a tightly knit professional élite. Their general attitudes undoubtedly reflected common backgrounds, shared professional experiences and a strong organizational esprit de corps. It has been convincingly argued by James Joll in his seminal inaugural lecture, 1914: The Unspoken Assumptions, that it is these beliefs rather than the facts of the immediate diplomatic situation which determined the options chosen. This view has particular pertinence for the study of a generation which came to maturity in the late Victorian or early Edwardian era and whose basic assumptions were far from shattered by the experiences of war.

The same men served Lord Curzon as had advised Sir Edward Grey. Apart from retirement, there was little change in the diplomatic establishment until 1919 when newly created departments and fresh regulations introduced to recruit men serving in the armed forces helped to relieve an acute shortage of diplomatic staff. It was the relatively large intake of new men during the 1920s which was to alter the balance of the inter-war service. Officials and diplomats were not released for war service (Duff Cooper and David Scott were exceptions in this respect) and no entrance examinations were held while the war lasted. Despite a four fold increase in the number of men and women working in the war-time Foreign Office, the diplomatic establishment of some fifty to sixty men remained constant.

Continuity in personnel and service as well as political changes which first enhanced and then diminished the prestige of the Foreign Office strengthened the Office ethos. Officials in the early twenties looked back at the pre-war period, with some degree of exaggeration, as a kind of Golden Age before the exigencies of war and the elevation of Lloyd George had challenged the primacy of the department in making foreign policy. There were divisions between older and younger officials, the latter more open to the new currents of the war period, but these rarely resulted in any fundamental cleavage in an establishment proud of its past and anxious about its future.

The British decision to enter a continental war in 1914 continues to provoke historical debate.[1] The Foreign Office, for its part, had no doubts about the necessity for such a decision. Its senior officials had only feared that Britain might desert her friends in their hour of need. Paradoxically, it was Britain's imperial weakness which had brought the country back into Europe. Clashes with France and Russia, particularly the latter's advances into the Far East and Central Asia, intensified Foreign Office awareness of rivals in areas where Britain was strategically weak. The Americans, still 'Cousin Jonathan' rather than

'Uncle Sam, had begun to flex their hemispheric muscles. In retrospect, the relatively long and costly Boer War can be seen as one of those generational turning points. Lord Salisbury's confident belief that Britain could safely defend her interests gave way to fears that Britain's responsibilities were greater than her resources. First the Unionists and then the Liberals found the costs of remaining the world's strongest power politically difficult and the search for diplomatic relief became increasingly more imperative. The Hay-Pauncefote treaty, the Anglo-Japanese alliance, the Anglo-French entente and the Anglo-Russian conventions were all intended to improve challenged imperial positions. Each involved a British compromise and imposed restrictions on her freedom of action which Lord Salisbury would have judged unnecessary and dangerous.

The men appointed to senior positions in the pre-war Office shared the apprehensions of their political chiefs. With some exceptions (Thomas Sanderson, an old war horse who retired in 1905), officials welcomed the new arrangements though some proved highly unstable and the price paid was higher than the Office acknowledged. Anglo-French relations, for instance, were punctuated with continuing imperial disputes. The French demanded, in 1905 and in 1911, British support against Germany. Respective foreign secretaries found that, even without alliances, they were tied in a new way to France. Grey continued to believe that in a semi-committed position, Britain could still act as the mediator of Europe. But the margin was far narrower than he assumed. The entente could not be broken unless Britain was willing again to face isolation or dependence on Berlin. France could not be allowed to act independently lest British interests be compromised. In the later stages of the Agadir crisis, in a colonial quarrel between France and Germany which might well have been resolved without any European changes, the British found themselves contemplating a war against Germany. And if war came, it would be the French (and Russian) armies which would have to provide the military power which the British could not muster.

Britain's position vis-à-vis Russia was even more vulnerable. Some have argued that the whole of Britain's diplomatic revolution should be understood in terms of the government's concern for the safety of India. The Russian agreements had been concluded after the Japanese victory and the destruction of the Russian fleet yet it was an understanding which conceded much to the superior Russian position in Central Asia. The conventions allowed an escape route from the need to raise 100,000 troops to defend the Indian border against a possible (though not probable) Russian attack yet they did not provide an effective check against further Russian advances into Persia. Having achieved an arrangement in Central Asia which had eluded his successors and which was much applauded at the Foreign Office, Grey never really enjoyed its fruits. His permanent under secretaries, Charles Hardinge and Arthur Nicolson, and George Buchanan, the ambassador at St Petersburg, argued that the whole British future in Asia depended on the maintenance and extension of the entente. Yet it proved difficult to find an identity of interests even outside Central Asia and problems in the Balkans and in Asiatic Turkey repeatedly strained the London to St Petersburg line.

The pressure mounted as it became clear from 1911 that the Russians were recovering from the shock of defeat in war and revolution at home. Nicolson predicted that the Russians would soon re-assert and re-establish their prominent position in the Balkans. But it was the fear of Russian expansion where it touched British imperial interests which set off a Foreign Office debate over how Russia was to be treated. As became apparent during the Balkan wars, there was only limited room to manoeuvre. Grey could not move too far from St Petersburg; the fears of Russian expansion linked the men of the Grey generation to those of Lord Salisbury's. There was, moreover, the equally threatening possibility that Russia might come to terms with Germany, an alternative which Nicolson and Buchanan were constantly invoking even in 1914 when the probability was slight.

The concern with imperial dangers was only one thread in the net which bound Britain to France and Russia. Nervousness about British strength made the Foreign Office sensitive to all threats, real and imaginary. There were those already watching Japan and the United States. The power of the former was still underestimated and the new ententes eased dependence on Tokyo. Counting on ties of blood and sentiment, the Foreign Office could accommodate America's growing strength with irritation but without undue alarm and even with some degree of condescension. The case was otherwise with Germany. It was unfortunate, indeed, that German diplomacy began to shift just at the time when British statesmen were becoming far less confident. The contrast between those who believed Britain could face isolation, and those who feared it is brilliantly illustrated by comparing the views of Thomas Sanderson and Eyre Crowe in 1907. The former permanent under secretary assumed that Britain had the largeness of vision and strength to make allowances for a young and strident competitor anxious to make its mark in a British-dominated world. Crowe was far less confident about Britain's ability to deal with a powerful state backed by a great army and a natural appetite for expansion. He made the case for firmness rather than for appeasement.

The problem is to say when and why the Foreign Office establishment began to think in terms of a German threat. The sources are, I believe, independent of, though linked with, the imperial difficulties sketched earlier. Sanderson charted the change in Foreign Office attitudes as early as 1902; others commented on the new 'anti-German current' found at Whitehall. Though it was repeatedly argued that Germany's 'legitimate' imperial and naval ambitions should be recognised, she had never been warmly welcomed at either table. British sensitivity to the 'German challenge' stemmed from many sources. German diplomacy did change during these years. The turn to Weltpolitik was accompanied by a series of diplomatic blunders which raised the European fever charts all over Europe. The British, for their part, were far more nervous not only about their imperial boundaries but about their prestige and strength. It was frequently alleged, and not by foreigners alone, that British diplomats of the Edwardian period tended to be more nationalist and even xenophobic than their more cosmopolitan predecessors. German bullying which Sanderson could dismiss as bad manners (similar comments about American diplomats were not uncommon) came to be seen in a more sinister light. The Germans had the strength to threaten or cajole their neighbours; they could isolate Britain and certainly challenge her traditional role as the balancer of Europe. Britain's new friends capitalised on her fears and used the German card to their own advantage. London took equal alarm when Germany moved towards or against Britain's entente partners. The Agadir crisis was seen as a 'trial of strength' in which concession meant defeat. If Grey was less alarmist than his chief advisers, he too came to see in Germany's imperial thrusts dangers to the European status quo. It was but a short step from Agadir to Crowe's dismissal of the details of the Austro-Serbian dispute in July 1914 and his acceptance of the view that 'the bigger cause of Triple Alliance versus Triple Entente is definitely engaged'.[2]

There was no evidence at the time that Germany was intent on upsetting the European equilibrium. Even Crowe had argued that 'the great German design is in reality no more than the expression of a vague, confused and impractical statesmanship, not fully realising its own drift' rather than a bid for the hegemony of Europe.[3] But the possibility of one becoming the other came to haunt the Foreign Office for its power to check any shift in the European balance was extremely limited. 'I fully believe in the theory of Germany's intention, if possible, to dominate Europe to which we are the only stumbling block', Hardinge wrote from India to Nicolson in 1911.[4]

On the one hand, the Foreign Office had lost the confidence in British power which had permitted Salisbury to play the diplomatic game with free hands. It feared isolation and was very much on the defensive. On the other hand, there was no question that but Great Britain was a Great Power with the largest and richest empire in the world and with a trade and navy second to none. This ambivalence in Foreign Office thinking about British strength explains, in part, the complexities of Grey's diplomacy. The Foreign Office recognised that Germany was a competitor but in ways which were difficult to measure and to meet.

Both before and after the war, British power was measured in naval terms. It seems difficult to believe that either Admiral Fisher or his subordinates really thought that the German challenge could succeed. The threat, nevertheless, provided a useful means of extracting funds from an economically minded Cabinet. Foreign Office officials, too, were united in their belief that Britain had to maintain and demonstrate a substantial measure of naval superiority if she were to sustain her claim to world power. The officials deplored any reduction in naval resources, as was clearly demonstrated during the Mediterranean discussions of 1912. Grey and his advisers were 'blue water' men. They never thought that Britain's military intervention on the continent could alter the balance of land forces. The Office was to return to this position in 1919; the Navy, after all, continued to draw the largest share of the defence appropriations right up until 1939. Despite warnings in 1909 and 1911 that the Admiralty's strategy was outdated and even consular reports in 1912 that Germany could withstand a war-time blockade, the Office never questioned the inherited assumption that 'sea power was more potent than land power'. It was naval strength which preserved England from attack, linked the empire, made Britain 'alliance worthy' and enabled her, rightly or wrongly, to continue her European role despite her dependence on others for the maintenance of the balance of power.

If war came, Britain would become the economic powerhouse for her allies (as the United States was to be from a more secure base). She would use her navy to keep the islands free from invasion but also to supply her friends and cut Germany off from those essentials which might enable her to cancel out the British contribution. The major concern of the Liberal cabinet at the start of the war was with its impact on her financial and trading position.

It was only in 1912, when assured of the ententes and her impressive margin of naval supremacy, that a détente with Berlin was possible and then only because the real issues were not discussed. The Foreign Office had never ignored the European importance of the Russian entente despite concern with its imperial focus. Grey knew that a strong Russia in Europe, rather than being a way of strengthening the balance of power, might well upset it and provoke Germany to act. British fears for her own position had tightened the net around Germany, adding to the nervousness of those in Berlin who felt that time was running out for the German empire. The post-1911 resurgence of Russian power only diminished and did not increase Grey's freedom of action. It had equally negative effects on both Germany and Britain and assured the continuing division of Europe into two camps.

When the final crisis came, it became clear how far Grey had ceded to others the initiative in deciding the crucial questions of peace and war. Once the terms of the Austrian ultimatum became known, officials reacted in entirely predictable ways. 'Our attitude during the crisis will be regarded by Russia as a test,' Nicolson cautioned Grey, 'and we must be careful not to alienate her.'[5] Eyre Crowe was far more concerned with Paris; moral bonds had been created which could not be dissolved. But Crowe, too, warned of the adverse consequences of either a German victory over France and Russia or a German defeat without British participation. Grey, himself, raised the spectre of isolation in his somewhat tortured defence:

> The real reason for going into the war was that, if we did not stand by France and stand up for Belgium against this aggression, we should be isolated, discredited and hated; and there would be before us nothing but a miserable and ignoble future.[6]

There was a strong moral element in Foreign Office thinking but there was also the fear of isolation and the possible loss of a world position. 'The theory that England cannot engage in a big war means her abdication as an independent state. . .' Crowe wrote. 'A balance of power cannot be maintained by a State that is incapable of fighting and consequently carries no weight.'[7] Britain was too weak to abstain from a continental war but strong enough, with allies, to prevent Germany from assuming the leadership of Europe. No one considered that a war without British participation might have weakened both sides thereby preserving Britain's world position at little cost to the mother country. Nor, as in

1871, that the British could have absorbed a change in the European status quo without feeling that her imperial position was under challenge.

It was not only a question of British weakness but also a case of German strength. 'That Empire', Grey wrote in <u>Twenty-Five Years</u>, 'was now, after forty years of consolidation and growth, the most mighty Power, actually if not potentially, in the world. Was it to dread war? On the contrary, was it not possible that war might be another stage in its growth?'[8] It was assumed that Germany was responsible for the unleashing of the conflict; Austria was deemed incapable of independent action. Fritz Fischer has argued the case for a premeditated war. Grey, at the time, believed that he had been deliberately deceived: 'Jagow did nothing, Bethmann Hollweg trifled and the military intended war and forced it. It was a huge and gratuitous crime, the outcome of pride and ambition.'[9] Even before the outbreak of war, a distinction had been drawn between the 'doves' and the 'hawks' at Berlin. It was the militarists, the term used indiscriminately to cover both the military and the naval establishments, who had seized control and forced the decision for war. It was the Prussian element in the German empire that had set Germany on its aggressive course. This over-simplified view of German behaviour, contested at the time by Crowe, became a Foreign Office orthodoxy. Germany had to be decisively defeated to discredit the Prussian military caste; this belief explains Office opposition to a negotiated peace and coloured its discussions of British war aims.

Even when it became clear at the end of 1914 that the war might be a long one (one or two years according to Nicolson) officials insisted there could be no thinking about peace until Belgium was restored and the 'menace of Prussian militarism' eradicated. Nor as the war dragged on through 1915 and 1916 did Office opinion shift. Grey was more shaken than his advisers; he did not discount the possibility of American mediation and a compromise peace. In the spring of 1916, Charles Hardinge, returning from India to his old position, and Sir Francis Bertie, the ambassador in Paris, joined in their condemnation of House's efforts and Grey's 'pacifism'. Hopes for a decisive defeat of the Germans were repeatedly revived; at the start of the Somme offensive officials spoke optimistically of a military victory which would cure the Germans and convince them of the futility of their annexationist dreams.

1917 was a bleak year with few hopes of military relief and the Russian collapse and revolutions. Hopes were not high either that the American entry into the war (about which there were some mixed feelings in Office circles) would have any immediate impact in terms of food, shipping, or, above all, manpower. Hardinge had lost one son, Tyrrell, two. Peace moves were very much to the fore. Nonetheless, Arthur Balfour, the Coalition foreign secretary, Robert Cecil, his nephew and a powerful assistant secretary at the Office, and Hardinge, still refused to consider a status quo peace or, as Lloyd George suggested, a peace made at Russian expense. Even a compromise peace must be seen to discredit the Prussian militarists if the fighting was not to have been in vain. And the possibility of the Central Powers in those parts of Russia where they could replace the Russians as a threat to the Indian lifelines had little appeal for men who had been so long concerned with just that danger.

After Passchendaele, those officials concerned with peace negotiations were forced to abandon hope for a decisive military victory. They looked instead to a sufficient margin of success at least to convince the Germans that their annexationist goals would have to be dropped. During the first six months of 1918, even these modest aims seemed excessive, yet the Office continued to drag its feet with regard to peace feelers and outside mediation. And with the turning of the military tide, officials returned to the hardline position of 1916, demanding that the war be continued until militarism and the spirit of expansion were totally crushed. Cecil and Hardinge, not natural allies, were in agreement on this point and their advice was reinforced by a stream of memoranda from the newly organised Political Intelligence Department. Its German experts, all recruited via the Intelligence Bureau in the Department of Information in early 1918, J.W. Headlam-Morley, Edwyn Bevan and George Saunders (the former _Times_ correspondent in Berlin and Paris), were slow to believe that the Germans would admit defeat and actually sue for peace.

An examination of British war aims illustrates a parallel insistence that Prussian militarism should be crushed so that Germany would abandon her world ambitions. In one of the very first Office papers outlining British war aims, William Tyrrell and Ralph Paget wrote:

> The preparations for this war, the impulse to this war, the aggressive designs connected with this war are all traceable to Prussian enterprise and it is not extravagant to hope that a defeated Prussia will considerably lose its power for evil.[10]

The two men argued in 1916 that the Allies were not out to crush Germany but to impair the hegemony of Prussia through the loss of Alsace-Lorraine, Posen and Schleswig (the national principle was to be the guide for post-war settlements) and that the peaceful German elements in the south should be strengthened by the addition of German-speaking Austria.

Similar proposals were made by Louis Mallet, Tyrrell and George Clerk, a key figure in the War Department which became the centre of Office political activity from 1914, in January 1917 when the military prospects were poor. 'We are not out to destroy a nation of 70,000,000 people in the centre of Europe and we do not believe that if such were one of the objects of this war we should be able to achieve it.'[11] The writers wished to restrict German ambitions to what she had gained by 1870. Britain must fight until Belgian independence was restored and the German colonies divided among the Allies, an effective blow at the 'military domination of Prussia'. Britain was to be left to continue her existence as an overseas empire without continental ambitions.

When Headlam-Morley of the P.I.D. prepared his summary memorandum on the German settlement for the Office in the autumn of 1918, his conclusions did not differ markedly from those of his predecessors. Again, Germany in Europe would be considerably reduced with France, Belgium, Denmark and Poland as the main beneficiaries.

Headlam-Morley supported a union between Germany and German Austria, a proposal seconded by Lewis Namier, another P.I.D. member. Men working on the eastern territorial settlements saw in the creation of Czechoslovakia, Poland and other successor states from the remnants of the Habsburg Empire a way of satisfying the criteria of self-determination and creating a barrier between Germany and Russia.

Some of the ablest men in the Foreign Office spent the war years handling blockade issues. A few not only came to appreciate the central importance of the economic weapon as a tool of war but understood that economic factors would play a key role in determining diplomatic relations in the post-war period. Eyre Crowe and Victor Wellesley, the heads of the Consular and Commericial departments, struggled unsuccessfully to strengthen the Foreign Office hand with regard to overseas trade. Their efforts gained only limited backing in the Office and were defeated as the Board of Trade and Treasury extended their control over those areas where trade, finance and diplomacy crossed. Even those alerted to such issues were often inconsistent in their views. By the end of 1916, for instance, Germany was beginning to feel the effects of the blockade; the 'turnip winter' was one of the worst periods of the war for those in Germany. Though officials were convinced of the key importance of the blockade in winning the war, the prospect of starving Germany into submission was hardly an attractive one and could well prove to be a more elusive goal than military victory. Success on the high seas, after the introduction of the convoy system, did not force the Germans to admit defeat.

The Office had taken only a modest part in mainly French-inspired efforts to ward off an expected post-war German trade offensive. During the last 18 months of the war, Cecil, Hardinge and the economic experts in the P.I.D. took up another French idea in the hope that by denying the Germans post-war access to certain vital raw materials her leaders would be forced to the peace table. The proposals were dropped in the face of domestic, Dominion and American opposition and only served to convince Woodrow Wilson that the British were out to feather their own nest.

The Office did consider various economic means to encourage civilian unrest in Germany and improve British trade prospects abroad but it was also highly conscious that such efforts might prove self-defeating. There could be no 'liberal' Germany if the country was crippled economically or denied the hope of future recovery and prosperity. On the question of indemnities and reparations, for instance, the Foreign Office took a moderate line, circulating, with approval, Maynard Keynes' memorandum urging that allied claims against Germany be limited to civilian damage and suggesting a capital payment over a few years rather than a long-drawn-out tribute.

Opinions were divided about the future of the German state. If during the summer of 1918 many were determined to impose a crushing military defeat on Germany, by the time of the Armistice negotiations, men like Headlam-Morley had come to believe that a real revolution had taken place inside Germany and that unduly harsh armistice terms would result in a social revolution which would spread to France, Italy and even Britain. Hardinge and Crowe, on the other hand, defended harsh terms even at the price of social revolution for only a clear recognition of defeat would topple the Junker regime. During the Peace Conference too, while Headlam-Morley hoped that Germany was on the way to becoming a liberal and constitutional state and counselled moderation, Hardinge and Crowe exhibited only the most limited faith in the possibility of German redemption. Countering arguments that a harsh peace would drive Germany into Bolshevism, Crowe, both during and after the Conference, maintained that the Germans were using the menace of revolution to undermine the unity of the Allies.

This debate was never fully resolved. Though the Foreign Office believed in a war against German militarism, its fears of German power went beyond the Prussian élite. Germany's performance during the war and the narrowness of the Allied victory, dependent as it was on the American role and intervention, were convincing proof, if proof was needed, of the enormous strength of the German state. Nothing, Arthur Balfour told the cabinet, 'which we and our Allies can accomplish will prevent the Germanic powers. . . from remaining wealthy, populous and potentially formidable'.[12] Even shorn of its Prussian leadership (the Office pressed relentlessly for the extradition of the Kaiser and the punishment of 'war criminals'), the return of Germany to 'great power' status could only be postponed.

In terms of its declared war aims, the Foreign Office might well have been satisfied with the results of the peacemakers' efforts. Belgium had been restored, though, in the Foreign Office view, somewhat shabbily treated by the French. The German navy had been cut (the scuttling of the fleet at Scapa Flow solved this problem) and her colonial empire disbanded in a manner which accorded with British interests. Though German disarmament had not been a war aim, Lloyd George won the anti-conscription battle and accepted in return Foch's figure of a German army restricted to 100,000 troops. The Foreign Office delegation warned that the abolition of conscription would not end German militarism but the key instrument of Prussian power had been massively blunted.

It was when it came to the territorial settlements that the ambiguity of the Foreign Office position became most apparent. Germany could not be crushed and would regain its strength. It was, therefore, essential to keep her checked and yet to avoid reviving the spirit of revenge. Foreign Office experts wavered between 'stabilisation and security' (David Stevenson's apt phrase). If steps were taken to reduce Germany's capacity for threatening others, it was equally necessary to avoid new Alsace-Lorraines. The doctrine of self-determination, warmly embraced by the younger men at the Office and by the members of the P.I.D. (though sceptically viewed by Crowe) proved a less satisfactory guide to the problem of stability than the Wilsonian idealists had intended.

It had been assumed at the Foreign Office that France would gain Alsace and Lorraine but there was little sympathy for French demands for independent or autonomous Rhenish states or even for a demilitarised Rhineland. The compromise Clemenceau accepted was considered something of a French triumph particularly as Lloyd George was loath to have British troops participate in occupation duties. In the light of later

American and then British behaviour, however, the French received less than might have been thought. In 1919 and again in 1921 and 1924, Eyre Crowe was to return to the idea of a British guarantee of the French position though always with qualifications. None of his suggestions commanded political support.

The future of the Saar proved another source of Foreign Office debate. Lloyd George determined the final terms; the details were worked out by Headlam-Morley who had in pre-conference days suggested that the Saar coalfields be transferred to the French. Crowe, on the other hand, was less than enthusiastic about the proposed division between economic and administrative control and exceedingly doubtful about the role reserved for the League. He was to have similar objections to the arrangements made for Danzig, East and West Prussia. The League solution, he believed, was 'a house of cards which could not stand'. Already at Paris, there was a division between the sceptics, Balfour (and later Curzon), Hardinge, Crowe and Tyrrell, and that small group which included Cecil, Eustace Percy, Harold Nicolson and Esmé Howard who thought that the League might be something more than an enlarged Concert of Europe.[13]

Foreign Office reluctance to extend Britain's continental obligations did not prevent relatively junior members of the Foreign Office delegation from taking an active part in the creation of new states and boundaries in central and southern Europe. Headlam-Morley, A. Leeper, H. Nicolson, E.H. Carr and others left their mark on the final treaty. The preparatory work for the conference suggested considerable support for the principles of self-determination despite considerable fears about the disappearance of the Habsburg empire. But though at Paris, these officials strongly supported claims for the newly created states, they were not always in agreement as to how their interests were best promoted and particularly with regard to Poland, pulled in opposite directions. British interests were not only political but commercial and financial. Ethnic claims had to be balanced by the British interest in stability (hence the disputes over Danzig, the Polish corridor and Upper Silesia) and future markets. Ideally, officials would have preferred some kind of Danubian Confederation which would have served both purposes but neither these hopes nor support for an Anschluss could be translated into practical politics. The new boundaries were largely shaped in accordance with French wishes; even within these limits, British aims and actions were often inconsistent. The lack of central direction, much resented by the Office staff, only underlined the ad hoc nature of many of the final compromises.

Critiques of the individual territorial clauses were mild compared with the denunciation of the economic and financial provisions of the treaty. Lloyd George had been caught up in the pre-election mood. It was more than a grass roots movement; the 'Germany must pay' slogans were backed by the Federation of British Industries, the Chambers of Commerce, the Institute of Bankers and even that liberal journal, The Economist. The prime minister shares the blame with the British delegates on the Reparation Commission for the failure to fix a workable reparations sum in Paris. The Foreign Office, however determined to limit the power of a future Germany, had never argued for its economic enfeeblement. In Paris, its members were excluded from the German reparations discussions but many were vocal in their condemnation of the suggested figures which were dismissed as unrealistic and damaging to European recovery. Headlam-Morley, who was later to criticise sharply Keynes' Economic Consequences of the Peace, warned that if Germany were ruined there would be no reparations at all. Harold Nicolson found the clauses 'immoral and senseless' and 'quite impossible to execute'. Others predicted that, deprived of hope, Germany would turn to Bolshevism or to an alliance with the Russians. There was little respect for either Lord Cunliffe or Lord Sumner; their actions confirmed Office opinion that political appointees should not draw up peace terms. Officials took an equally negative view of the high reparation payments at first demanded from Bulgaria and Austria. In each case, fears for the future viability of the states concerned as well as hopes for future trade dictated a more lenient approach to financial questions than to territorial settlements.

Members of the Foreign Office delegation left Paris, fatigued, disgusted and generally disgruntled. Some had come with high hopes for a new Europe and had their illusions badly shaken. Their number, however, was relatively small. The great majority of the Foreign Office delegation was possibly more disturbed by the way the peace was made than by the actual terms of the settlement. The Foreign Office had failed to regain its position at Paris; relations with 10 Downing Street were to deteriorate further as Lloyd George began to bully the new foreign secretary, Lord Curzon, who even at his best was a difficult chief to serve. Changes within the Foreign Office strengthened the positions of those who had pressed for a harsh treaty. They were not averse to the fact that the Versailles settlement imposed strategic and economic restraints on Germany which went well beyond the destruction of its Prussian military élite. It served British as well as French interests that the treaty should delay and even damage Germany's capacity to return to its pre-war strength and that the French should be given the opportunity to shift the power relations between the two continental states.

The debate about Germany continued. Lord Curzon had little confidence in the new German leaders. 'You cannot like them, but you do not know whether your feelings are those of distrust or positive dislike', he told his colleagues.[14] Crowe, now permanent under secretary, deplored Treasury and Downing Street tendencies to substitute an entente with Germany for that with France. He and Sydney Waterlow, head of the Central department, dismissed warnings from Berlin that the harsh disarmament and reparations clauses would bring down the German government and assure the triumph of Bolshevism. The senior men agreed that 'the leopard does not change his spots'. Crowe spelled out these views when contesting a General Staff memorandum of 1920 arguing that the policy of 'pin-pricks' and occupation would revive the spirit of German militarism and nationalism.

> What I think is false is the conclusion that with the cessation of these clauses, the military and nationalist spirit will disappear. I think that on the contrary, when Germany returns to more normal conditions there will be a

steady growth of the feeling, traditional in German thought, that national spirit and military strength are the pride of a healthy and self-confident state. There is likely to be a hearkening back to the idea of general national service under arms and the more normal and prosperous the German state, the stronger will become that feeling.[15]

There was little question in Crowe's mind of the need for eternal vigilance.

What the Foreign Office feared were the many sources of future tension created by the peace treaty which would necessitate continuing British intervention on the continent. The Foreign Office would have preferred a self-regulating settlement which might have replaced the old balance of power, leaving Britain free to look to her imperial concerns. If the Treaty had weakened Germany, it had also strengthened Britain. Her empire had been enlarged, the mandates for Palestine and Mesopotamia with its vast oil reserves, and the changes in the Persian Gulf created a new and potentially rich sphere of influence. Lord Curzon could well boast that the 'British flag never flew over a more powerful or a more united empire'.[16] The latter had come to the defence of the mother country; British naval supremacy had paid handsome dividends. But neither in 1919 nor in subsequent years did the Foreign Office hierarchy ignore the signs of British weakness which, as before the war, made it difficult to sustain a world role.

The empire was far less stable than that arch-imperialist, Lord Curzon, proclaimed. Civil war in Ireland and rumblings elsewhere were already over-taxing Britain's much reduced military resources. If British fears about the spread of Bolshevism in Europe began to subside when the Poles turned the Red Army back before Warsaw, the strong anti-Bolshevik feeling at the Foreign Office did not abate. There was again the haunting spectre of a German-Russian agreement (Tyrrell thought Rapallo 'the most important event' since the Peace Treaty) and revived Russian imperialism now dressed in Bolshevik clothing. The Office remained fearful of the Russian threat to India's internal security and there were clashes south of the Caspian, in northern Persia and in Turkestan. Lord Curzon was soon fighting familiar battles.

Nor were the Russians the only competitors in sight. The battles with the French in Turkey and the Middle East were as fierce, if not fiercer, than imperial clashes before the war. At best the Ottoman inheritance was a mixed blessing and the rise of Mustapha Kemal inflicted a series of defeats on the British which led to Lloyd George's fall and gave to Lord Curzon his one great diplomatic success at Lausanne. Across the Atlantic, the difficulties with the United States could not be ignored for they touched Britain at her most vulnerable points, her economy, her Far Eastern empire and her naval strength. Though war with America was unthinkable, the acceptance of naval parity had deeply worrying implications for an Edwardian generation. 'If it became widely known that we had abandoned the One-Power Standard our diplomatic postition throughout the world would be weakened', Mr. Churchill wrote in 1922, 'and it would indicate to the Dominions that a new centre had been created for the Anglo-Saxon world.'[17]

There was yet one other sign of weakness which alerted the Foreign Office to the dangers of complacency. Some officials and diplomats undoubtedly shared Edward Grey's pre-war belief that Britain was living through a long social revolution. By 1920, the brief post-war boom was over; unemployment figures soared to over two million. The subject was to become the dominating political issue. Even before 1921 when these views spread to the whole political spectrum, the Office establishment argued that the economic rehabilitation of Germany and Austria was an essential ingredient for a British recovery. The prosperity of Europe, as well as its stability, would depend on the re-integration of Germany into the European system despite all the attendant dangers.

The Office did not wish to police Europe. The continental commitment, in military terms, had been too costly, and as had already been recognised in 1918-19 had become politically unacceptable. There was little sympathy at the Office with the isolationists who thought that Britain could afford to turn its back on Europe or even with those, like Maurice Hankey and at times, Lord Curzon, who would have preferred a strong imperial orientation. There were, moreover, few 'Atlanticists' in the post-war Office. It was not Eyre Crowe alone who believed that Paris was much closer and far more reliable than Washington, D.C. Nor was there really much sympathy, with but few exceptions, with the new League structure either as a guarantor of the European status quo or as an appropriate agency for future disarmament.

This left the French. During the early twenties, the Office was far more sympathetic to a French guarantee than its political masters. Yet Anglo-French relations reached their nadir point in these very years. It was not just a question of personalities and the clashes between Lloyd George, Lord Curzon and the French leaders, above all, with Poincaré, 'the uncrowned king in the Pantheon of French bêtes noires'.[18] There were continual quarrels over Germany, central Europe, Turkey, Syria, Palestine, Tangier and the League which drove the two governments apart. Even that Francophile, Eyre Crowe, refused to consider a guarantee or an alliance without a substantial quid pro quo.

> The French are clearly very difficult to please... I believe they want the alliance against Germany. But when it comes to dropping her anti-British policy in the rest of the world, France, true to her traditional practice, wants to see her support in each field in return for separate rewards. Much as I am in favour of a comprehensive understanding with France to which Great Britain should contribute in the shape of an alliance against German unprovoked aggression, I should hesitate to recommend it in such terms.[19]

'Or at this time', Curzon added. French behaviour at the Washington Conference was almost the last straw. The Admiralty was busy discussing the French submarine menace; the Committee of Imperial Defence its bombing potential against London. The best the Foreign Office could do was to back that wing of the Cabinet pointing to the disastrous consequences of a breach with Paris. When, once again, Crowe tried and produced a 43-page memorandum supporting an alliance, he tied the offer to settlement of quarrels with Paris. And when at Cannes in January 1922, Lloyd George made his alliance bid, the terms proved too high for French acceptance. The Office had worked itself into a paradoxical position. It believed that France would remain a second-rate power and that Germany would surge ahead. It knew that the French would not change their attitude towards Berlin unless certain of British underwriting, yet Britain would not offer a guarantee or alliance unless France changed its tune.

Lord Esher wrote to Maurice Hankey on 7 March 1918:

> You have got in the Office men who have all their lives been imbued with the doctrines of Vienna. They are the oldest of old bottles, and how on earth do you suppose that the extra-ordinary new wine - with a Bolshevist flavour - is going to stand being corked up by men with that mentality?[20]

Esher underestimated the strength of those factors which had already forced the Office to recognise that Britain could no longer play its nineteenth-century role. Nor could the new forces be ignored at Paris. Nonetheless, its most articulate members did believe that Britain was strong enough to preserve the balance of power in Europe and its empire overseas. This view was held despite the fact that Britain had used first France and Russia and then the United States to maintain that dual role and was not fundamentally stronger in 1919 than it had been in 1914. Few at the Foreign Office believed that Britain need relinquish its position in either sphere. Throughout the twenties, the Office held to its belief that Britain could hold the balance between France and Germany, despite the hostility of Bolshevik Russia and American abstention. This confidence depended on a resurgence of British strength which proved illusory and a belief in German restraint which some senior officials strongly doubted. Britain was still defending a weak position with old tools. The war had not really shattered inherited assumptions.

Notes

1.   J.A.S. Grenville, 'Foreign Policy and the Coming of War' in D. Read (ed.) Edwardian England (London, 1982), K. Wilson, 'British Power in the European Balance 1906-1914' in D. Dilks (ed.) Retreat from Power (London, 1981) vol. 1 and his forthcoming book; K. Hildebrand, 'Zwischen Allianz und Antagonismus Das Problem Bilateraler Normalität in Den Britisch-Deutschen Beziehungen des 19. Jahrhunderts (1870-1914)' in H. Dollinger, H. Gründer, A. Hanschmidt (eds.) Weltpolitik Europagedanke Regionalismus (Münster, 1982).
2.   G.P. Gooch and H. Temperley, British Documents on the Origins of the War, XI, no. 101, minute by Eyre Crowe. Cited hereafter B.D.
3.   B.D. VII, Appendix A.
4.   F.O. 800/92, Hardinge to Nicolson, 29 March 1911.
5.   B.D. XI, No. 101.

6.   Lord Grey, Twenty-Five Years (London, 1925) vol. II, pp. 15-16.
7.   B.D. XI, no. 369.
8.   Grey, Twenty-Five Years, vol II, p. 24.
9.   F.O. 800/65, Grey to Sir R. Rodd, 6 March 1915.
10. Cab. 29/1 quoted in V. Rothwell, British War Aims and Peace Diplomacy, 1914-1918 (Oxford, 1971) p. 43.
11. Cab. 16/36, quoted in Rothwell, op, cit. p. 47.
12. Cab. 29/1/7, memorandum by Balfour.
13. See the interesting piece by Esmé Howard, 'British Policy and the Balance of Power', American Political Science Review, xix, 2. I owe this reference to Brian McKercher.
14. Cab. 32/9 (3) p. 26, 5 Oct. 1923.
15. F.O. 371/4757, 14 November 1920.
16. Hansard, House of Lords, vol. 32, col. 162, 18 Nov. 1920.
17. Cab. 9 (22), Conclusion 2, 1922. I owe this reference to Professor Donald Watt.
18. J. Douglas Goold, 'Lord Hardinge as Ambassador to France and the Anglo-French Dilemma over Germany and the Near East, 1920-1922', The Historical Journal, vol. 21, 4, p. 923.
19. F.O. 371/6995, minute by Crowe, 14 June 1921 and addition by Lord Curzon.
20. Hankey Mss., Lord Esher to Lord Hankey, 7 March 1918.

MASS CULTURE AND THE STATE IN GERMANY, 1900-1926

Robin Lenman

German efforts to limit the supposedly fearful effects of mass culture did not begin in earnest until after the turn of the century. They were preceded by a lengthy and largely unsuccessful attempt in the 1890s to broaden the obscenity paragraph (184) of the Criminal Code which finally came to a halt in the spring of 1900 amid a storm of protest from artists, writers and other sections of the educated public.[1] For the Reich and Bavarian governments in particular, this so-called Lex Heinze episode was a traumatic experience, and discouraged ministers for a long time from supporting any new initiative which might be construed as an attack on artistic and literary freedom. Nevertheless, two important ideas emerged from it: firstly, that legal action might be desirable against material which was felt to be harmful or offensive without being actually obscene; secondly, that publications which, for political or other reasons, could not be denied to adults, might still need to be withheld from young people. These notions became crucial in the campaign against mass culture which got under way in the decade and a half before the First World War and continued into the mid-1920s.

For present purposes, a working distinction needs to be drawn between 'mass' culture on the one hand and 'popular' culture on the other. Whereas the latter might be seen as primarily participatory, or at any rate responsive to influence or modification by those involved with it, the former has been defined as 'an impersonal commodity of the masses',[2] made possible by industrial methods of manufacture and distribution, and stereotyped for consumption by a passive, anonymous and undifferentiated (usually urban) public. From the legislator's point of view, these differences were important. In 19th-century Germany a wealth of regulations, most of them embodied in the police codes of the individual states, existed to control popular culture: singing, dancing, puppet-shows and öffentlichen Lustbarkeiten of all kinds. There were even attempts, like the Bavarian Government's campaign against Hasenfeldtreiben in the 1890s,[3] to suppress certain forms of it altogether. But the products of mass culture, especially pulp literature and the cinema, required other control mechanisms than those of the traditional police state, including in the long run even a degree of self-regulation.

Considering the extent of German influence on early American comics,[4] the comic strip seems to have played a surprisingly insignificant role in Germany itself before the First World War. But other forms of low-grade literature or Schund (trash) were immensely popular, although the industry had had to adjust to a major shift in demand in the last years of the 19th century.[5] The 1870s and 1880s had been a boom period for the serialised Hintertreppenroman, usually

51

printed in a hundred or more instalments and peddled to servants up the back stairs. Cheap and crudely produced, its content was either primitive fiction or sensationalised accounts of establishment catastrophes like the Mayerling affair or the death of Ludwig II. But by the late 1880s the serial's popularity was declining in favour of the single-story Groschenheft, with increasing emphasis after 1900 on the one-hero Western or thriller series. Modelled on the American dime novel, the Groschenheft was more attractively produced and more expensive (20-25 pf., despite the name) than the older serial, and was probably read by middle-class adolescents as well as the working class.[6] Although contemporary circulation figures seem to have been based largely on guesswork, and sometimes on deliberate scare-mongering, this kind of publishing could be highly profitable, with entrepreneurs like Adolf Eichler of Dresden, who bought the rights for the hugely successful Nick Carter and Buffalo Bill series, making considerable fortunes. In 1913, the Reich Government calculated that one of the most famous serials, Der Scharfrichter von Berlin had sold 2,200,000 copies, while the Nick Carter and Buffalo Bill stories could achieve sales of 80,000 copies a week.[7]

The cinema was equally popular, developing rapidly from a mere variety attraction in the 1890s into a major form of mass entertainment in its own right.[8] 1907 saw the first attempt to form a national distribution network, and by the outbreak of war there were 2446 permanent cinemas in the Reich. There was also a growing production industry, mainly concentrated in Berlin, although the majority of films shown before 1914 were imported. By about 1909, intellectuals and serious actors were becoming increasingly interested in the medium, and its artistic and educational potential was gradually being recognised.[9] But the founder of Munich's first cinema, the Bavaria Bioscop, was a former book-pedlar,[10] and from at least as early as the turn of the century films were inevitably being denounced as the ultimate form of Schund. 'The seamstress who loves a count, the gruesome secrets of a castle, are just as interesting today as before', wrote the author of a pioneering sociological study. 'But people no longer have enough leisure to wait for the hundred instalments . . . In a cinema show one can live through the same sensations for a few pence in a short time'.[11] Before long the cinema had also taken over the pulp-book heroes, Nick Carter, Buffalo Bill and eventually even Fantômas, whose films (unlike the original serials) almost certainly reached Germany before the war.[12]

Although educated disapproval of popular literature and entertainment already had a long history, it was intensified in the late 19th century by concern about the growth of cities, Socialism and modernity in general, and by a variety of biological anxieties. After 1900, trash in its various forms was increasingly perceived as a threat to Germany's military strength and racial vitality. These new fears merged with longstanding assumptions about the effects of Schund on immorality, crime, suicide and juvenile problems of all kinds: teachers' experience, wrote the Bavarian Interior Minister in November 1910, showed that trash 'over-stimulates the imagination (of young people), takes away their sense of truth and reality, makes them inattentive and idle, coarse and violent';[13] and similar views were expressed, often in much more extreme language, by churchmen, bourgeois politicians and morality campaigners all over the Reich. The S.P.D. was almost equally disapproving (the Socialist Münchener Post described pulp literature as 'printed meths');[14] mainly out of general cultural conservatism[15] rather than from any idea that Schund, with its glorification of violence, escapism and implicit acceptance of a hierarchical social order, might actually tend to stabilise existing society and lubricate the working of the capitalist system.

The post-1900 campaign against trash differed in certain respects from the anti-obscenity crusade of the 1890s. Whereas the latter had become closely identified with the Catholic Church and the Centre Party, the former had a somewhat broader following, attracting men like Georg Kerschensteiner[16] (who could relate the appeal of Schund to the dullness of school) and other liberal figures. There was some awareness, too, in the wake of the Lex Heinze fiasco, that radical proposals which seemed to threaten the arts were likely to be counter-productive, if only because of governments' nervousness about adopting them. But the trash and obscenity debates resembled each other in that both were bedevilled by intractable problems of definition. Many conservatives made no distinction at all between trash and pornography, and lumped both of them together with 'unpatriotic', Socialist and freethinking literature of all kinds. (They were unconcerned, of course, about the possibly harmful effects of contemporary militarist and racist propaganda.) Attitudes to popular fiction were thoroughly unclear, and the case of Karl May demonstrated that one man's trash was another man's adventure story.[17] Even distinctions between Schund and art were problematical, given the European avant-garde's current fascination with 'low' culture (in 1914, Apollinaire described Fantômas as being 'from an imaginative point of view one of the richest works in existence'),[18] and conventional rejection of both it and advanced modernism was a classic example of 'the middle against both ends'.[19]

Germany's press legislation also caused formidable problems. On the one hand, not only newspapers but all other printed material, as well as photographs and later even films, were defined as 'press products' and therefore protected by the Press Law of 1874. On the other, many newspapers could easily be equated with Schund. From about 1870 onwards, innumerable small scandal-sheets had come into being, feeding on sensation and competing with the serial-publishers by printing 'horror-novels aimed at the dregs of the population'.[20] They were later superseded by large-circulation illustrated dailies which offered a similar combination of ghoulish news coverage and low-grade fiction, but on a much greater scale. Whereas the scandal-sheets had been vulnerable in practice to various forms of police harassment, the so-called 'boulevard papers' were virtually immune to attack, taking full advantage of the safeguards created in 1874, the practical difficulty of controlling newspapers, and the fact that in several states press offences had to be tried by jury. Press freedom soon became an absolute noli me tangere for large sections of German society and an inescapable fact of life for the authorities. Even Bismarck was wary of tampering with the Press Law,[21] and detailed case studies of controversial papers like Simplicissimus show that after 1900 governments were highly reluctant to risk confrontations with the press, except in conditions of national emergency justifying a state of siege.[22]

By about 1908, however, regardless of the difficulties, the anti-Schund campaign was gathering momentum on several fronts. Booksellers organised boycotts of their more unscrupulous (or perhaps prosperous) colleagues, while reform societies and publishers searched for 'acceptable' forms of light and juvenile fiction. As Rudolf Schenda has pointed out,[23] the commercial incentives were considerable, and large quantities of Schund-substitutes reached the market before the war, ranging from Reclam's slot-machine editions of the classics to the most dubious kind of patriotic-militarist adventure story. Under pressure from the campaigners, the authorities also became more active. 1908/9 brought decrees in several states encouraging school boycotts of pulp-literature outlets, and offensive material was banished from the state railways.[24] There was also renewed use of the 'gross mischief' clause (360/11) of the Criminal Code against press products. This tactic, which enabled prosecutors to evade the jury, had caused an outcry in the 1890s, and in conjunction with so-called 'flying jurisdiction' had been a serious hazard.[25] But 'flying jurisdiction' had been virtually abolished in 1902, and it was probably symptomatic of a changing climate of opinion that the use of Paragraph 360/11 on a modest scale against Schund seems to have gone largely unopposed.

Yet administrative and minor judicial measures taken at state or local level failed to satisfy the reform lobby and were inadequate to deal with an industry which had become national and indeed international in scope. Both at this time and later, the cultural, confessional and until 1918 also legal (or at least procedural) diversity of the German states was as serious an obstacle to controlling Schund as the problems of definition already described. As a result of the international treaty signed in Paris in May 1910,[26] a central police office was eventually set up in Berlin to co-operate with foreign governments and also to assist the individual German prosecuting authorities in coordinating their activities. But it had already become clear that new national legislation was needed, and the Reich Government finally presented a Bill to the Bundesrat in April 1913.[27] It took the form of a modest addition to the Reich Trade Regulations prohibiting the display of pictures and other publications in shops or public places 'in a manner liable to cause offence by morally endangering youth'. One of its objectives was to remove the anomaly by which the police could vet the wares of street pedlars but not those of kiosks and other fixed outlets through which, by this time, most low-grade literature reached the public. But its most interesting feature was its strictly limited scope; since no attempt was made to ban material that was not obscene, and the Introduction explicitly denied any intention to attack art or literature, or to interfere with 'every adult person's freedom to choose his own reading-matter as he likes'.[28] This was significant for the future. In the meantime, artists and writers were nevertheless quick to denounce the proposed 'shop-window law' as a new Lex Heinze, and a considerable protest campaign was building up by the time the Bill's progress was halted by the outbreak of war.

The events of July 1914 also put paid to proposed Reich legislation on the cinema. Here, however, rather more had been achieved by the individual states. This was possible because, although films in themselves were deemed to be 'press products', protected by the 1874 Press Law, the projection process could be regarded as a kind of performance: a potential threat to public order subject (like the theatre) to the police-state licensing and censorship controls permitted by the Trade Regulations and the police codes. A film censorship office was created by the Berlin police in 1906 and by 1914 was handling 1½ million metres of film a year,[29] and similar systems came into being in Bavaria, Brunswick, Württemberg and other states. Yet it was some time before censorship rulings in capital cities like Berlin and Munich became binding in the provinces, and in 1914, despite the acknowledged efficiency of the Alexanderplatz office, there was no question of films passed in Berlin being automatically accepted outside Prussia. Despite the film industry's strong interest in unified control, therefore, both general censorship criteria and important practical questions like the regulation of children's performances varied from state to state; and there were also signs of the South German suspicion of Weltstadt tolerance which was to complicate both the film and anti-Schund legislation of the 1920s.

Much more work needs to be done on the relationship between war, propaganda, militarism and mass culture. What seems clear, however, is that the First World War gave a strong stimulus to the German cinema and to certain branches of popular publishing, and further complicated the issue of legal control. While state of siege regulations allowed the military authorities to clamp down summarily on material considered to be subversive or demoralising, an orgy of war-publishing took place and large quantities of sadistic and racist Kriegsschund seem to have been tolerated.[30] The still comparatively weak German film industry benefited from the elimination of foreign competition and eventually also from much more positive government interest in the cinema.[31] By the summer of 1916, after serious initial problems, nationalist businessmen like Hugo Stinnes and Alfred Hugenberg had become actively involved in using film to enhance Germany's foreign image, and over the next eighteen months both the civilian authorities and the High Command (particularly Ludendorff) also became increasingly enthusiastic. December 1917 finally saw the formation of the Universum Film Aktiengesellschaft (UFA), a collaborative venture between business and the state designed to promote film propaganda while the war lasted and to secure a powerful international position for German film-makers after hostilities had ended.

The moral disequilibrium of the immediate post-war months and the accompanying spate of exploitative films and pulp-literature encouraged a vigorous revival of the anti-Schund movement and was not without an effect on the German National Assembly. Therefore, although Article 118 of the Weimar Constitution guaranteed freedom of expression and rejected censorship in general (stage censorship had already been abolished in November 1918), it explicitly sanctioned future laws to control the cinema and protect young people against 'dirt and trash'.

The speed with which a film censorship Bill was introduced reflected both the apparent urgency of the problem and the high degree of consensus among the main political parties.[32] The debates concentrated mainly on technicalities, and above all on the issue of centralisation versus Land control, since the Württemberg government representative's claim that 'The Swabian people is fighting for the soul of its youth'[33] reflected serious concern in Southern Germany about possibly over-permissive attitudes in the Reich capital. Although it created a national censorship system, the Film Law of 12 May 1920 was designed to allay these fears by allowing Land appeals against its rulings and permitting extra local safeguards for the protection of young people. Censorship offices were to be set up at the main centres of the film industry (in effect, Berlin and Munich), with an appeals tribunal in Berlin. In general, the Law set out to be as modern and enlightened as possible, not only creating panels of lay censors from the fields of education, the arts and the film industry, but even stipulating that their official colleagues should have a 'pedagogical and artistic' background.

Although political film censorship was explicitly renounced by the 1920 Law, and in general the German system seems to have been no more illiberal in operation than those of France or Britain, some serious controversies inevitably arose (for example over Eisenstein's 'Battleship Potemkin'), and helped to make the process of devising a law against pulp literature even more contentious. Public concern about high juvenile crime-rates, inner-city gang warfare[34] and other problems made it impossible to evade the issue, yet all the old questions of definition remained unanswered and political consensus was almost totally lacking. When the Reich Interior Ministry finally presented a Bill in 1925, the Right and the Catholic Parties strongly supported it, while the Left remained firmly opposed: the S.P.D. more in sorrow than in anger, the Communists stridently exploiting the whole issue to denounce capitalist cultural exploitation, the corrupting effect of militarist and racist propaganda and the hypocrisy of the bourgeois press.[35] The Liberals were characteristically divided, although Theodor Heuss of the D.D.P. made one of the most impressive speeches in favour of the Bill.[36] Outside Parliament, a galaxy of intellectuals attacked what they saw as yet another assault on art and literature. There was also, once again, the problem of balancing Länder and Reich, with fears of cosmopolitan decadence on the one hand and of regional bigotry on the other. In its final form, the Law of 18 December 1926 inevitably amounted to a compromise. Land ministries and Youth Offices (but not individuals, associations or churches) could apply for publications to be placed on a national list of items to be restricted from display and from distribution to young people under 18, although the 1913 principle was upheld that adults were free to read what they liked. Applications were to be considered in Berlin and Munich by panels rather similar to those created by the Film Law, with an Oberprüfstelle in Leipzig for appeals. Although the total exemption of newspapers (everything, therefore, from the sensational dailies to Der Stürmer) left a serious loophole in practice, this was on the whole a worthy attempt to balance freedom of expression with the interests of youth, and it was not without influence on the West German legislation of the 1950s and 1960s.[37] In the late Weimar period, however, compared with the immensely destructive effects on young people of political extremism and the Depression, its benefits can only have been marginal.

* * * * * *

Approaches to the 'problem' of mass culture often showed little understanding of the limitations of popular literacy, the nature of popular or juvenile taste or the aridity of urban life and conventional schooling. Like the anti-masturbation campaigns of the 18th and 19th centuries,[38] the struggle against 'dirt and trash' was fuelled by moral hysteria and far-fetched assumptions about human behaviour. Just as pornography and eroticism were believed to threaten Germany's libidinal economy by undermining the family and diverting energy away from healthy nationalism,[39] the unbridled fantasy stimulated by Schund was blamed for juvenile delinquency, social indiscipline and even 'degeneration'[40]. Attempts to combat this peril can perhaps be seen as part of a much broader movement in the early 20th century to come to grips with and control an emerging mass society: in the name not only of traditional culture and authoritarian-national values but also, especially after the First World War, of deceptively progressive-sounding notions of 'rationalisation', 'social hygiene' and Volksgesundung.[41] Yet the concrete outcome was surprisingly tame: after 1900, no further legislative action was taken against obscenity, while the 1926 Schundgesetz turned out to be a distinctly limited measure. Evidently a wide gulf existed between the aspirations of morality campaigners and would-be social engineers and the views of the legal and bureaucratic establishment, which was clearly becoming more and more acutely aware of the legal and practical obstacles to comprehensive repression. What in fact seems to have been taking place in this period was a process of transition away from the traditional 'police-state' attitude of German governments towards the mass of the population, its amusements and its moral welfare, and towards a much more pragmatic and modest concern for the protection of youth. Rather than any liberalisation of official outlook, the principal reason for this appears to have been the sheer scale of the problem, resulting from modern technology and marketing methods, which threatened to explode control mechanisms devised for very different kinds of 'press product' or for the conventional stage. (The effect of video and cable-television developments on post-1945 obscenity legislation and media-censorship arrangements is likely to be similar.) More, perhaps, than has sometimes been realised, however, artists, writers and their allies in parliament and the press also played a significant part: if not by discouraging state intervention altogether, at least by making protests embarrassing enough to moderate official proposals.

After 1933, moderation was cast to the winds. Hitler had denounced Schund in Mein Kampf,[42] and the Nazi regime rapidly intensified state counter-measures as part of its general campaign against freedom of expression. Later efforts to drive the Hollywood cinema out of Europe[43] can also be seen at least in part as a move to shut off a major source of cosmopolitan mass culture. All this was entirely predictable, given the right-wing extremist undertones of much anti-Schund agitation since the turn of the century. Yet the relationship between mass culture and National Socialism was not simply a negative one. As a film addict, Karl May enthusiast and lifelong reader of illustrated newspapers, Hitler himself could be described as a product of Schund rather than of classical culture, while his world-view and political self-presentation gave him much of the allure of a pulp-book saviour: a kind of Captain America for the German lower middle class. At the same time, even totalitarian repression could not eliminate the taste for fantasy, adventure and escapism, or the social conditions which fostered it, and 'positive' substitutes for Schund must therefore have been necessary. The exact nature of these substitutes and their links with official ideology and propaganda need to be investigated as a further step towards clarifying the relationship between the Third Reich and the modern industrialised world.

Notes

1.   See R. Lenman, 'Art, society and the law in Wilhelmine Germany: the Lex Heinze', Oxford German Studies viii (1973), pp. 86-113.
2.   D. Macdonald, 'A theory of mass culture', in B. Rosenberg & D.M. White (eds.), Mass Culture: The Popular Arts in America (New York & London, 1964), p. 59.
3.   See Ian Farr, '"Haberfeldtreiben" et société rurale dans l'Oberland bavarois à la fin du XIXe siècle: quelques réflexions provisoires', in J. Le Goff & J.-C. Schmitt (eds.), Le Charivari (Paris, 1982), pp. 285-295.
4.   See G. Metken, Comics (Frankfurt & Hamburg, 1970).
5.   See especially R. Schenda, Volk ohne Buch: Studien zur Sozialgeschichte der populären Lesestoffe 1770-1910 (Frankfurt/M., 1970); and R.Fullerton, 'Creating a mass book market in Germany: the story of the "colporteur novel" 1870-1890', and 'Toward a commercial popular culture: the development of pamphlet fiction in Germany, 1871-1914', Journal of Social History x (1977), pp. 265-83 and xii (1978/9), pp. 489-511.
6.   E. Schultze, Die Schundliteratur (Halle, 1909), pp. 34-40.
7.   Bundesrat, 1913 Session, Nr. 60 (20 April 1913), p. 6.
8.   See R. Taylor, Film Propaganda: Soviet Russia and Nazi Germany (London, 1979); W. Bredow & R. Zurek (eds.), Film und Gesellschaft in Deutschland: Dokumente und Materialien (Hamburg, 1975).
9.   See A. Kaes (ed.), Kino-Debatte: Texte zum Verhältnis von Literatur und Film 1909-1929 (Tübingen, 1978).
10.   Staatsarchiv für Munchen, Munich: Pol. Dir. 1088.
11.   E. Altenloh, Zur Soziologie des Kino (Leipzig, 1913), p. 98.
12.   See the Fantômas number of Europe, 590/1 (June/July 1978); and F. Lacassin, Louis Feuillade (Paris, 1964).
13.   Bayerisches Hauptstaatsarchiv, Munich: MK 19 102 (memo. of 11 Nov. 1910).
14.   Nr. 65, 19 March 1912.
15.   See W.L. Guttsmann, The German Social Democratic Party 1875-1933: From Ghetto to Government (London, 1981), pp. 188-215.
16.   See Diane Simmons, Georg Kerschensteiner (London, 1966).
17.   See H. Wollschläger, Karl May, Grundriss eines gebrochenen Lebens (Zürich, 1976).
18.   F. Lacassin, 'Fantômas ou l'opéra de treize sous', Europe 590/1, p. 5.
19.   L. Fiedler, 'The middle against both ends', in Rosenberg & White, Mass Culture, pp. 537-47.

20. C. Harrer, Die Geschichte der Münchener Tagespresse, 1870-1890 (Munich, 1940), p. 149.
21. M. Stürmer (ed.), Bismarck und die preussisch-deutsche Politik, 1871-1890, pp. 259f: Bismarck to Herbert Bismarck, 2 Oct. 1888.
22. See R. Lenman, 'Censorship and society in Munich, 1890-1914', Oxford D. Phil, thesis, 1975.
23. Die Lesestoffe der kleinen Leute (Munich, 1976), pp. 78-104.
24. Schultze, Die Schundliteratur, pp. 60-66.
25. Lenman, 'Censorship and society', p. 33.
26. Reichsgesetzblatt 1911, pp. 209-215.
27. Bundesrat, 1913 Session, Nr. 60 (20 April 1913).
28. Ibid., p. 4. See also L. Leiss, Kunst im Konflikt. Kunst und Künstler im Widerstreit mit der Obrigkeit (Berlin, 1971), pp. 84, 100f.
29. Verhandlungen der National-Versammlung (VdNV), Bd. 341 (Anlagen), Nr. 2317, p. 2489. See also Bredow & Zurek, Film und Gesellschaft, pp. 67-72.
30. Schenda, Lesestoffe, pp. 78-104.
31. See Bredow & Zurek, Film und Gesellschaft, pp. 19-27, 73-101.
32. For the debates, see VdNV Bd. 328, session 58; 330, sess. 92, 100; 333, sess. 162; 341 (Anlagen), Nr. 2317. For the Law, Reichsgesetzbl. 1920, pp. 953-8.
33. VdNV, Bd. 341, Nr. 2317, p. 2492.
34. See E. Rosenhaft, 'Organising the Lumpenproletariat: cliques and Communists in Berlin during the Weimar Republic', in R. Evans (ed.), The German Working Class 1888-1933 (London, 1982), pp. 174-219.
35. For the debates, see Verhandlungen des Reichstags (VdRT), Bd. 391, sess. 238-41, 245; Bd. 409 (Anlagen), Nr. 2372. For the Law, Reichgesetzbl. 1926, i, pp. 505f. See also Leiss, Kunst im Konflikt, pp. 85-90.
36. VdRT, Bd. 391, pp. 8233-7 (27 Nov. 1926).
37. See K. Koszyk and K.H. Pruys (eds.), dtv Wörterbuch der Publizistik (Munich, 1969), pp. 173ff.
38. See J. van Ussel, Sexualunterdrückung. Geschichte der Sexualfeindschaft (Reinbek, 1970), pp. 137-163.
39. See G.L. Mosse, 'Nationalism and respectability: normal and abnormal sexuality in the 19th century', Jnl. of Contemp. Hist. (1982), pp. 221-46.
40. Ibid., p. 230.
41. This view was put forward during discussion of papers presented by Detlev Peukert and Cornelia Usborne to the conference on Weimar culture and politics held at Liverpool University in September 1982.
42. 1938 edition, p. 34.
43. See M. Phillips, 'The German film industry and the New Order', in P. Stachura (ed.), The Shaping of the Nazi State (London, 1978), pp. 257-81.

INDUSTRY AS A POLITICAL FACTOR IN THE WEIMAR REPUBLIC

Hartmut Pogge von Strandmann

Nearly thirty years ago the Vierteljahrshefte für Zeitgeschichte published an article which portrayed the Weimar Republic as an historical problem.[1] Research into that period of German history was then at its beginning and the author singled out two main causes for the failure of the Republic, which to his mind needed further investigation: the breakdown of democratic order and an unwillingness to accept an international situation based on the Peace Treaty of Versailles. Both causes were interrelated and could be traced back to the revolutionary beginnings of 1918/19 as well as to the end of the Republic. Referring to the beginning of the Republic the author quoted Eric Kollmann's earlier article in which the latter had stated that the Republic had in 1918 been unable to adapt modern industrial capitalism to new forms of democracy.[2] Because the Republic was based on the liberal ideas of a nation state which were developed in the 19th century, Germany became the prototype for counter-revolutionary developments in the inter-war years. Whereas Kollman was aware of the fact that industrial capitalism, with its tendencies towards power concentrations and the formation of monopolies, strongly influenced politics, the author merely questioned the 'possibilities and conditions for democracy in a modern mass state'.[3] He regarded the Weimar Republic as a failed democratic experiment 'under the conditions of an industrial mass state'. But not much further attention was paid to the economy, let alone to its industry.

In 1980 the same author listed five factors as being responsible for the decline of the Republic.[4] One of them was the economic situation which, with its clash between production and distribution interests, posed difficult problems of cooperation for parties and parliament. None of these five factors was systematically analysed and causally linked to the fall of the Republic. Instead he blamed the breakdown of the Great Coalition of 1930 and the desertion of the Republic by its republicans for the demise of Germany's first republic. However these explanations are insufficient because the supposed desertion of one group reveals nothing about the reaction of the others. Moreover the structural weaknesses of the Republic and the anti-democratic currents within Weimar society were not explored. But generally the author is in line with a number of historians who have followed the notion of primacy of politics and used a traditional approach to research on parties, pressure groups, cabinets, individuals and 'high politics'.

Whilst adhering to historical tradition, but remaining very much aware of the importance of the economy for the conduct of politics, K.D. Bracher discussed in 1955 the role of industry in his by now classic study Die Auflösung der Weimarer Republik.[5] He also pointed to some gaps in our knowledge in this respect which needed to be filled. However most of his later work does not deal with an economically based power structure.

Only gradually did general history turn to economic problems and deal with historical ones in particular.[6] Erdmann's original approach was changed into a suitably analytical one. Industrial influences on politics and society were examined within the context of what such influences meant for state and society. Ten years ago the Bochum Symposium about the industrial system and political development in the Weimar Republic focused, as Hans Mommsen put it, on the 'social history of industry' with its effect on the Republic's political set-up.[7] One of the tasks of the symposium was to illuminate the structural background of the collapse of Germany's first parliamentary democracy which was seen as a crisis of a liberal-capitalist economy. Generalisations were however difficult to verify as other parliamentary democracies were not affected in the same way nor did the depression lead in those countries to a successful rise of fascism. There were other reasons why the economic crisis in the early 30s exacerbated the political difficulties of the Weimar Republic. One of them was the destabilizing role industry assumed on the political stage in Berlin. A number of historians have recognised this factor without however asking how it had come about.[8] Instead of trying to find causes they focused on the question of whether industry's political importance was the consequence of capitalist development or whether mass unemployment and the payment of reparations had provided the economy in general with a vantage point in politics. The first question was of interest to historians because of the possible causal connection between capitalism and fascism in general and the link between the NSDAP and big business in particular.[9] The level of industrial funding for Hitler prior to 1933 was to give an answer to it and provide some proof of the causal connection.[10] Some substantial headway seems to have been made, but the analytical value of several explanations is reduced because of pre-stated ideological assumptions. But whatever the strength of determinist arguments for the role of industry in politics may be, they tend to overlook the particular drive by industry into politics, a process which accelerated during the Wilhelmine era.

In the discussion about organised capitalism and state monopolistic capitalism the concept of corporative pluralism was put forward and this seems to have provided historians with a framework for analysing the links between industry and politics before 1914.[11] Thus a number of studies have concentrated on the political activites of economic pressure groups and business associations in Wilhelmine Germany.[12] However none of these groups achieved political leadership before 1914. As pluralism in Imperial Germany did not imply equality between the various political factors, several industrialists were not satisfied with the amount of political influence they had. This meant that those forces which did not wield political power commensurate with their economic weight seized the opportunity after 1918 to become a predominant political factor. This was particularly true for industry.

Gerald Feldman has made a comparison between agrarian Junkers and heavy industrialists who changed roles after 1918. Heavy industry took over the position of the so-called Grossagrarier and thus 'laid claim to political primacy for die Wirtschaft and assumed a role in diplomatic negotiations, domestic political affairs, and administrative functions that has no real parallel in other capitalist societies of the period despite efforts to characterize it as part of the "Americanization" of German life'.[13] Although Feldman overestimated the influence of the Grossagrarier in the last few years before the First World War it is certainly true that industrialists played an even larger part on the political stage after 1918.

How did this change come about? There seem to have been a number of factors which stood in the way of such a shift of emphasis. Before 1914 the divergence of industrial interest seems to have been even more wide-ranging than after the war. Industry was divided not only between the steel producers on the one side and those involved in manufacturing industry on the other, but also between the big corporations and the small and medium-sized companies. The horizontal and vertical differentiation of the industrial camp had one further consequence. Whom did the industrial associations represent? As the growing industrial concerns began to employ their own political representatives there emerged a dual approach to lobbying in the capital. Certain questions were left in the hands of the secretaries of the industrial associations whereas in a number of cases the concerns approached politicians and civil servants directly. Direct lobbying was not undertaken because of dissatisfaction with the work done by the officials of the interest groups. Obviously there were advantages to be gained from direct lobbying such as speed of information and secrecy with which rivals could be defeated. However direct lobbying did not mean that the industrial associations only represented the interests of their smaller members. In fact the large concerns exerted a strong influence within the associations and tried to control their policies. Consequently life was not easy for the secretaries of the industrial associations. In addition there was the dichotomy between heavy industry and manufacturing industry which on occasions was superseded by cooperation between the large companies of both camps, as in the case of the Bülow Tariffs in 1902.[14]

Within the economy industry's position was rising, yet its political influence was reduced by disunity within industry.[15] There was however a widespread feeling, also expressed, among others, by Max Weber, that economic power ought to have a corresponding influence in politics. The rise of industry during the last years before the First World War as well as the ascendancy of the large corporations led to the demand for greater involvement in political decision-making.[16] In Britain and the United States industrial influence in politics had gradually grown and did not pose any serious problems as far as lobbying, membership of legislative assemblies and influence on governments were concerned. Despite Germany's rise as an industrial power, industry was less well represented in parliaments and governments than in the other two countries.[17]

What seems to have been different in Germany before 1914 was the demand put forward by a few leading industrialists for greater involvement in politics and for politics to be geared more to industrial needs. Although one of these bids came from the steel and coal industrialist August Thyssen, the awareness that they lacked political power was more widespread in the electro-technical, machine-building and chemical industries than in the heavy industrial sector.[18] It was also light industry which resented the political power of agriculture although its economic superiority and social influence were declining. Another concern of light industry which was shared by a number of leading industrialists from the heavy industrial sector was the power of the civil service. The frustrating situation industry in general experienced over the issue of tax reforms in 1909 led to the joint foundation of the Hansa League. However the united front only lasted for two years, because the steel industrialists then left.[19] But even while the united front existed the political scene in Berlin had not been dramatically altered Nevertheless there were a number of industrialists for whom the existing involvement in decision-making was not sufficient. The development of Germany into an industrial state was to mean for industrialists like Kirdorf, Rathenau, Siemens, Stinnes and Thyssen that industry ought to become the predominant factor in politics.

What was the justification for this belief? Ever since the public debate of Industriestaat versus Agrarstaat in the 1890s, when the former concept had carried the day, a number of industrialists had desired an equivalent to their growing economic weight in politics. They identified to a large extent with the state and wanted their interests to be tantamount to those of the state. Alongside the concept of raison d'état a new concept emerged: raison d'industrie (Wirtschaftsräson). Nevertheless the political role of industry continued to be a limited one, although foreign and domestic politics depended increasingly on its efficiency. Yet industry had more resources at its disposal to make itself felt in politics than any other group: money, organisational efficiency, access to decision-making bodies and the ownership of several newspapers. Of course for many industrialists, especially for those of smaller and medium-sized enterprises, the existing situation was satisfactory so that there was no need for them to increase their power within society. They were also content with the restricted power the liberal and conservative parties possessed. The fact that some leading industrialists were aware of the time-lag between the rise of economic power and the translation of it into political power was frustrating, but did not lead to concerted efforts to alter the situation in their favour.

This is not to argue that Wilhelmine Germany was still an agrarian economy or that any so-called pre-industrial élites ran the country. Whether agriculture, banking, or industry was concerned, the economy was by all definitions a capitalist one. But what was at stake was the translation of industry's perception of its political needs into political practice. Obviously the representation of their interests by parliamentarians or pressure groups was regarded by some as insufficient. These industrialists wanted only a greater share of power and were therefore against any radical reform of the political status quo.

Before the First World War no major change occurred in the relationship between state and industry, but once war had broken out this situation altered. The longer the war lasted, the more the war effort became dependent on industry and its degree of efficiency. The first indication of industry's greater concern with the war came from a number of leading industrialists like Rathenau, Stinnes and Thyssen who supplied the Chancellor with war aims memoranda which he incorporated in his well-known guideline on war aims, the September Programme.[20] On a more practical level the Prussian Ministry of War was compelled to set up a special department under the leadership of Rathenau to organise the supply of scarce raw materials important for the war effort.[21]

The production of weapons and ammunition led to a necessary cooperation with the army and navy which was initially resented by a number of industrialists. However they were virtually forced into a kind of symbiosis despite industry's 'complaints about the utter chaos and confusion in the structure and operation of the procurement agencies'.[22] Two years later the cooperation between industry and the Prussian War Ministry had reached an impasse and heavy industry demanded a complete overhaul of the organisation of war production. Feldman has called the subsequent introduction of the so-called Hindenburg Programme in 1916 the 'triumph of heavy industry', but in many ways it was a pyrrhic victory.[23] The shortage of labour, the lack of coordination and the unwillingness to collaborate more closely with the War Office severely reduced the effectiveness of the Hindenburg Programme. In the end there were not enough resources and certain target figures in production could not be reached due to bottlenecks in the supply of men and materials. Yet in certain sectors an excess of production was achieved for which there were not enough soldiers at the front.

Whatever the failures and successes of the Hindenburg Programme, the economic and political position of heavy industry and the large corporations of the electro-technical and chemical industries had been substantially enhanced. In all of this industry had followed a policy which had largely been dictated by the pursuit of self-interest, but it was strongly believed that the dependence on war contracts was sufficient to justify the amount of war profits industry had been able to net. Industry claimed that its attitude was compatible with its views about identical interests between state and industry. Thus it was able to brush aside any criticism.

During the war the alliance between army and industry helped the latter into the prominent political position it desired. The main beneficiaries were heavy industry and the electro-technical and chemical industries. However this new power position was matched by the rising power of a state bureaucracy which tended to put the interests of the state above those of industry and to develop economic controls. Consequently the relationship between state and industry during the war and afterwards underwent a substantial revision. But apart from being accused of making large war profits industry came out of the war, its prestige intact. Although, some insiders criticised industry and German technology for the loss of the war, industry's belief in its own superiority proved to be stronger. Even the rivalry between heavy industry and the manufacturing sector did not change this picture.

How much industry's feeling of self-importance had grown during the war may be gathered from a remark Rathenau made to the economist Franz Oppenheimer in 1918.[24] He naively compared the German economy with an industrial plant both of which he considered he would be able to run successfully on similar lines. The hypothetical switch from micro-economics to macro-economics came easily and shows how much confidence men like Rathenau had in their own ability to run the country and decide the economic and political fate of Germany. Towards the end of the War a number of leading industrialists from both industrial camps seized the initiative and after some protracted negotiations concluded a pact with organised labour to establish guidelines for a Demobilization Office to be controlled by interest groups and to carry more weight than the existing government bureaucracy. Its other aim was to forestall any revolutionary effects on the structure of industry. When the revolution finally broke out in November 1918 industry was in a position to control social and economic policies and this the Provisional Government had to accept when it endorsed the Stinnes-Legien Agreement of 15 November.[25] The subsequent creation of the Zentralarbeitsgemeinschaft (Central Working Association) indicated that there was, from a pragmatic point of view, considerable willingness at the time from industry to collaborate with trade unions within a new political framework.

This newly conceived cooperation was to replace the traditional idea of social conflict with one based on social harmony, but it was recognised that this could not last unless there was a substantial change in the political structure. As traditional party allegiances began to take shape, the concept of collaboration proved illusory although for reasons of expediency it was maintained for several years. Seen in the context of a bid for political power it is remarkable that industry was able to be so flexible while it was attempting to replace its war-time partner, the army, with the trade unions. Although this move was designed to be a defensive measure it was also the best guarantee against any radical change in economic policy.

The initiative of the small group of leading industrialists who thrashed out the Stinnes-Legien Agreement, had further repercussions. It was this particular group which acted as the spearhead in bringing about a unified industrial pressure group, the Reichsverband der deutschen Industrie (Reich Association of German Industry - RdI), which comprised heavy industry as well as the electro-technical, machine-building and chemical sectors. One particular aim of the association was to increase the political 'power of German industry'.[26] A few weeks earlier Rathenau had tried to set up the Demokratische Volksbund as a rallying point for those members of manufacturing industry who felt obliged to become active in politics. However nothing came of it, especially when the old liberal parties were refounded.[27]

By this stage industry was not short of institutions through which it kept in contact with the sphere of politics. The large concerns had their own liaison men in Berlin. Thus Krupp, Stinnes and the Gutehoffnungshütte to name but a few were well represented in the capital. The Hamburg shipping company, the Hamburg-Amerikanische-Packetfahrt-Aktiengesellschaft (HAPAG) even kept a political salon in Berlin which was run by its 'political director', Arndt von Holtzendorff.

K.D. Buse has recently shown that the HAPAG round table was not simply a lobbying institution.[28] He ascribes to the salon the role of a 'transfer mechanism' by which economic interests were translated into politics and political views found their way into the business world. Buse defines this interaction as 'dual dynamism'; that is to say he abandons the notion that business is the active and the state the passive side. It is a two-way process, to which both sides contribute.

A well-known publicist valued the Holtzendorff-Tisch very highly, especially as divergent interests were brought together:

> Every chancellor, every minister, every party leader . . .
> the leading business-men and intellectuals, everyone who
> held a significant post met there with each other, not all
> together, but in groups . . . preferably eight in number . . .
> there many appointments and institutions were decided
> upon.[29]

Among the industrialists and bankers who were frequently invited were Rathenau, Warburg, Cuno, Raumer, Dernburg and Schacht. Moderate Social Democrats included Ebert, Noske, Südekum, Hermann Müller and Bauer. Others were only invited on one occasion, but in any case, the two sides met on an equal footing although in the long run employers had a considerable advantage over Social Democrats in their contacts with the state bureaucracy. Obviously the HAPAG's interests were not identical with those of industry. Nevertheless meetings of this kind took place in similiar circumstances in the Deutsche Gesellschaft, the Mittwoch-Gesellschaft and the Mittwoch-Abend. The last three were founded during the war, but carried on afterwards, mostly until 1933. To what extent this type of 'dual dynamism' helped to stabilise the early phase of the Weimar Republic is difficult to determine, but the willingness to discuss and exchange opinions and information meant that any strong feeling of hostility between industry and politics as well as other sectors in the economy were overcome by some move towards a consensus.

At the Holtzendorff gathering heavy industry and trade unions were absent. Whether the Zentralarbeitsgemeinschaft, where the latter two met, was a substitute for the Holtzendorff round table, as Buse suggests, is doubtful. It looks much more likely that the polarization between heavy industry and the leaders of manufacturing industry had come to the fore again after a brief interlude in the autumn and winter of 1918/19. Peter Wulf suggests that the cooperation between the leading industrialists lasted in fact until the second half of 1919 when reparation demands caused the old groupings to become more differentiated again.[30]

In the event the steel producers did not make use of the Holtzendorff discussion group as they had their own liaison men in Berlin. They probably favoured the Mittwoch-Gesellschaft instead and gradually began to drift away from the concept of a consensus within industry which included the trade unions. Politically they stood to the Right of the participants of the Holtzendorff table, and although they were willing to tolerate the new situation after 1918 they did not want to identify themselves with the Republic. Light industry on the other hand was more forthcoming and the policy of fulfilment of the Rathenau-Wirth cabinet found more support among the representatives of the processing industry than among Ruhr industrialists. The latter, under the leadership of Hugo Stinnes, objected increasingly to any notion of fulfilment until Stinnes concluded his own agreement with the French industrialist Lubersac about reparation deliveries in kind.

Manufacturing industry appeared to be more willing to cooperate with the state whereas heavy industry expressed its concern about the 'health of the economy' (Wohl der Wirtschaft) and aimed for a return to the conditions that existed before 1914. Putting the interests of industry above those of the state resulted in Stinnes together with other Rhenish-Westphalian industrialists effectively torpedoing the plan to make their foreign currency reserves available for the government to raise a loan in 1921.

Peter Wulf has pointed out that industry's growing strength led to a weakening of the government.[31] Obviously this development could have been averted if the government had been able to give priority to the principle of the 'health of the economy' and conduct its domestic and foreign politics accordingly. But the effectiveness of such cooperation would have been based on a consensus between industry and government which by 1921/22 only existed in certain spheres. As far as the parties were concerned, by 1921 they were no longer in a position to enforce policies against industry's will. Thus the failure of the credit action in autumn 1921 was a milestone for industry as it gradually increased its predominance in Weimar politics.

There were of course areas where the 'industrial will' did not prevail right away. From 1920 the steel industry had attacked the eight-hour day and since heavy industry dominated the Reich Association of German Industry the elimination of the eight-hour day became a constant industrial demand. The chance for success finally came in the wake of the Ruhr crisis of 1923, when heavy industry was able to drop this limitation on working hours. Even then the powerful Rhenish and Westphalian industrialists needed Berlin's support for the measure.[32]

As a result, manufacturing industry had to follow suit when the pre-war double shift and the 58-hour week were re-introduced. Thus industry had been able to go back on an agreement which it had concluded during the revolutionary days of November 1918. Feldman has rightly underlined this new triumph of heavy industry which had been able to persuade the politicians and its customers that its interests had to be put higher than those of any other groups in society.[33] The justification for this attitude was the argument that industrial concern for the 'health of the economy' would benefit state and society. Of course this could be achieved more easily if government and industry pursued identical aims.

Heavy industry's argument was not unanimously accepted. On the government's side it was the Chancellor, Wilhelm Cuno, the former managing director of HAPAG, who advocated the separation of economics from politics so that industry could benefit from 'free initiative'. His line was welcomed by industrialists, but his statement in December 1922 that 'the relationship between economic circles and the government should also be one in which the government takes the lead and the business community supports the government' was not met with approval.[34]

In fact before the occupation of the Ruhr in 1923 industry tried to work out a political programme which would give the policies of the RdI even greater consistency.[35] The demand for low wages, low taxes and low social expenditure was given priority over foreign policy as well as monetary issues. The abolition of the eight-hour day figured prominently, but so did the wish that no government should operate independently of industry.

In addition Silverberg drafted a programme entitled the 'Reconstruction of the German Economy'.[36] In it he pleaded for the primacy of industry, the abolition of all state interference and a substantial cut in social legislation. In short he aimed at diminishing the effects of the revolution and the immediate post-war period. Like many other industrialists he favoured a return to the pre-war situation, whilst retaining industry's new position.

In order to carry out his programme he maintained that industry would need the existence of a strong state which would acknowledge industry's sphere of political, economic and social autonomy. The strength of the state would be measured by the willingness and ability of the government to work primarily for the 'health of the economy' as the paramount goal of any policies. However action on Silverberg's programme had to be postponed until after the occupation of the Ruhr.

The Ruhr occupation and the subsequent stabilisation of the German currency revealed to some extent the limitations of industrial power. Industry could neither prevent the French action nor impose its order of priorities on events in 1923 and 1924. In November 1923 Stinnes's argument, that a revaluation should not be carried out until a reparation settlement had been reached, was rejected and the mark was stabilised. Several industrialists had been under the illusion that they had benefited from the inflationary process after the war and thus objected to stabilisation. Although this attitude may have changed between 1920 and 1923, Dieter Lindenlaub has recently demonstrated that industry did not benefit from inflation as was assumed by Feldman and Wulf.[37] In the summer of 1922 at the latest, industrialists were becoming aware of the negative effects of inflation, but were not able or were perhaps unwilling to induce the government to change course. Subsequently all efforts to stabilise prices and to reduce public indebtedness, which in 1923 alone had trebled in size, were jeopardised by the Ruhr occupation. The stabilisation of the currency had become imperative and had to be carried out before other economic and political problems could be tackled. Although the government took the initiative in solving some of the economic consequences of the Ruhr crisis, the ensuing measures of 1923/4 were based again on a cooperation between government and industry. This included the Dawes Plan, the Locarno Treaty and the introduction of national and international cartel policies.[38]

The subsequent economic upsurge forced heavy industry to put its own house in order and leave manufacturing industry more room to manoeuvre. In any case the translation of industrial power into political influence seems to have been less urgent after Stinnes's death when a period of relative stability ensued. The improving economic condition led Silverberg, in September 1926, when the RdI leadership was in the hands of the leading personality of the chemical industry, Carl Duisberg, to plead for a renewed cooperation between big industry, trade unions and the state.[39] He pledged support for the Republic and was even willing to accept social democracy, albeit only in a minor role, but then went on to criticize the existing social policy, the arbitration rules for settling labour disputes and the collective contract. As a late convert to some of Rathenau's ideas, Silverberg hoped to put a stop to any further developments in the direction of a welfare state and state interventionism by cooperation with the trade unions in a gigantic cartel.[40]

The reaction among the machine-building, electro-technical and chemical industries was favourable to Silverberg's main thrust of argument, while heavy industry objected to any alliance with the trade unions or the SPD. According to Neebe neither industrial camp won the upper hand in this debate. But during the Ruhr lock-out in November 1928 the first shots in a renewed campaign against the economic powers of the state were fired, when the Ruhr industrialists objected to the mandatory system of state arbitration.[41]

Silverberg's change of sides indicated a major shift to the Right from which the new calls for a Reichsreform emanated. The aim was to reduce any danger of 'state socialism' in the face of a coming recession. It was also hoped that parliamentary government would be weakened and the social democratic stronghold in Prussia would be destroyed.[42] Consequently industry worked for the dissolution of the Great Coalition in 1930. Nevertheless most leading industrialists, with the exception of Thyssen and Vögler, accepted the Young Plan. While this reparation settlement appeared to be temporary and preferable to any return to Stinnes's earlier policies, the end of the Great Coalition was regarded as a crucial milestone on the road to an authoritarian government. In this situation Max Schlenker, a leading heavy industrialist, renewed the call upon the 'German entrepreneur to push forward politically in order to secure a position due to him at the helm of the state'.[43] Despite this renewed initiative to move into politics, Neebe maintains that the existing division between light and heavy industry foiled any attempt of either industrial camp to impose its strategies and crisis management upon the other. The lack of any unified action weakened the industrial position in politics.

Neebe has set his 'stalemate' against Bernd Weisbrod's thesis that heavy industry was in the position of a 'veto-group'.[44] However the two interpretations are not mutually exclusive. The 'veto'-position heavy industry assumed from time to time may have contributed to a stalemate' within the industrial camp, but heavy industry's organisational strength gave greater weight to the political actions of the steel and coal industrialists. The latter group was not united over every issue, but at least it was held together by a common dislike of any cooperation with the SPD. Earlier in 1930 some industrialists had come out in favour of a renewal of the Great Coalition, but Chancellor Brüning, backed by a number of leading industrialists, ruled out any such plan. To these industrialists a compromise with the rising National Socialists was in the end preferable to any arrangement with the Social Democrats, who in 1932 committed in the eyes of several industrialists the arch sin of reviving socialisation plans for work creation schemes.

Neebe has argued that despite the growing opposition to the Weimar Republic, industrial influence in politics declined from 1930 onwards, leaving the government with a larger degree of autonomy.[45] He emphasizes that the National Socialists came to power against the background of a divided industrial camp and that Hitler's triumph meant a victory for the heavy industrial grouping round Thyssen. The renewed ascendancy of this particular industrial faction appears to have been a consequence of the rising power of the NSDAP rather than its pre-condition. Thus the rapprochement between certain leading industrialists and the NSDAP was aided by the economic situation.

Rhenish and Westphalian heavy industry was very much affected by the crisis which led it to criticise the political leadership. Furthermore, by turning increasingly against Social Democrats and trade unions, industry helped to destabilise the system which put it automatically closer to the NSDAP, although several industrialists like Reusch favoured Papen and a conservative authoritarian regime. The divisions within the industrial camp may have been important, but at the end of the Weimar Republic they were not decisive. As hardly any leading industrialist seems to have wished that the Republic would survive the economic crisis, the variation in their degree of rejection of the existing political system was not ultimately important. Thus it was not so much a question of different industrial influences cancelling each other out; instead they competed with each other for the top position within a general trend towards the Right. The winner of this race was Thyssen, but by 1933 only a few industrialists objected to the National Socialists coming to power.[46]

Had the leading industrialists been as united as in 1918 and had they not turned against the SPD and trade unions, industry would have remained the leading economic-political factor, a position it had assumed in the 1920s. By turning against the political system, industry undermined the Weimar Republic which it had helped to stabilise for reasons of political and economic expediency. Because industry asked for interventionist measures to reflate the economy, because it was disunited and did not have a clear political concept, it abdicated its leading position. What remained were long-term intentions which were overtaken by the effects of political radicalisation and the rise of the National Socialists as well as the Communists.

Under these circumstances the convergence of Conservatives and National Socialists was accepted by industry although not actively supported by all of its leading members. Industry's search for a 'strong state' during the crisis was regarded as an alternative to the Weimar Republic. How strong that new state was to be was unclear, except that it had to be anti-socialist, anti-liberal and in favour of putting industrial interests first. Although Hitler fulfilled the first two expectations of a 'strong state', he did not let industry assume the political position it desired. To some extent industry's political position after 1933 was similar to that it had held before 1914.[47] After 1933 industry began to resume its investments on an increasing scale because it was felt that the political framework was propitious. However before 1914 industry had wanted to increase its political role because it had become the leading economic factor and industrial empires of substantial size had come into existence. After 1918 industry played the leading role it had worked for, but felt unable to change the 'weak state' of the Weimar Republic into a state which in the eyes of the industrialists inspired economic confidence. Thus neither Wilhelmine Germany nor the Weimar Republic nor the Third Reich were, albeit for different reasons, 'ideal states' for the political aspirations and concepts of industry. This was to change under the rule of democratic conservatism after 1948/49.

Notes

1. K.D. Erdmann, 'Die Geschichte der Weimarer Republik als Problem der Wissenschaft', in Vierteljahrshefte für Zeitgeschichte, 1955. See for a traditional interpretation of the historiography of the Republic's collapse, H. Schulze, 'Das Scheitern der Weimarer Republik als Problem der Forschung', in K.D. Erdmann and H. Schulze (eds.), Weimar. Selbstpreisgabe einer Demokratie. Eine Bilanz heute, Düsseldorf 1980.
2. E. Kollmann, 'The historical significance of the Weimar Republic', University of Toronto Quarterly, 1947.
3. Erdmann, p. 8.
4. K.D. Erdmann, 'Vom Scheitern einer Demokratie - Forschungsprobleme zum Untergang der Weimarer Republik', in Stifterverband für die Deutsche Wissenschaft, Annual General Meeting 1980. See for an inadequate treatment of the economic sector in general, K.D. Erdmann, 'Versuch einer Bilanz', in K.D. Erdmann and H. Schulze (eds.), Weimar.
5. K.D. Bracher, Die Auflösung der Weimarer Republik. Eine Studie zum Problem des Machtverfalls in der Demokratie, Villingen 1955, pp. 199-228.
6. The bibliography edited by K.D. Bracher, H.A. Jacobsen and M. Funke (eds.), Bibliographie zur Politik in Theorie und Praxis, new edition, Düsseldorf 1976, still clings to a primacy of politics.
7. H. Mommsen, D. Petzina, B. Weisbrod (eds.), Industrielles System und politische Entwicklung in der Weimarer Republik, Düsseldorf 1974, pp. 15 and 22.
8. See the recent studies by B. Weisbrod, Schwerindustrie in der Weimarer Republik. Interessenpolitik zwischen Stabilisierung und Krise, Wuppertal 1978. R. Neebe, Grossindustrie, Staat und NSDAP 1930-1933, Göttingen 1981.
9. H.A. Turner, Faschismus und Kapitalismus in Deutschland. Studien zum Verhältnis zwischen Nationalsozialismus und Wirtschaft, Göttingen 1972. See also his two articles, 'Grossunternehmertum und Nationalsozialismus 1930-1933', in Historische Zeitschrift, 221, 1975 and 'Hitlers Einstellung zu Wirtschaft und Gesellschaft vor 1933', in Geschichte und Gesellschaft, 1976. D. Stegmann, 'Zum Verhältnis von Grossindustrie und Nationalsozialismus 1930-1933. Ein Beitrag zur Geschichte der sogenannten Machtergreifung', in Archiv für Sozialgeschichte, 13, 1973. D. Stegmann, 'Kapitalismus und Faschismus in Deutschland 1929-34. Thesen und Materialien zur Restituierung des Primats der Grossindustrie zwischen Weltwirtschaftskrise und beginnender Rüstungskonjunktur', in Gesellschaft. Beiträge zur Marxschen Theorie 6, Frankfurt 1976. R.

Kühnl and G. Hardach (eds.), Die Zerstörung der Weimarer Republik, Köln 1977. V. Hentschel, Weimars letzte Monate. Hitler und der Untergang der Republik, Düsseldorf 1978. D. Abraham, The Collapse of the Weimar Republic. Political Economy and Crisis, Princeton 1981. G.D. Feldman, 'Aspekte deutscher Industriepolitik am Ende der Weimarer Republik 1930-1932', in K. Holl (ed.), Wirtschaft und liberale Demokratie, Göttingen 1978. See also the two books mentioned in fn. 8.

10. See for the latest scholarly contribution to this complex, T. Trumpp, 'Zur Finanzierung der NSDAP durch die deutsche Grossindustrie. Versuche einer Bilanz', in Geschichte in Wissenschaft und Unterricht, 4, 1981.

11. H.A. Winkler (ed.), Organisierter Kapitalismus. Vorassetzungen und Anfänge, Göttingen 1974. C.S. Maier, Recasting Bourgeois Europe. Stabilization in France, Germany, and Italy in the Decade after World War I, Princeton 1975. Weisbrod, pp. 19-25.

12. S. Mielke, Der Hansa-Bund für Gewerbe, Handel und Industrie 1909-1914. Der gescheiterte Versuch einer antifeudalen Sammlungspolitik, Göttingen 1976. H.P. Ullmann, Der Bund der Industriellen. Organisation, Einfluss und Politik klein-und mittelbetrieblicher Industrieller im Deutschen Kaiserreich 1895-1914, Göttingen 1976. V. Hentschel, Wirtschaft und Wirtschaftspolitik im Wilhelminischen Deutschland. Organisierter Kapitalismus und Interventionsstaat, Stuttgart 1978. G. Eley, Reshaping the German Right. Radical Nationalism and Political Change after Bismarck, New Haven and London 1980.

13. G.D. Feldman, Iron and Steel in the German Inflation 1916-1923, Princeton 1977, p. 464.

14. H. Nussbaum, Unternehmer gegen Monopole. Über Struktur und Aktionen antimonopolistischer Gruppen zu Beginn des 20. Jahrhunderts, Berlin 1966. H. Pogge von Strandmann, 'Widersprüche im Modernisierungsprozess Deutschlands. Der Kampf der vararbeitenden Industrie gegen die Schwerindustrie', in D. Stegmann, B.J. Wendt, P.C. Witt (eds.), Industrielle Gesellschaft und Politisches System. Beiträge zur politischen Sozialgeschichte. Festschrift für Fritz Fischer zum 70. Geburtstag, Bonn 1978.

15. Ibid. H. Pogge von Strandmann, Unternehmenspolitik und Unternehmensführung. Der Dialog zwischen Aufsichtsrat und Vorstand bei Mannesmann 1900 bis 1919, Düsseldorf 1978.

16. H. Pogge von Strandmann, 'Walther Rathenau. Grandmaster of Capitalism' (typescript).

17. P. Molt, Der Reichstag vor der improvisierten Revolution, Köln 1963. H. Jaeger, Unternehmer in der deutschen Politik (1890-1918), Bonn 1967. A. Roth, Business Background of Members of Parliament, London 1963.

18. W. Treue, Die Feuer verlöschen nie. August Thyssen-Hütte 1890-1926, Düsseldorf and Vienna 1966, p. 186.

19. See the books by S. Mielke and H.P. Ullmann as in fn 12.

20. See for this topic, F. Fischer, Germany's Aims in the First World War with an introduction by James Joll, London 1967, pp.108 ff.

21. See the relevant passage in the forthcoming English edition of Rathenau's diaries, H. Pogge von Strandmann (ed.), Walther Rathenau.

Industrialist, Banker, Intellectual, and Politician. Notes and Diaries 1907-1922, Oxford 1984.
22. G.D. Feldman, Army, Industry and Labor in Germany 1914-1918, Princeton 1966, p. 57.
23. Ibid., pp. 149 ff.
24. Walther Rathenau. Briefe, vol. 1, Dresden 1927, p. 384, Rathenau to Franz Oppenheimer, 14 March 1918.
25. G.D. Feldman, Army, Industry and Labor, pp. 519-533. G.D. Feldman, 'German Business between War and Revolution. The Origins of the Stinnes-Legien Agreement', in G.A. Ritter (ed.), Entstehung und Wandel der modernen Gesellschaft. Festschrift für Hans Rosenberg zum 65. Geburtstag, Berlin 1970. See also H. Potthoff, Gewerkschaften und Politik zwischen Revolution und Inflation, Düsseldorf 1979, pp. 29-40.
26. Veröffentlichungen des Reichsverbandes der Deutschen Industrie,i, May 1919.
27. H.M. Barth, Der demokratische Volksbund. Zu den Anfängen des politischen Engagements der Unternehmer der Berlinger Elektroindustrie im November 1918, Berlin 1966. H.J. Meinik, 'Walter Rathenau und die Sozialisierungsfrage', unpubl. thesis, Berlin 1973, pp. 35-45.
28. D.K. Buse, 'Economic Interests and Lobbying in the Early Weimar Republic: Holtzendorff's Political Salon', in Social History, xiv, 1981.
29. Ibid., p. 455. E. Jäckh, Der goldene Pflug. Lebensernte eines Weltbürgers, Stuttgart 1954, pp. 189 ff.
30. P. Wulf, Hugo Stinnes. Wirtschaft und Politik 1918-1924, Stuttgart 1979.
31. Ibid., p. 293.
32. G.D. Feldman, Iron and Steel, pp. 438 ff.
33. Ibid., p. 444.
34. Ibid., p. 334.
35. Ibid., pp. 321 ff. R. Neebe, pp. 26-33.
36. Ibid., p. 29. Silverberg's programme dates from 26 December 1922.
37. D. Lindenlaub, 'Maschinenbauunternehmen in der Inflation 1919-1923. Unternehmenshistorische Untersuchungen zu einigen Inflationstheorien', in G.D. Feldman, C.L. Holtfrerich, G.A. Ritter, P.C. Witt (eds.), Die Deutsche Inflation. Eine Zwischenbilanz, Berlin, New York, 1982. Lindenlaub's forthcoming book bears the same title.
38. G.D. Feldman, Iron and Steel, pp. 443 ff.
39. R. Neebe, pp. 36 ff.
40. Ibid., p. 39.
41. Ibid., pp. 41-46.
42. B. Weisbrod, 'Industrial Crisis Strategies during the Great Depression', unpubl. lecture delivered to the American Historical Association's 95th Annual Meeting in Washington DC, 28-30 December 1980.
43. R. Neebe, p. 60.
44. B. Weisbrod, Schwerindustrie, pp. 26 ff. R. Neebe, pp. 200 ff.
45. Ibid., pp. 72, 89, 97.
46. V. Hentschel, Weimars letzte Monate, p. 138. T. Trumpp, p. 235.
47. In 1913/14 there existed a broad agreement on political matters between some leading agrarians and leading members of heavy industry.

Industry as a Political Factor in the Weimar Republic

The clash between heavy industry and agriculture in 1932/33 provides little evidence for D. Abraham's thesis of a re-emerging 'ruling bloc'.

NAZISM AND EUGENICS: THE BACKGROUND TO THE

NAZI STERILIZATION LAW OF 14 JULY 1933

Jeremy Noakes

'Eugenics has become fashionable. Public opinion has now become so familiar with a set of minimum eugenic demands, politicians in parliaments and governments have been convinced of the necessity of bio-political measures by such important rational considerations and such effective pressure from public opinion that the first legislative steps cannot be long delayed.'[1]

Theodor Geiger - one of the ablest German sociologists of his generation and, significantly, himself a eugenist, albeit a critical one - was writing at the time of the Nazi take-over of power. He was correct in his assumption that legislative steps could not be long delayed: within months the new Nazi government had introduced a law for the compulsory sterilization of those with defects considered to be hereditary. This was to be the first move in an elaborate policy for 'improving the racial health' of the German people, a policy which went in tandem with the measures against the Jews and which was to culminate in the so-called 'euthanasia' programme against the handicapped which began in 1939.[2] There was a certain logic in the fact that the gassing techniques first used to murder the handicapped were then applied to exterminate the Jews. For both the eugenics programme to improve German racial hygiene and the programme of anti-Semitism ultimately derived from a common perspective, a perspective which viewed man and society not simply in biological terms, but from a particular Social Darwinist standpoint.[3] Much attention has been devoted to the background to Nazi anti-Semitism; far less work, however, has been done on the eugenics aspect of Nazi racial policy and very little has appeared in English.[4] This essay attempts to sketch in the background to this particular aspect and indicate its importance.[5]

In his statement on the imminence of eugenics legislation Geiger did not have the Nazis and their policies specifically in mind. He was referring to a much wider consensus on the need for action in the eugenics field. To understand both the specific character of Nazi ideas on eugenics and the form of their implementation it is important to see them in a broader context of a movement which had gained widespread support by the early 1920s - and not just in Germany. For eugenics had influential followers in the United States, Switzerland, Britain and elsewhere.[6] Its advocates expressed a wide range of views on policies to be followed; they had in common, however, a number of basic ideas which formed the core of eugenics as an ideology.

Eugenics had originated in Britain with the work of Sir Francis Galton, a nephew of Charles Darwin and a Victorian Privatgelehrte of some distinction.[7] Like many of his contemporaries, Galton had been deeply influenced by the publication of Darwin's Origin of Species (1859).

In 1869, in his book Hereditary Genius, he applied Darwin's arguments to the human race and went on to argue that ability - both mental and physical - was hereditary. He developed this thesis further in Inquiries into Human Faculty and its Development (1883) which first introduced the term 'eugenics' to describe a programme for improving the human race by genetic means. Galton did not envisage eugenics as being confined merely to 'questions of judicious mating'[8] but conceived it as a new science which covered 'those agencies under social control which may improve or impair the racial qualities of future generations either physically or mentally', i.e. it was seen as relevant to the whole field of social issues - health, crime, education, sex and the family, welfare and so on. It was not, however, until the 1890s and, in particular, the pre-war years that eugenics began to attract a wide following.[9] In 1904 Galton funded a research fellowship in eugenics at University College London. In 1907 a Eugenics Education Society was founded to educate public opinion and in 1910 a journal was founded - the Eugenics Review.

In Germany too this period saw the emergence of eugenics as part of a wider Social Darwinist movement.[10] Rather than deriving directly from the influence of Galton - although he came to be widely read in Germany - this appears to have been an indigenous development stemming from the influence of Darwin's ideas in Germany. In 1900, a competition was sponsored by Alfried Krupp in which the substantial sum of RM 50,000 was offered as a prize for the best response to the question: 'What can we learn from the principles of the theory of evolution in relation to domestic political developments and the legislation of states?'[11] The winner was a doctor, Wilhelm Schallmeyer, whose work had the title: 'Heredity and Selection in the Life of Nations. A Study in Political Science on the Basis of the New Biology' and advocated a programme of eugenics or what the author called 'service to the race' (Rassedienst). It was published in 1903 and over the next few years went through several editions, becoming the standard German book on eugenics until the early 1920s.[12]

If anyone had the right to the title of pioneer of eugenics in Germany, however, it was Alfred Ploetz who, after practising as a doctor for a few years, devoted the rest of his life to the movement.[13] In 1895, he published a book with the title: The Efficiency of our Race and the Protection of the Weak. An Analysis of Racial Hygiene and its Relationship to the Humane Ideals, and particularly to Socialism, in which he introduced the concept of 'racial hygiene' (eugenics) and advocated its implementation.[14] In 1904, Ploetz founded a journal - the Archiv für Rassen und Gesellschaftsbiologie - which had acquired some 1200 subscribers before 1914, mainly academics and doctors, and which he was to edit until 1937. A year later, he established a society - the Gesellschaft für Rassenhygiene (from 1916 Deutsche Gesellschaft für Rassenhygiene) which again, by 1914, had acquired a small but select membership of some 350 with branches in Berlin, Munich, Freiburg, and Stuttgart.

How then can one account for the growth of this eugenics movement? A variety of explanations may be suggested. First, there was a new intellectual climate created by new theories of man's development.[15] By finally removing the guiding hand of God from nature and by formulating a dynamic biology of development through natural selection, Darwin's theory of evolution had - as Galton and his fellow eugenists saw it - placed the awesome responsibility for the future of the species in man's own hands.[16] One further development was necessary, however, in order to complete the scientific background to eugenics - a new interpretation of the role played by heredity in man's development. According to Lamarck's theory, which dominated nineteenth century ideas of heredity and was accepted by Darwin, characteristics acquired by the individual through his interaction with his environment are inherited. Towards the end of the century, however, a number of major biological discoveries - the rediscovery of Mendel's laws of genetics in 1900, de Vries' work on mutations, and August Weismann's work on cell structure - discredited Lamarck's theory. The most radical statement of the independence of heredity from the environment was Weismann's theory of an autonomous, immutable germ plasm, a concept which had a great impact on the development of eugenics. Moreover, these important discoveries in genetics encouraged a new emphasis on the role of genetic factors in determining human behaviour. Now, not only did Galton's view that human ability was hereditary seem to be confirmed, but it became plausible to regard deviant social behaviour (criminality, alcoholism, prostitution and so on) as - to a greater or lesser extent, and the consensus favoured the former - genetically determined. The implications of this new climate of opinion for the view of man and of his position in society were enormous. There was clearly a strong temptation to regard individual human beings as, in effect, a collection of genes (Erbmasse), as biological material of either a positive or a negative kind, whose significance as individuals weighed little compared with that of the future of the 'race'. The race could be conceived in broad terms as the human race or in narrower terms as a specific race or a nation, and eugenists differed sharply in their emphasis here, but the implications for the individual were far-reaching whichever concept was adopted.[17]

It would be a mistake, however, to explain the eugenics movement simply in terms of the context of scientific ideas within which it emerged, important though it was. The response of the eugenists to these biological discoveries and the way in which they interpreted and applied them was determined to a large extent by their own professional and social concerns, attitudes, and prejudices. For a second explanation, then, one can focus on professional concerns.

Research into the German eugenics movement is only at an early stage and we do not yet have an analysis of its membership. Evidence of eugenics movements elsewhere, however, suggests that eugenists tended to be members of the professional middle class, particularly medical men and academics.[18] Certainly, the authors of the eugenics literature which appeared in Germany in increasing quantities from 1900 onwards tended to fall into that category. Practising doctors, particularly psychiatrists, lawyers and others engaged in dealing with crime, and academics in the fields of biology, zoology, and anthropology were particularly prominent. The emergence of eugenics must be seen against the background of a change in the orientation of certain professions and the emergence of new professions and academic disciplines in response to needs created by the social changes introduced by industrialization and urbanization. For example, from the late nineteenth century onwards, the medical profession began to acquire more and more social responsibilities as part of the growing welfare apparatus of the state and the municipalities. In addition to their own practice, many doctors began to take on duties in such spheres as schools, prisons, infant welfare, the combatting of sexual diseases and tuberculosis. This process encouraged doctors to see their role in a broader context than simply that of an individual doctor-patient relationship. This was, of course, particularly true of those doctors who became part of the developing state or municipal medical bureaucracies. Doctors began to acquire a sense of medicine as a social function and to develop a sense of social responsibility, a concern with 'social hygiene', which encouraged an active interventionist outlook.

It is not yet clear exactly how the eugenics movement fitted in to this process. On the one hand, the eugenists' emphasis on the significance of hereditary factors could well have alienated those involved in trying to improve the social environment of disadvantaged groups. On the other hand, the new activist social role which had emerged for professionals could also provide a fertile climate for eugenic ideals which appeared to offer a 'scientific' solution to social problems; social hygiene sometimes came to be supplemented by 'racial hygiene'.[19] It has been shown that in the United States many converts to eugenics came from social workers who, frustrated by the intractability of the problems with which they were faced, sought an explanation of their clients' failure to respond to treatment in theories of hereditary degeneracy.[20] Eugenics was influential among some amateurs involved in the field of social welfare, including a number of leading figures on the Left. Thus, the 'League for the Protection of Mothers', founded in 1905, attracted the support both of leading eugenists and of some leading members of the SPD, who shared their concern for 'the improved breeding of the race' (Eduard David).[21] If the nineteenth century had seen man applying science to control and improve his environment, now it seemed he could use it to improve mankind itself, solving many of the social ills with which it had long been plagued. This was a heady doctrine and some of its advocates acquired an almost messianic quality. They demanded a revaluation of values in a biological direction. Indeed, Galton was not alone in insisting that eugenics 'must be introduced into the national consciousness as a new religion'.[22]

But academics and doctors were not simply professional men with professional preoccupations, they were also members of a particular stratum in society - the educated upper middle class or Bildungsbürgertum. This was a group which, by the first decade of the twentieth century, was beginning to feel itself threatened by a number of social developments, notably the creation of a 'mass' urban society combined with the emergence of a powerful new rival moneyed élite, neither of which shared their values.[23] They both despised and feared the democratizing, levelling aspects of a mass society and what they saw as the crude materialism of the new élite. Specifically, they were concerned that the traditional professional élite was being undermined by the influx of 'new men' from the commercial middle class as a result of the expanding numbers within the professions. Significantly, according to his biographer, Galton regarded two features of modern civilization as especially harmful to the race - 'wealth and urbanism'.[24] Eugenics emerged within a <u>fin de siècle</u> climate of pessimism in which 'degeneration' (<u>Entartung</u>) was seen on all sides.

What were then the main preoccupations of eugenists?[25] Firstly, they were concerned about the decline in the rate of population growth, which had begun to affect Western European countries by the turn of the century, and which they attributed to the lower fertility of urban society. More particularly, they were worried about what they saw as a degeneration of the race, which they attributed primarily to a decline in the birth rate of the upper social groups - a consequence of the increased use of birth control methods - and, as a result, an increase in the proportion of 'inferiors' (<u>Minderwertigen</u>) within the population. The tendency to equate social superiority with eugenic superiority was present from the start. Thus, much of Galton's work was concerned with differential rates of fertility between different social groups and this became a major focus of concern for most (though not all) German eugenists.[26]

Secondly, there was also a concern that modern improvements in social welfare would mainly have the effect of encouraging the below average half of the population to procreate with the result that their genetic proportion would increase. Similarly, it was feared that modern advances in medicine would have a similar dysgenic or 'counter-selective' effect by interfering with nature's 'elimination' (<u>Ausmerzung</u>) of the unfit. The consequence would be a degeneration of the race. There was also a growing resentment at the economic cost of providing welfare for the handicapped and 'asocials' who were regarded as 'worthless life' (<u>lebensunwertes Leben</u>), 'burdens' (<u>Ballast-existenzen</u>), or 'inferiors'. Instead, it was felt that resources should be concentrated on the eugenically favoured sections of society. There was a particular fear that the number of mental defectives was large already and was in danger of increasing still further because of their allegedly greater libido and lack of inhibitions. In 1911, the weekly magazine, <u>Die Umschau</u>, held a competition with the aim of eliciting data on the question 'What do the inferior elements cost the state and society?'[27] The prize was won by Ludwig Jens, an official of the General Asylum for the Poor in Hamburg, who produced the anticipated large sum by including virtually all welfare costs within his figure. Two years later, in an article reviewing this question, Professor Kaup of the Seminar for Social Hygiene in Munich insisted that 'on the question of the isolation of the inferiors there is no place for sentimentality. Our healthy offspring have a right to protection from corruption from the genetically damaged and every progressive nation has the duty to avoid the burden of the costs of inferiors as far as possible.'[28] There is, in fact, a distinct air of paranoia about much eugenics literature and it may not be entirely fanciful to suggest that, for some, fear of the threat posed by the levelling effects of a modern urban society found unconscious expression in the traumatic vision of fecund hordes of mental defectives, criminals, and asocials breeding in the slums of the big cities and eventually swamping 'civilization'.

In response to these threats eugenists proposed a number of courses of action: firstly, the keeping of biographical records of families, particularly those who were either gifted or 'distinctly below the average in health, mind, or physique';[29] secondly, positive measures to encourage the procreation of the eugenically favoured by means of child benefits, tax reforms, and propaganda, particularly expert eugenics advice to engaged couples. And, finally, negative measures to discourage the dysgenic from procreation by means of marriage controls, confinement in asylums, or sterilization.

There were differing opinions within the eugenics movement over the relative importance of 'positive' or 'negative' eugenics, but there was a growing tendency to stress the priority of negative eugenics. Galton himself was representative of this changing mood. By 1908, he had come to the conclusion that the first object of eugenics was 'to check the birth rate of the unfit'; indeed, he emphasized the need for 'stern compulsion' to prevent the 'free propagation of the stock of those who are seriously afflicted by lunacy, feeble-mindedness, habitual criminality and pauperism...'[30]

This concern with 'negative eugenics' made an early appearance in Germany. Its most extreme exponent was a business man, Alexander Tille, who, in 1895, demanded the creation of social conditions under which those who were from birth more gifted and successful received more nutrition 'while the more inadequate anyone is the less he should get to eat so that the inadequate infallibly perish.'[31] Tille, however, was something of an outsider. More significant was the growing pressure from academics and practising medical men. Since the isolation of 'inferiors' in asylums was extremely costly, sterilization offered itself as a solution which prevented the procreation of the unfit at minimum cost to the community and also appeared less harsh, and therefore unpopular, than confinement. Already in 1889, a doctor in government service (Medizinalrat), Paul Näcke, described it as a 'sacred duty of the state' to introduce legislative measures to facilitate the sterilization of certain classes of 'degenerates'.[32] On 13 April 1897, a Heidelberg gynaecologist named Edwin Kehrer carried out the first sterilization to prevent the procreation of 'inferior' offspring - in breach of §§ 224-225 of the Penal Code, which defined such an act as an attack upon the person for which the penalty was a minimum of two years' imprisonment.[33] In 1903, at the Ninth International Congress to combat Alcoholism held in Bremen, a young psychiatrist, Ernst Rüdin, advocated the sterilization of incurable alcoholics, a proposal which was, however, indignantly rejected.[34]

The focus of interest on the sterilization of 'inferiors' was sustained by the example of developments in the United States where the eugenics movement was achieving widespread influence.[35] Here the practice of sterilization was encouraged by the development of a new technique - vasectomy - by a Chicago doctor, A.J. Ochner, a simple operation which avoided the need for castration with its drastic side effects.[36] This technique was applied in 1899 by Dr. Harry Sharp, the prison doctor in Jeffersonville, Indiana, and it was at Sharp's suggestion that in 1907 the State of Indiana passed a Sterilization Law designed to deal with hardened criminals, rapists, and the mentally handicapped. Two years later Washington State followed suit and subsequently a number of others. The German public was informed about American developments by Geza von Hoffmann who, as an Austro-Hungarian Vice-Consul, had studied the practice of eugenics in the United States.[37] On his transfer to Berlin, he became an active member of the Deutsche Gesellschaft für Rassenhygiene and published an influential book which exaggerated the extent of sterilization in America, creating the false impression that it was commonplace.

In 1914, the Deutsche Gesellschaft für Rassenhygiene incorporated in its 'Principles' the demand for 'legal regulation of the procedure in cases where abortion or sterilization appear medically desirable'.[38] In July 1914, the Reich government, alarmed by the growing discussion about sterilization, introduced a draft bill to clarify the situation.[39] It laid down that sterilization and abortion could only be carried out if there was an 'immediate threat to life or limb' i.e. neither social nor eugenic grounds were sufficient. The bill, however, fell victim first to the war and then, after its revival in 1918, to the Revolution.

The effects of the First World War introduced a new sense of urgency into the discussion of eugenics and of the whole question of population policy. The enormous war casualties not only reduced the numbers of the population directly, but the loss of large members of young men clearly threatened the future birth-rate which was already in decline. By the end of the 1920s, concern about the birth-rate was reaching panic proportions. In December 1927, for example, the right-wing journal, the Süddeutschen Monatshefte, devoted a long article to the problem, describing it as 'the most fearful of the many symbols of the decline of our culture'.[40] It was attributed to a combination of urbanization ('the victory of the city over the peasantry') and the emancipation of women, and the article predicted 'the fall of the white race'. Pressure for official action to deal with the problem became intense.

General concern about the birth-rate in the aftermath of the war almost certainly contributed to a marked growth in the academic respectability of eugenics as a science during the Weimar period. In 1923, a leading eugenist, Fritz Lenz, was appointed to a personal chair (Extraordinariat) in racial hygiene at Munich University. In 1927, the Kaiser Wilhelm Society, Germany's leading academic foundation, established a Kaiser Wilhelm Institute for Anthropology, Human Heredity, and Eugenics in Berlin-Dahlem under the directorship of Professor Eugen Fischer, the author of a pre-war study of the so-called Rehobother Bastards in South West Africa.[41] Under the direction of Hermann Muckermann, S.J., the Eugenics department of the Institute launched a series of investigations into the differential birth-rates of particular social and occupational groups - villages and small towns in Westphalia, professors, secondary and primary school teachers, and the Prussian police.[42]

The most influential figures involved in the population debate, however, were a director in the Reich Statistical Office, Dr. Friedrich Burgdörfer, and a senior official in the Prussian Ministry of Social Welfare, ORR Dr. A. Ostermann.[43] Burgdörfer not only produced the statistical material on which the fears about a population decline were based, but was extremely active in communicating his fears to a wider public through lectures and publications.[44] Dr. Ostermann was deputy chairman of the Bund für Volksaufartung und Erbkunde, founded in 1925 to represent a group of moderate eugenists who had broken away from the Deutsche Gesellschaft für Rassenhygiene because of its growing association with the racist movement. Ostermann supported the line taken by Muckermann which stressed the need for positive eugenic measures, in particular the need for an active policy of marriage guidance on eugenic principles.[45] On 19 February 1926, at his prompting, the Prussian government initiated the opening of marriage advice centres in major cities to give medical advice to engaged couples.[46]

Pressure from the Prussian government and elsewhere finally persuaded the Reich Minister of the Interior, Carl Severing, to establish a Reich Committee for Population Questions attached to the medical department of his ministry.[47] The inaugural meeting was held on 20 January 1930, and attended by 27 civil servants, academics, and representatives of various branches of the medical profession.[48] Severing had decided that the leading eugenists should be excluded, although the meeting was attended by Burgdörfer and Ostermann and the first paper was given by Professor Alfred Grotjahn, a pioneer eugenist and former SPD Reichstag deputy. Grotjahn, however, simply stressed the need for changes in tax and welfare legislation to encourage births along the lines being adopted in France and Italy, and also for a propaganda campaign through the Zentrale für Heimatdienst. The more immediate and pressing problems of the depression and the political crisis, however, prevented this committee with its emphasis on the quantitative aspect of population policy from developing any initiative, with the result that Grotjahn soon resigned.

The First World War had not only increased concern about the declining number of births but also about their quality. Professor Robert Gaupp of Tübingen summed up the factors behind this concern in a speech to the Annual General Meeting of the German Association for Psychiatry on 2 September 1925:

> The emphasis on quality rather than quantity in the composition of the nation is psychologically connected with the reduction in our food-producing area, the complications of our economic existence and our competitive struggle with an unfriendly international environment, closely connected also with the mass annihilation of our genetically most valuable elements, to some extent also with the theory of the threatened 'coarsening (Verpöbelung) of our race' through late marriage and birth control particularly among educated and responsible people who have lost (in the inflation) not simply their property but, even before then, their determining influence on the shaping of German events.[49]

This concern prompted a renewed interest in negative eugenics. In 1922, the Deutsche Gesellschaft für Rassenhygiene issued a set of principles which, while emphasizing measures of positive eugenics, also urged the authorization of voluntary sterilization on eugenic grounds.[50] For some, however, this did not go far enough, and a number of doctors were prepared to take independent action, despite the fact that §§ 224-225 remained in effect.

The most notorious example of this was the District Health Officer for Zwickau in Saxony, Dr. Boeters. In 1924, the consultant surgeon at the Zwickau hospital, Professor H. Braun, announced to his colleagues that, at Dr. Boeters' instigation, he had recently sterilized a girl and three boys who were mentally handicapped with the approval of their parents and without any legal repercussions.[51] In the same year, Boeters published in the Ärztliche Vereinsblatt a draft law for 'the prevention of worthless life through surgical methods'. Significantly, the categories of those liable for compulsory sterilization under this so-called Lex Zwickau included not only hereditary blindness, deafness, epilepsy, and imbecility, but also the 'morally dissolute'. Moreover, women who repeatedly produced illegitimate children were to be examined for 'hereditary defects' and, according to §9 of the draft regulation for implementing the law, 'hereditary defects' were to be assumed in the event of 'alcoholism, morphine or cocaine addiction, incorrigible reluctance to work, as well as for tramps and gypsies'.[52] The law produced a mixed but generally hostile response from the medical profession and from lawyers and, when it was submitted to the Reichstag in October 1925, was rejected. To encourage other doctors to go ahead, however, Boeters announced defiantly that the local public prosecutor had failed to take action over the 63 voluntary sterilizations of 'degenerates' which he had initiated in Zwickau during the years 1921-1925, three of which had been carried out with the express approval of the guardianship court.[53]

In his views on sterilization Boeters was an extreme figure within the German medical profession. Nevertheless, the practice of sterilization on eugenic grounds was by no means restricted to Zwickau as became clear from the response to a questionnaire sent out in 1930 by Professor Fetscher of Leipzig to 95 cities with a population of more than 50,000 inhabitants.[54] Of these, 19 either failed or declined to reply, 53 had not carried out sterilizations at public expense, seventeen had done so, and six either wished or intended to do so. In the 17 which recorded a positive response, between 1928-9 eighteen women and eleven men had been sterilized on eugenic or social grounds, seven of the cases being specifically approved by the guardianship court. Fetscher concluded that many more eugenic sterilizations had been carried out at the expense of the insurance companies.

The early 1930s saw a marked increase in the influence of eugenics which was both reflected in and, to some extent, a consequence of the activities of the Deutsche Gesellschaft für Rassenhygiene.[55] Whereas in 1929 there were only eight branches of the society, by 1931 six new branches had been founded, several other branches were in the process of formation, and the membership had approximately doubled to 1085. Moreover, this did not include those who were organized in the Bund für Volksaufartung which, in 1932, was to merge with the Deutsche Gesellschaft für Rassenhygiene. A statistical analysis showed that 'the overwhelming majority of the membership came from academic circles, including a significant number of professors'. The society organized a massive programme of lectures, of which the main burden was born by

Hermann Muckermann, a popular speaker. Most significant were lectures to doctors' associations and other such bodies influential in fields relevant to eugenics. In 1931, the Prussian Ministry of Welfare organized two large courses for medical officials at the Kaiser Wilhelm Institute for Anthropology, Human Heredity, and Eugenics which consisted of sixty lectures each, most of which were given by members of the society. The extent of the acceptance of eugenics became further apparent in May 1931, when a conference of Protestant churchmen involved in social welfare supported eugenic ideas, advocating a shift in the emphasis of welfare towards those 'who can be expected to return to work (ihre Leistungsfähigkeit wieder erlangen).'[56] While they rejected 'the destruction of worthless life', they approved of voluntary sterilization on eugenic or social grounds, defined as 'anticipated asocial offspring'.

One factor in the growing interest in eugenics after 1929 was almost certainly concern at the social implications of the economic crisis. Geoffrey Searle has suggested in the parallel case of Britain during these years that 'many worried middle class intellectuals of a conservative cast of mind turned with interest to a creed which purported to explain the catastrophically high level of unemployment and offered a remedial programme couched in impressively scientific language.'[57] In particular, there was concern about the increasing numbers of mental patients in asylums and the financial cost involved at a time when public expenditure was being cut back.[58] Sterilization offered an opportunity to release some of these patients without the danger of them producing 'asocial offspring' and to divert the resources saved to those welfare cases which offered more potential benefit to society, assessed in narrow terms of economic performance (Leistung). It also 'satisfied the urge to do something drastic and unusual while leaving social and economic institutions intact.'[59]

The combination of growing pressure for the use of sterilization with the uncertain legal position produced a series of legislative initiatives. In 1925, the Reichstag introduced a clause (§ 238) in the draft of a new Penal Code which asserted that 'Operations and treatment which are in accordance with the practice of a conscientious doctor are not injuries to the person or maltreatment within the meaning of this law'.[60] The draft did not, however, become law. In 1927, a proposal made by Professor Grotjahn of Berlin at a meeting of the Prussian Health Office to introduce a clause specifically permitting voluntary sterilization on eugenic grounds was rejected. The chairman of the Reichstag Committee for Criminal Law, Geheimrat Kahl, declared that he would resist the incorporation of eugenic ideas into the law 'not just with one arm but with both arms'.[61]

By the beginning of the 1930s, however, the views of the octogenarian Geheimrat Kahl were becoming those of a minority. On 2 July 1932, the Committee for Population Questions and Eugenics of the Prussian State Council of Health, consisting of lawyers, psychiatrists, doctors and civil servants, held a conference to debate the issue of 'Eugenics in the Service of the National Welfare'.[62] They unanimously adopted a set of proposals which, after further polishing by a drafting committee, were presented to the Prussian government on 30 July. The key proposal was a draft Reich Sterilization Law for the voluntary sterilization of those with hereditary defects.[63] At the same time, Ostermann, who had played a key role in the formulation of this draft law, helped to persuade the German Doctors' Association to pass a resolution along similar lines, referring specifically to its voluntary character.[64] This was followed in November and December 1932 by similar declarations by the Württemberg and Prussian Chambers of Doctors. The next step was clearly up to the Reich government to whom the Prussian draft was forwarded. On 30 January 1933, however, a new Reich government was formed by the Nazis and the Conservatives under Adolf Hitler. What was their response?

Nazi ideology combined both the racist and the eugenic components of the German Social Darwinist tradition and, although the main emphasis was on the former with anti-Semitism the dominant theme, eugenic ideas formed an integral part of the Nazi Weltanschauung.[65] The main source of eugenic initiatives within the Nazi movement before 1933 was the Department of National Health (Amt für Volksgesundheit).[66] It is doubtful, however, whether any of the plans and proposals prepared here had much, if any, impact on future legislation.[67] The man who - initially at any rate - was to have the dominant influence on Nazi eugenics legislation in general and on the sterilization issue in particular was something of an outsider before 1933. Dr. Arthur Gütt had been active in the völkisch movement in East Prussia in the mid-1920s, but had then dropped out of active politics.[68] He became a medical officer of health, ultimately in Wandsbek near Hamburg and, in the summer of 1932, began to correspond with members of the Nazi Party's Department of Health on matters of 'racial hygiene'. He joined the party on 1 September. During February 1933, he forwarded a nineteen-page memorandum entitled 'State Population Policy' to two acquaintances - Wilhelm Kube, Gauleiter of Kurmark and Dr. L. Conti, who had just been appointed a special commissioner for medical affairs within the Prussian government.[69] Conti was clearly impressed with the memorandum and, in view of the shortage of qualified medical officials who were Nazis, used his influence to secure Gütt's appointment to a senior post in the medical department of the Reich Ministry of the Interior from 1 May. Gütt's memorandum was not only a comprehensive re-statement of the main themes of the eugenics movement in its racist version, but also a detailed programme of action and, with his ministerial appointment, Gütt was now in a position to put his ideas into effect.

Firstly, he almost certainly played a key role in the dissolution of Severing's Reich Committee for Population Questions on 1 June and its replacement by a new 'Committee of Experts for Population and Race Questions'.[70] The only member of the Severing committee who was retained was Burgdörfer. The other eleven members included the father of German eugenics, Alfred Ploetz, Walther Darré, the Nazi Minister of Agriculture and author of New Aristocracy from Blood and Soil, the notorious Professor of Racial Science at Jena, Hans Günther, and the head of the Nazi doctors' organization, Gerhard Wagner. Apart from Burgdörfer, only one member was a genuine 'expert' - Professor Spiethoff of Jena, a specialist on sexual diseases. Nevertheless, the new committee was to play an influential role in future population measures.

The guidelines laid down at its inaugural meeting on 28 June, first by the minister Frick, and then by Gütt as chairman, followed closely the proposals contained in Gütt's memorandum.[71]

Secondly, among Gütt's proposals in his memorandum was one for the state regulation of sterilization and abortion on the understanding that 'a strict scientific basis for its initiation' and a 'legal process' for its implementation could be guaranteed. On arriving at the Ministry, however, he found the draft law prepared by the Population Committee of the Prussian Health Office and he proceeded to use this as the basis for a Nazi sterilization law, though with some significant alterations.[72]

The key first paragraph of the Nazi law read as follows:[73]

1.   (i)   Anyone who has a hereditary illness can be rendered sterile by a surgical operation if, according to the experience of medical science, there is a strong probability that their offspring will suffer from serious hereditary defects of a physical or mental nature.

    (ii)   Anyone is hereditarily ill within the meaning of this law who suffers from one of the following illnesses:
a) Congenital feeble-mindedness.
b) Schizophrenia.
c) Manic depression.
d) Hereditary epilepsy.
e) Huntington's chorea.
f) Hereditary blindness.
g) Hereditary deafness.
h) Serious physical deformities.

    (iii)   In addition, anyone who suffers from chronic alcoholism can be sterilized.

This differed from the Prussian draft principally in the more detailed specification of the illnesses involved and also in excluding carriers of hereditary illness who had been included in the Prussian draft.[74] This clause was not, however, the most important difference between the two drafts.

At the Prussian conference in July 1932, the representatives of the Nazi party, notably Dr. Conti, had protested against the voluntary aspect of the proposed law.[75] In his own memorandum Gütt had not referred to this aspect but now compulsion became a central feature of the new law. Thus, whereas §1 Section 1 of the Prussian draft had insisted on the prior agreement of the person to be sterilized, §12 Section 1 of the Nazi law laid down that once the decision to sterilize had been taken, it could be done 'against the will of the person to be sterilized'. The compulsory aspect of the law was reinforced by the implementing decree of 5 December 1933, which laid down that if, when treating a patient, a doctor or other medical personnel became aware that he or she was suffering from an hereditary illness or chronic alcoholism, it was their duty to inform the local medical officer of health.[76] The medical officer would then, if necessary, request sterilization if he could not persuade the patient or his legal guardian to make the request himself.

The request for sterilization would then be considered by a new court established by the law (§§5-10) - the Hereditary Health Court, which was attached to a magistrate's court. It consisted of the magistrate as chairman, a medical officer of health, and another qualified doctor, experienced in the field of eugenics. It was up to the court to collect and review the evidence, hear witnesses, and, if it wished to, require the presence or medical examination of the person involved. It would then reach a majority decision. There could be an appeal to a Higher Hereditary Health Court, attached to a Land Court, with a similar composition and process. 205 Hereditary Health Courts and 26 Higher Health Courts were established.

The law, which had the title 'The Reich Law for the Prevention of Hereditarily Diseased Offspring' (Gesetz zur Verhütung erbkranken Nachwuchses) was approved by the Cabinet on 14 July 1933 at Hitler's express wish and over the protest of the Vice-Chancellor, Franz von Papen, who was concerned about Catholic opposition.[77] It came into effect on 1 January 1934. The law represented the culmination of more than thirty years' activity by the German eugenics movement. The young psychiatrist, Ernst Rüdin, who had proposed the sterilization of alcoholics in 1903 had now been able to play an active part in the realization of his proposal. In terms of Nazi goals, it represented a modest first step. Those involved were acutely aware of public sensitivities and particularly of the hostile attitude of the Roman Catholic Church. Thus, it is probably significant that the word 'sterilization' was omitted from the title of the law.[78] Similarly, efforts were made to avoid the impression that the activities of the Hereditary Health Courts represented a penal process.[79] Instead, sterilization was portrayed as a 'truly beneficial deed for the hereditarily sick family'.[80] The regulations were on the surface tightly drawn, although their actual implementation was to show only too clearly the problematic nature of the whole enterprise, based as it was on highly dubious scientific foundations.[81] This aspect lies outside the scope of this essay, but an indication of the impact of the law is provided by statistics collected by the Reich Ministry of Justice. They show that, by the middle of 1937, almost 200,000 people had been sterilized, of whom 102,218 were men and 95,165 were women.[82] This compares with the admittedly conservative estimate of 12,145 sterilizations for the whole of the United States for the period 1907-1932.[83]

Although the Nazis were in a minority in pressing for compulsory sterilization not just among the population but also among eugenists, nevertheless they had the logic of the theory of eugenics on their side. Moreover, most of the opposition to compulsion among eugenists had been based on fear of its unacceptability to public opinion. For this reason, many people found it easy to accept the new law once it had been passed and put into operation. Even before 1933, support for the idea of compulsory sterilization could be found in some surprising quarters. Thus, for example, the women's supplement to the SPD newspaper, Vorwärts of 10 April 1930, commenting on the new Danish Sterilization Law of 1929, remarked that, however promising this law was as a beginning, it balked at the decisive question: namely, the compulsory sterilization of inferiors (Minderwertigen), preferably when still young. It is clear that, precisely because of their inferior intellects and characters and their attitude of protest towards society, they are incapable of bringing themselves to request sterilization or to agree to it. Compulsory sterilization is all the more necessary in such cases, naturally not without a thorough medical examination.[84]

After thirty years of eugenics propaganda, reinforcing deep-rooted forms of prejudice against the handicapped and 'asocials', and in the context of a general trend to devalue individual rights in the name of some collective, there were few left who even accepted, let alone were prepared to take an uncompromising stand on, the principle of the essential dignity of every individual human being, however biologically inadequate or 'socially useless' he might appear to be.[85] Thus, Theodor Geiger spoke for many when, in criticizing the opponents of compulsory sterilization, he asserted that:

concern about personal freedom rests on the liberal ideal of personal self-determination, an ideal which both in fact and in law has been too eroded to be maintained as a principle. Heroic collectivism is overcoming this attitude to life and making it appear superfluous. If a measure is recognized as socially necessary and useful, there is no point in criticizing it with such arguments.[86]

While it would be wrong to lay the direct blame for what was to come on the eugenists, they certainly helped to create a climate of opinion within the medical profession and elsewhere in which such horrors as the 'euthanasia' programme were possible.[87]

Notes

1. Cf. T. Geiger, 'Soziologische Kritik der eugenischen Bewegung' in Veröffentlichungen aus dem Gebiet der Medizinalverwaltung XL.4. (Berlin 1933) p.3.
2. On Nazi sterilization as a prelude to the 'euthanasia' programme see Y. Ternon and S. Helman, Les Médecins Allemands et le National-Socialisme (Paris 19) pp. 155 ff.
3. On 'Biologismus' see G. Mann, ed., Biologismus im 19. Jahrhundert. Vorträge eines Symposiums von 30. bis 31. Oktober 1970 in Frankfurt am Main (Stuttgart 1973). On the complexity of the impact of biological ideas see the impressive article by P. Weindling, 'Theories of the Cell State in Imperial Germany' in C. Webster, ed., Biology, Medicine, and Society 1840-1940 (Cambridge 1981).
4. Limited space forbids a full bibliography. Among the most useful post-war studies of Nazism and eugenics are G. Bock, '"Zum Wohle des

Volkskörpers..." Abtreibung und Sterilisation im Nationalsozialismus' in Journal für Geschichte 2 (1980) Heft 6 pp.58-65; G. Lilienthal, 'Rassenhygiene im Dritten Reich. Krise und Wende' in Medizinisches-Historisches Journal 14 (1979) pp.114-134; K. Novak, Euthanasie und Sterilisierung im "Dritten Reich". Die Konfrontation der evangelischen und katholischen Kirche mit dem "Gesetze zur Verhütung erbkranken Nachwuchses" und der "Euthanasie" - Aktion (Göttingen 1977); R. Pommerin, 'Sterilisierung der Rheinland-bastarde'. Das Schicksal einer farbigen deutschen Minderheit 1918-1937 (Düsseldorf 1979); and Y. Ternon and S. Helman, op. cit. In English on German eugenics there is: D. Gasman, The Scientific Origins of National Socialism. Social Darwinism in Ernst Haeckel and the German Monist League (London 1971) and L.R. Graham, 'Science and Values: The Eugenics Movement in Germany and Russia in the 1920s' in American Historical Review 82.5 1977 pp. 1133-1164.

5. Its impact on several aspects of Nazi social policy has been neglected. For its effects on women see the important article by G. Bock, 'Frauen und ihre Arbeit im Nationalsozialismus' in A. Kuhn and G. Schneider, eds., Frauen in der Geschichte (Düsseldorf 1979) pp.113-149. The author hopes to consider its implications for some other groups in a study of social outcasts in the Third Reich.

6. For a useful review of sterilization legislation see J. Blasbalg, 'Ausländische und deutsche Gesetze und Gesetzentwurfe über Unfruchtbarmachung' in Zeitschrift für die gesamte Strafrechtswissenschaft 52 (1932) pp. 477-496.

7. On Galton see C.P. Blacker, Eugenics. Galton and After (London 1952); D.W. Forrest, Francis Galton: the Life and Work of a Victorian Genius (New York 1974).

8. Cf. F. Galton, Inquiries into Human Faculty and its Development (London 1883) p.24.

9. Cf. G. Searle, Eugenics and Politics in Britain 1900-1914 (Leiden 1976).

10. On German Social Darwinism see H. Conrad-Martius, Utopien der Menschenzüchtung. Der Sozialdarwinismus und seine Folgen (Munich 1955) and H.G. Zmarzlik, 'Der Sozial-darwinismus in Deutschland als geschichtliches Problem' in Vierteljahrshefte für Zeitgeschichte 11.3 (1963) pp.246-273.

11. Cf. H. Conrad-Martius op. cit. pp.74f.

12. It appeared as Vererbung und Auslese im Lebenskampf der Völker: Eine staatswissenschaftliche Studie aut Grund der neueren Biologie (Jena 1903). The 1918 edition has an account of the competition and its rather acrimonious aftermath in the 'Vorwort' pp. III-VIII.

13. On Ploetz see W. Doelecke, 'Alfred Ploetz (1860-1940), Sozialdarwinist und Gesellschaftsbiologe', Med. Diss. Frankfurt 1975.

14. Die Tüchtigkeit unserer Rasse und der Schutz der Schwachen (Berlin 1895).

15. Cf. G. Mann, op. cit.

16. In Galton's view 'it suggests an alteration in our mental attitude and imposes a new moral duty' Cf. F. Galton, op. cit.p.218.

17. On the conflict within the German Social Darwinist movement on the question of 'race' see G. Lilienthal, op. cit. pp. 116ff., and L.R.

Graham, op. cit. pp. 1129ff. The term 'racial hygiene' adopted by Ploetz as a synonym for 'eugenics' initially did not have any racialist connotations. But during the 1920s, the choice of the term 'racial hygiene' or 'eugenics' began to become a sign of commitment for or against racist views.

18. On the social basis of the movement in Britain see D. MacKenzie, 'Karl Pearson and the Professional Middle Class' in Annals of Science 36 1979 pp. 125-143. For a rather different view see G. Searle, 'Eugenics and Class' in C. Webster, ed. op. cit.pp. 218ff. On the United States see M.H. Haller, Eugenics: hereditarian attitudes in American thought (New Brunswick); K. M. Ludmerer, Genetics and American Society: a historical appraisal (Baltimore 1972); D. Pickens, Eugenics and the progressives (Nashville 1968).

19. Professor Alfred Grotjahn (1869-1931), Professor of Social Hygiene at the University of Berlin, a leading figure in the fields of both social and racial hygiene and, significantly, for a time an SPD Reichstag deputy, is a good example of the tendency for the two fields to overlap. Cf. A. Grotjahn, Erlebtes und Erstrebtes. Erinnerungen eines sozialistischen Arztes (Berlin 1932).

20. Cf. M.H. Haller, op. cit. pp.

21. Cf. M. Jannssen-Jurreit, 'Sexualreform und Geburtenrückgang - über die Zusammenhange von Bevölkerungspolitik und Frauenbewegung um die Jahrhundertwende' in A. Kuhn and G. Schneider, eds., op. cit. pp. 65ff. See also L.R. Graham, op. cit. pp. 1140ff. Social Darwinism and eugenics also influenced sections of the British Left, though how and to what extent is a matter of dispute; see B. Semmel, Imperialism and Social Reform (London 1960) and D. MacKenzie, op. cit. and G. Searle, 'Eugenics and Class'.

22. Quoted in C.P. Blacker op. cit. p.104.

23. Cf. F. Ringer, The Decline of the German Mandarins. The German Academic Community 1890-1933 (Cambridge Mass.1969).

24. Cf. C.P. Blacker op. cit. p.90. In Germany Social Darwinism produced a similar quasi-religious fervour, notably in 'Monism', the movement founded by Ernst Haeckel, cf.D. Gasman, op. cit.

25. The following represents a summary of the dominant themes in eugenics literature from Galton onwards. Although individual eugenists varied in their particular emphasis on the question of positive or negative eugenics and although different themes were sometimes given different weight at different times, the same preoccupations recur regularly throughout the period 1890-1945.

26. Geiger, for example, was very critical of such assumptions,cf. op.cit. pp. 32ff. But this was very much a minority view.

27. Cf. J. Kaup, 'Was Kosten die minderwertigen Elemente dem Staat und der Gesellschaft' in Archiv für Rassen und Gesellschaftsbiologie 1913.10 p. 723.

28. Ibid, p.747.

29. For Galton's proposal see C.P. Blacker, op. cit. p.106. As early as 1891 Schallmeyer had advocated that the state should institute a scheme of Erbbiographien for every individual. Cf. M. Jannssen-Jurreit op. cit. p.63.

30. Quoted in Blacker op. cit. p.126.

31. Quoted in F. Bolle, 'Darwinismus und Zeitgeist' in Zeitschrift für Religions-und Geistesgeschichte XIV 1 (1962) p.152. On Tille, who was Geschäftsführer of the Verband deutscher Industrieller and from 1903 onwards Syndikus of the Handelskammer and of several industrial organizations in Saarbrücken, see H. Conrad-Martius op. cit. pp.214ff.

32. Cf. H. Frank, Nationalsozialistisches Handbuch für Recht und Gesetzgebung (Munich 1935) p. 813.

33. Cf. F. Lenz, Menschliche Auslese und Rassenhygiene (Eugenik) (Munich 1931) p.270.

34. H. Frank op. cit. p. 813.

35. On the sterilization movement in the United States see D.K. Pickens, 'The Sterilization Movement: the Search for Purity in Mind and State' in Phylon 28 (1967) pp.78-94 and J.H. Landman, Human Sterilization. The History of the Sexual Sterilization Movement (New York 1932) pp. 52ff.

36. Cf. J.H. Landman op. cit. pp.52ff. The equivalent operation for women - Salpingectomy - was, however, a more difficult exercise.

37. Cf. K. Novak, op. cit. p.40.

38. Cf. Lenz op. cit. p. 273.

39. 'Entwurt eines Gesetzes gegen Unfruchtbarmachung und Schwangerschaftsunterbrechung' Cf. J. Blasbalg, op. cit. p. 489.

40. Cf. R. Korherr, 'Geburtenrückgang' in Süddeutschen Monatshefte 25 Jg. Heft 3 Dezember 1927.

41. Cf. A. von Harnack, ed. Handbuch der Kaiser Wilhelm-Gesellschaft zur Förderung der Wissenschaften (Berlin 1928) pp. 116ff. and E. Fischer, 'Kaiser Wilhelm-Institut für Anthropologie, menschliche Erblehre und Eugenik' in Max Planck, ed. , 25 Jahre Kaiser Wilhelm-Gesellschaft zur Förderung der Wissenschaften Vol II (Berlin 1936) pp. 348-356. On Fischer see A. Ploetz, 'Lebensbild Eugen Fischers' in Archiv für Rassen- und Gesellschaftsbiologie 30 (1936) pp.85-87.

42. See E. Fischer op.cit. and Prussian Ministry of the Interior to Oberpräsidenten, Regierungspräsidenten etc. 22.1.1931 in Bundesarchiv Koblenz (in future BAK) R 86/2370. The SPD minister, Carl Severing, gave his blessing to the investigation of the police.

43. On Burgdörfer and Ostermann see the material in the files of the Reichgesundheitsamt (BAK R 86) and BAK R 43 I/1978 and G. Lilienthal, op.cit. p.117.

44. E.g. his pamphlets 'Der Geburtenrückgang in Deutschland. Seine Folgen und seine Bekämpfung' (1928) and 'Volk ohne Jegend' (1932). In the former, Burgdörfer demanded 'biologically oriented legislation' to solve the birth problem, but for him it was primarily a problem of numbers. In his view, improvements in quality, though desirable in principle, would only complicate the legislation (p.15).

45. In February 1932, the Prussian Ministry of Welfare sent copies of two of Muckermann's eugenic pamphlets to the Regierungspräsident in Wiesbaden for distribution to medical officers. See Prussian Ministry of Welfare to the Reg.Präsident in Wiesbaden 13.2.1932 in Hauptstaatsarchiv Wiesbaden 405/3158.

46. This Erlass and its inadequacy is referred to by Muckermann in 'Die Eugenik im Dienst der Volkswohlfahrt' in Veröffentlichungen aus dem Gebiet der Medizinalverwaltung XXXVIII.5. (Berlin 1932) p.19.

47. See Prussian Ministerpräsident to the Reich Chancellor 31.0.1928 in BAK R 43 I/1978.

48. See the minutes of the meeting in BAK R 86/2369 Vol. II and Reichsgesundheitsamt to ORR Dr. Goldmann (RMdI) 13.12.1929 in ibid.

49. Cf. Robert Gaupp, Die Unfruchtbarmachung geistig und sifflich Kranker und Ninderwertiger (Berlin 1925) p.16.

50. Cf. O. Kankeleit, Die Unfruchtbarmachung aus rassenhygienischen und sozialen Gründen (Munich 1929) p.81.

51. Cf. H. Braun, 'Die künstliche Sterilisierung Schwachsinniger' in Zentralblatt für Chirurgie 51.3. (1924) p.105.

52. Cf. O. Kankeleit, op.cit. pp.78ff. and J. Blasbalg, op.cit. pp. 490ff.

53. Cf. Dr. Boeters, 'Die Unfruchtbarmachung Geisteskranker, Schwachsinniger und Verbrecher aus Anlage' in Zeitschrift für Medizinalbeamte und Krankenhausärzte (1925) p.341.

54. Cf. R. Fetscher, 'Die Sterilisierung aus eugenischen Gründen' in Zeitschrift für die gesamte Strafrechtswissenschaft 52 (1932) pp. 419-420.

55. For the following see 'Aus der Gesellschaft für Rassenhygiene (Eugenik)' in Archiv für Rassen und Gesellschaftsbiologie 26 (1932). pp.94ff.

56. Cf. 'Erklärung der Treysaer Konferenz vom 20. Mai 1931 zu den Gegenwartsfragen der Eugenik' in BAK R 43 II/721a.

57. Cf. G. Searle, 'Eugenics and Politics in Britain in the 1930s' in Annals of Science 36 (1979) p. 168.

58. The distinguished lawyer, Professor Eduard Kohlrausch of Berlin, claimed that 'it is financial motives in particular which have made the problem of eugenic sterilization topical at the present time.' Cf. E. Kohlrausch, 'Sterilisation und Strafrecht' in Zeitschrift für die gesamte Strafrechtswissenschaft 52 (1932) p. 404.

59. Cf. Searle, 'Eugenics and Politics in Britain in the 1930s' op.cit. p.169.

60. Cf. F. Lenz op.cit. p.278.

61. Ibid. p. 277.

62. The minutes of the conference are in 'Die Eugenik im Dienst der Volkswohlfahrt' in Veröffentlichungen aus dem Gebiet der Medizinalverwaltung XXXVIII 5. pp. 3-112.

63. The draft law is in ibid. pp.107ff.

64. Cf. G. Lilienthal, op.cit. pp.119-120.

65. See, for example, Hitler's comments in Mein Kampf (London 1969) pp. 232,365ff.

66. For the Hauptamt für Volksgesundheit see Der Reichsorganisationsleiter Adjutantur: Gliederung der Reichsorganisationsleitung 18.7.1932 in BAK Sammlung Schumacher 374.

67. See the list of projects in 'Übersicht über die bei der Innenpolitischen Abteilung-bezw. der Rechtsabteilung der Reichsleitung des NSDAP in München vorhandenen Vorarbeiten und Unterlagen' and the complaint about the new regime's neglect of this work in v. Heydebrand u.d. Lasa to Lammers 29.3.1933. Both documents are in the Preussisches Geheimes Staatsarchiv Berlin-Dahlem Rep. 77/10.

68. See Lebenslauf 12.3.1933 in Berlin Document Center (in future BDC). Personal file Dr. Arthur Gütt.

69. Cf. 'Staatliche Bevölkerungspolitik' von Dr. Arthur Gütt, Medizinalrat, Wandsbek in ibid. This was a revised version of a memorandum composed by Gütt in 1924 and sent to Ludendorff among others. See M. Stürzbecher, 'Die gesundheitspolitische Konzeption Arthur Gütts im Jahre 1924' in Berliner Ärzteblatt 84 (1971) pp.1072-1082. See also the correspondence in Gütt's personal file in the BDC.

70. Cf. 'Berufung eines Sachverständigenbeirats für Bevölkerungs-und Rassenpolitik.' WTB 2.6.1933 in BAK 43 II/720a.

71. For Frick's speech and the minutes of the meeting see 'Niederschrift uber die erste Sitzung des Sachverstandigenbeirats für Bevölkerungs-und Rassenfragen am 28. Juni 1933' in ibid.

72. Although there are two Reich Interior Ministry files covering the operation of the Sterilization Law between 1935 and 1939 (BAK R 18/5585 and 5586), the file covering the actual drafting and the first year of the operation of the law is missing. This makes reconstruction of the drafting of the law difficult. However, in view of Gütt's key position within the medical department of the Ministry and the fact that he subsequently published the authoritative commentary on the law (together with Professor Ernst Rüdin, then director of the Kaiser Wilhelm Institute in Munich, and a lawyer, Dr. Falk Ruttke), it sems plausible to attribute primary responsibility to him. Certainly Hans Frank does so in his account of the genesis of the law in op. cit. pp. 815ff.

73. Cf. Reichsgesetzblatt I 1933 p. 529.

74. For a comparison of the two drafts see H. Frank op.cit. pp. 815ff.

75. He had also protested at the way in which the racial question was ignored. Cf. 'Die Eugenik im Dienst der Volkswohlfahrt' op.cit. p. 59.

76. Cf. Gesetz zur Verhütung erbkranken Nachwuchses vom 14 Juli 1933. Bearbeitet und erläutert von Dr. med. Arthur Gütt, Dr. med. Ernst Rüdin, Dr.Jur. Falk Ruttke (Munich 1934).

77. Cf. 'Auszug aus der Niederschrift über die Sitzung des Reichsministeriums vom 14. Juli 1933' in BAK R 43 II/720.

78. Dr. Falk Ruttke, one of the authors of the official commentary, later instructed the members of the Nazi Doctors' League always to use the official title of the law and not to refer to it as 'the Sterilization Law'. See F. Ruttke, 'Das Gesetz zur Verhütung erbkranken Nachwuchses vom 14 Juli 1933 und seine Durchführung' in F. Ruttke, Rasse, Recht und Volk. Beiträge zur rassengesetzlichen Rechtslehre (Munich/Berlin 1937).

79. Cf. 'Begründung' in Gütt, Rüdin, Ruttke, op.cit. p. 61. It had been the original intention of the Ministry of the Interior to include in the law clauses permitting the sterilization of habitual criminals and the castration of sexual criminals, but this was successfully resisted by the Reich Ministry of Justice no doubt in order to avoid giving the law any penal connotations. These clauses were then included in the Law against Dangerous Criminals of 24 November 1933 (§§ 42a and 42k). However, significantly, Gütt specifically emphasized the close connexion between the two laws in A. Gütt, 'Ausmerze und Lebensauslese in ihrer Bedeutung für Erbgesundheits-und Rassenpflege' in E. Rüdin, Rassenhygiene im volkischen Staat (Munich 1934) pp. 114-115.

80. Cf. 'Begründung' op.cit. p. 60.

81. The hereditary basis of various illnesses is still a highly

of the sterilization of those born blind and indeed of the whole mentality of eugenics see the pamphlet published by the main German organization for the blind and written by its secretary while the law was in gestation - R. Kraemer, Kritik der Eugenik vom Standpunkt des Betroffenen (1933).

82. Cf. 'Übersicht über die Durchführung des Gesetzes zur Verhütung erbkranken Nachwuchses' gez. Schlegelberger in BAK R 18/5585.

83. Cf. J.H. Landman, op. cit. p. 289.

84. Cf. Vorwärts-Beilage Frauenstimme Nr. 169 10 April 1930.

85. The most vigorous opposition to the Sterilization Law came from the Roman Catholic Church, although a measure of compromise was reached. Cf. Novak op.cit.

86. Cf. T. Geiger, op.cit. p.46. See also T. Geiger, Erbpflege. Grundlagen/Planung/Grenzen. (Stuttgart 1934) pp. 93ff.

87. Many of the leading eugenists who before 1933 had been more or less sceptical about racist ideas, notably anti-Semitism - Ploetz, Fischer, and Lenz, for example - rapidly adapted themselves to the new regime. The temptation of at last acquiring full government support to realize their programme proved irresistible. Already in 1931, after making some muted criticism of the racial aspects of Nazi ideology, Lenz had concluded that 'Hitler is the first politician of real influence who has recognized racial hygiene as a central task of all politics and who wants to intervene actively to encourage it.' Cf. F. Lenz, 'Die Stellung des Nationalsozialismus zur Rassenhygiene' in Archiv für Rassen-und Gesellschaftsbiologie 25 (1931) p.308.

After submitting this article I have been able to consult the archives in Potsdam which I discovered contained the Reichsministry of the Interior file on the drafting of the Sterilization Law which was missing in Koblenz. It does not substantially modify the general line of argument, but does provide interesting detail.

THE ART OF THE IMPOSSIBLE:

GERMAN MILITARY POLICY BETWEEN THE WARS

David Schoenbaum

By the end of World War I, it was clear to the victorious allies and even the German military that the German army was, after all, vincible. But it had been a close thing. Skeptical in 1914 that they could maintain a major, i.e. a two-front, war beyond the heroic exertions of its opening campaign, Germans had astonished themselves no less than their many enemies. In the summer of 1917, it looked as though the German submarine force, itself a strategic afterthought, might actually starve Britain out of the war. As late as spring 1918, German armies were again marching on Paris. In Eastern Europe they were roaming virtually at will. In November 1918, when they threw in the towel, Germans were still ensconced in positions in Belgium and northern France they had held since the war began.

Large numbers of Germans refused to believe that they had really lost at all. In considering the post-war order, the allies ruled out any thought of German military business as usual. A long memo for presumptive negotiators in September 1918 from Robert Lansing, the U.S. secretary of state, concluded with a threefold injunction. The American peace delegation was to respect national self-determination, assure universal access to the seas, and keep constantly in mind 'the imperative need of rendering Germany impotent as a military power.'[1]

In direct evidence of allied respect and even awe for German military professionalism, the peace provisions systematically disarmed the Reich with such effect that the new republic's 100,000-man cadre was hard-pressed to deal even with domestic insurrection. Frequent and ingenious efforts to circumvent the treaty provisions in surreptitious cooperation with the Soviet Union were largely outstanding for their fruitlessness. In 1923, a real moment of truth came and passed without a shot as French forces occupied the Ruhr in reprisal for delayed reparations.

Operational planning testified to a rich fantasy life.[2] But as late as the mid-30s, German officers acknowledged with singular consistency and sobriety that they were unprepared for a real war, which could only mean a defensive one, even on one front against Poland. Generals are paid to anticipate worst cases, and disposed by temperament and professional habit to say 'Can't do' more often than is generally supposed. But even post facto, there is little reason to question the Reichswehr's professional judgment. This is not to say that Germany was defenseless or even militarily insecure. As will be seen, the contrary position can be plausibly argued. But neither contemporary actors nor most subsequent historians, German or foreign, have done so. Traditional arguments have revolved instead around two positions: that a disarmed Germany after 1919 was ipso facto defenseless, and that a rearmed Germany was ipso facto aggressive.

Both positions are historically explicable, particularly in the perspective of the huge rearmament that followed Hitler's appointment as chancellor in 1933. In only a few years, rearmament had turned the new Germany into a military power even more formidable than the old one. But neither position is self-evident. The transformation has understandably preoccupied and puzzled historians. If anything, the puzzlement has grown with the passage of time and the erosion of conventional wisdom. A generation of post-war debate produced alternative explanations for Germany's extraordinary recovery from a military nadir, and the epoch-making successes that followed in 1939-41. The first makes Hitler the causative agent, a conscious actor with a programmatic vision and an effective timetable that led from purposeful rearmament to aggressive war. The other, acknowledging the curious bottlenecks and shortfalls in the German peacetime economy and the demonstrable discrepancies between real policy and its putative timetable, suggests that the Third Reich's successes were the triumph of bluff and improvisation.[3]

Neither position is entirely persuasive. But Hitler is the common denominator, the necessary and even sufficient condition in both. The military has generally been understood as an accessory, irrespective of its motives and growing reservations. In practice, even accessory status sufficed at Nuremberg to sentence two senior generals to death, and two senior admirals to life and 10 years respectively. Yet even in the afterglow of wartime solidarity, when the rearmament of Germany seemed about as likely as, say, the rearmament of Japan, the victorious allies carefully refrained from assigning corporate responsibility. The general staff was not (italics in the original) declared a criminal organization, a contemporary German reporter informed his readers the morning after the verdicts.[4]

Historians of Germany have laboured since World War II on the political history of the military under the Empire, the Weimar Republic and the Third Reich.[5] Historians of the military have laboured again on the institutional history of the services, their operational planning and, most obviously and relevantly, their conduct of war.[6] The Schlieffen plan alone, that veritable paradigm of German military history, has retained a seemingly inexhaustible fascination.[7] While a well-preserved and well-organized mound of documentation has certainly facilitated serious study of the German navy and its curious history,[8] the absence of anything comparable has been no obstacle to serious study of the German air force.[9] Since the appearance of their memoirs and apologias in the early post-war years, even the generals have held the attention of investigators curious to know 'Why were the Germans so much better at soldiering than we were? How did they achieve their combat excellence?'[10] The aftermath of Vietnam has only increased their reputation in America, though not the Federal Republic. Recent strategic revisionists have discovered German military examples with a warmth recalling the enthusiasm of Enlightenment philosophers for China and Iran.[11]

What historians have often overlooked is the issue that might imaginably have mattered most to Clausewitz, till recently, at least, a military philosopher more often apostrophized than read. It might also be the issue most relevant and interesting to posterity. The question is what armed forces exist to do and whether armaments are useful. Even taking Clausewitz at his classical word that combat is the military equivalent of cash payment,[12] the scope and utility of armed forces, like the scope and utility of banking, have come a long way since the days of the Prussian reformers. The implications of his most cogent and memorable proposition, that 'war is a branch of political activity, not autonomous',[13] are broader still. Book Eight, Chapter Three, of On War, where Clausewitz sketches the variety of possibilities that followed from this even in his lifetime, fully deserves Bernard Brodie's characterization as an 'austerely condensed intellectual tour-de-force.'[14] But it has only recently had much impact on historians, otherwise accustomed to Visa cards and political horizons beyond anything Clausewitz dreamed of.

Recent studies by Geyer and Deist are as significant for the originality of their questions as they are for what they report about the direction and impact of the German military in the 20s and 30s.[15] If they refer to Clausewitz, it is no coincidence. In Deist's case, the acknowledgement of Clausewitz is not only immanent but slightly ironic. A student of Gerhard Ritter, Deist is employed at the Military Historical Research Office (MGFA) in Freiburg. The MGFA, an agency of the West German defense ministry, is a lineal descendant of the historical division of the general staff, whose dedication to military history, both authors confirm, was as short-sighted as it was exemplary. Geyer and Deist address issues that traditional military history, German and otherwise, has often foreclosed or dismissed. What were, in fact, the lessons of World War I for German soldiers? What were Germany's security interests? To what extent were armed forces really able to satisfy them, and how did the military do its job? Was rearmament consistent with German interests? Was war the extension of German policy or the other way round?

Geyer's answers are voluminously documented and richly suggestive. The ultimate problem of the German military between the wars, he argues, was neither a lust for blood, a simple affinity for totalitarianism nor political naiveté, though all three unquestionably existed. The real existential dilemma had to do with what Marxist historians call 'false consciousness.' Military thought lagged behind social reality. German soldiers - though they were hardly unique in this - failed to grasp the radical transformation of their own professional environment. Their subsequent guilt and tragedy derived from their efforts to make a recalcitrant world match their professional expectations. As a result, they deceived themselves, kept bad company, and did a fundamental disservice to the world and their country.

The irony is that none of this was inevitable. Like the foreign policy of the republic they ambivalently served, the soldiers were revisionist virtually by definition. But there were other routes to the goal than unilateral rearmament and war. From its conception, Gen. Seeckt's postwar army was dedicated to rearmament by any means, and recovery of Germany's pre-war status. But Germany, somehow, was also to be a world power. Ideology took a back seat in the meanwhile. If cooperation between junker generals and Bolshevik commissars broke down in 1924, it was because something better turned up. A fundamentally pragmatic view of the Soviet Union - quite different, incidentally, from an almost hysterical view of Poland - is among Geyer's secondary themes.

The military's raison d'être, traditional military victory in the service of a traditional foreign policy, understandably misled both contemporaries and historians, who saw it as a kind of nostalgic Wilhelminism. The reality, as Geyer describes it, was more complicated and more interesting. In many ways, the military really had learned important things in 1914-18. Largely purged of its proverbial arrogance, the post-war army was modern and even radical in ways that rather recall the heroic days of Scharnhorst and Gneisenau. There seems to have been remarkably little attention to rank. Professional debate was candid and vigorous. 'Von' or no 'von', the majority of officers lived like civil servants, not junkers. While eloquent about their inclination to subordinate civil society to the presumed needs of a nation in arms, Geyer acknowledges the 'professionalism' of their concern. The prevailing view of national security and national interest may very well have been extravagantly irresponsible and ill-advised. It must nonetheless be understood on its own terms. In contrast to the militarism of the old regime, Geyer emphasizes, the 'cold militarism' of the post-war era was something other than a figleaf for domestic conservatism.

What caused the trauma of 1923 was not simply that the French incursion tested traditional professional premises, but that the premises failed the test. Reichswehr planners conceded that there was no way to stop, or repel, the occupiers by military force. Their operational plans for 1924-25 testify to the very hopelessness of the enterprise: retreat to redoubts in central Germany, gas attacks on occupied areas, destruction of roads, bridges and telephone lines, grassroots guerrilla warfare and terrorism 'on the basis of colonial experience, particularly in South West Africa.' There was to be 'no consideration for the population, if that's what victory requires.'[16] In effect, the national interest required that Germany be treated like a colony. It was necessary to destroy the country in order to save it.

The paradox was that the Ruhr occupation, calamitous as it was for the Germans, was also a disaster for the French. The German tailspin threatened France's neighbors, frightened its allies, and destabilized its government and economy.[17] The realities of the postwar system may have meant the bankruptcy of national defense, at least as German soldiers traditionally understood it, but they also meant its salvation. The French were no longer strong enough to act unilaterally. Their allies were no longer prepared to sign blank checks. After an inflationary binge like none before it, Germany's economy was exhausted, impoverished, undercapitalized. Neither American bankers nor German officers wanted the chaos to go on.

And so there was a deal, a whole package of deals. There was a commitment to 'peaceful' change, to economic recovery and even domestic conciliation - at least within limits. There was also a new defense minister, Wilhelm Groener, who happened to be a soldier of credibility and reputation. As contemptuous of politics as the next German general, Groener nonetheless managed to pull off successive political prodigies. He persuaded the defense establishment that the new interdependence of diplomacy and international finance was not only a fact of life. It was a potential advantage for German security and the economic recovery crucial to rearmament. He persuaded the army to plan for contingencies it could actually handle, and exploit the possibilities of collective security. He persuaded the navy to join a strategic consensus, and accept a coordinated role in a coherent policy. He persuaded a democratic government, including a Social Democratic chancellor, to budget and thereby legitimate rearmament, beginning with a battleship whose military utility was as obscure as its political purpose was transparent.[18]

What he failed to persuade were colleagues, who regarded his views as unnatural, and a rampaging Right, who regarded him with reason as an obstacle to themselves. As the international economy and republican stability crumbled, Groener's position crumbled too. He was eased out of office by a former protégé, Kurt Schleicher. A political general in every imaginable sense, Schleicher pursued the main chance in both the domestic and international debris, linking general disarmament proposals and reparations concessions, authoritarian government and the domestic labour movement, in improvisations of frantic virtuosity. His colleagues turned their thumbs down on Schleicher too. 'The stumbling block for the Reichswehr was not Schleicher's "political" career,' Geyer says, 'but rather that his politics, nationalistic and above all cynical as it was, was more important to him than the purely military interest.'[19]

In early 1933, 'purely military' interest, like beauty, was a category that existed in the mind of the beholder. The new military leadership defined the institutional interest as the professional mainstream had defined it all along: economic recovery, unilateral rearmament and a reserve force to deter any threat while rearmament was in progress. The Reichswehr assumed as a matter of self-definition that what was good for the institution was good for the country. But now there was a chancellor who shared their views and promised to deliver the goods. The Reichswehr acquiesced in the Third Reich in incremental, even painless, stages. Hitler agreed to rearm it, the Reichsbank agreed to make the credits available, the industrialists agreed to produce and deliver according to the regular budget and current plans. The new government assumed responsibility for internal order, and withdrew from the disarmament talks in Geneva as the generals requested. To its considerable relief, the military could again go about its traditional business.

By 1936, Geyer concludes, the military had got its wishes like the fisherman's wife in the Grimm brothers' story. Hitler had preserved its sovereignty by wiping out the autonomy of his paramilitary formations in 1934. He resolved impending personnel problems by resuming conscription in 1935. He acknowledged the strategic problems of defending the Ruhr against presumptive attack by remilitarizing the Rhineland in 1936. Yet things were more threatening than before. The British were rearming. The French were exchanging meaningful glances with the Soviet Union. The economy, already stretched between military orders and its dependence on foreign trade, was overheating. As rearmament progressed, a reality no general would challenge, security receded. Aggressive war or a coup d'état were becoming the only options. War had become an extension of rearmament, Geyer argues, and policy an extension of war.

Deist's story complements Geyer's. His concern, again like Geyer's, is 'the fundamental and total breakdown of the relationship between armaments and politics,' already addressed and defined in an article by the late Hans Herzfeld.[20] Groener is Deist's base-line. Virtually alone among German military leaders before and after, Groener understood the relationship between means and ends. He had grasped the implications of social and industrial mobilization in the course of World War I, Deist contends. A disciple of the legendary Schlieffen, successively responsible for mobilization and demobilization, he had spent the post-war years re-examining first principles from his study and the ministry of transport. His promotion to the ministry of defense was an opportunity to impose reality on military colleagues still inclined to believe in the redeeming grace of heroic generalship, despite the static horrors of the western front. His colleagues speculated on tactical virtuosity and the magic of new technologies. Groener's solutions, while only partially realized, lay in deliberate coordination of forces, supply and political support linked to realistic objectives.

While Groener's colleagues regarded him with deep ambivalence, Deist believes he left a significantly stronger Reichswehr on his dismissal than the one he found. Whatever their reservations about his political premises, his colleagues had at least acknowledged his economic ones. The rearmament Hitler promised them shortly after taking office should presumably have been - at least in its early stages - the defensive rearmament in depth that Groener envisaged.

But it all came out differently. By September 1939, Germany fielded an army substantially larger than the one that went to war in 1914, and an air force without precedent.[21] But the army's yawning gap between personnel and equipment had only been closed by the windfall of Czech materiel acquired by a predatory foreign policy. On the eve of what the planners themselves assumed would be a world war, there was an estimated two months' fuel for the air force. The navy had its own problems. Demonstrably unprepared for the climactic shoot-out with Britain that had made the sailors' eyes sparkle since the days of Adm. Tirpitz, Adm. Raeder conceded in September 1939 that surface forces 'were still so far behind the British fleet in terms of numbers and strength that - even at full stretch - they could only demonstrate their readiness to die honorably and thus pave the way for a new fleet.'[22]

The regime's preferred self-image - spartan dynamism embodied in columns of blue-eyed youth with gothic faces - was true and untrue. For both technical and political reasons, the German war economy compared badly with the British war economy.[23] Certain problems were endemic in the system. The most basic of them, the regime's distrust of its fellow citizens, was itself a basic strategic consideration. Deeply suspicious of the population's idealism and toughness alike, the leadership treated living standards with great caution.[24] The competition between exports and military orders was just a part of Germany's economic dilemma. Consumer demands, labour mobility and the inflationary pressures of wages and benefits only added to the headaches of military planners, aware like Gen. Georg Thomas, the nominal coordinator of economic mobilization, that 'England was not going to be conquered with radios, vacuum cleaners and kitchen appliances.'[25] In Nazi Germany, labour conscription, fiscal austerity and rationing were an effect of total war, not, as theorists had assumed, its condition.

The basic rearmament, as Deist describes it, was another story. With seemingly unlimited labour and plant capacity, negligible competition for resources and funding, and unqualified political support, the army had already grown by 1936 from the stipulated 100,000 of the Treaty of Versailles to half a million. Starting from zero, the air force had grown even more spectacularly. It had even grown more or less coherently, a fact all the more remarkable for the accelerated tempo, the floods of new personnel, the unfamiliar technologies and the relative underdevelopment of the industry.

But rearmament and revision of the peace treaty were only the beginning, not the end of Hitler's foreign policy. For the moment, German diplomacy and propaganda deterred preemptive attack and avoided isolation. But the bottlenecks were already visible by the mid-30s. The Four Year Plan, the option for autarky and accelerated rearmament in 1936, was a quantum jump. It was as though Germany could break the encirclement of economic dependency by denying it existed. Coûte que coûte, German forces were to be operational by 1940. The economy and the services were to organize themselves accordingly. The military, increasingly uneasy but impressed by Hitler's foreign policy and grateful for a regime that met its traditional expectations of internal stability, cooperated. There was no reason not to. Having established policy, Hitler kept hands off its coordination and practical implementation. There was again no reason not to. Identity of aims is debatable, according to Deist. But complementarity of aims is indisputable.

The laissez-faire from the top was itself a basic cause of the murderous confusion that followed. Because the services were encouraged to go their ways and hurry up about it, they not only competed with one another for funds, resources and industrial capacity, but planned for different wars. Hitler's goals and tempo intensified the competition without imposing limits or direction. Projections and planning goals pursued one another in wild flights of unreality - 85% of existing world oil production by 1941 to maintain a combat-ready air force, for example, with storage facilities yet unbuilt.[26] 'Since Hitler did not even consider an economic solution to the problems, the only other possibility was that of predatory wars,' Deist observes.[29] The means and ends had been transposed. 'It was no longer only necessary to rearm in order to wage wars but also necessary to have war in order to continue rearming.'[28]

As the cult of Hitler sank in the totality of defeat, there was understandable speculation on what might have happened if he had only listened to the generals. But the speculation misses the point. In the real world where Hitler and the generals chose to go about their business, armed force was of only limited utility, even when employed with the military brilliance of German professionals. Even France, even Stalingrad, the respective benchmarks of German operations, pale in significance before the enormous goals the Germans set themselves. The object was to change the world in a fundamentally open-ended way with fundamentally limited resources. Irrespective of the speed, mass, concentration, mobility or morale of the forces available, the limits were inherent in the German situation. 'Cannae', the climactic objective of German military thought, was inconclusive in 1870 and inaccessible on the western front in 1914 against the forces of modernized, industrial adversaries. Tannenberg, another benchmark in German military history and a plausible approximation of the 'Cannae' the generals sought, was inconclusive again, even against a hugely underdeveloped adversary led by incompetent drunks.[29] Given the German goal - world power by world war - it is hard to see how things could have come out differently on the eastern front in 1941-45, no matter how the generals deployed their forces, and even if Hitler had deferred to their every word. There could be no Cannae on the eastern front. The alternative was the war of attrition the generals had set out to avoid.

It is instructive to compare the German dilemma with the British one that was, in its way, its mirror image. The problems of Britain's defense, and above all the British army, between the wars had to do with fundamental incompatibilities of force structure, strategic priority and economic resources. The influence of Col. Blimp, the strategist so often blamed for the débâcles that followed, has been significantly overrated. Britain's dilemma as a victor in World War I was that its responsibilities grew without any commensurate growth in its capacity to meet them. Even had Britons given their army pride of budgetary place, and employed Liddell Hart, the army's most eloquent critic, to equip and deploy it, it is unlikely that new weaponry and tactics would have stopped the Germans or prevented World War II. In part, this was because of strategic choices that gave the Middle East and East Asia priority over Europe. In part, it was because of an economy unable to support the new army and provide the new weapons in adequate numbers. 'British responsibilities,' to quote Correlli Barnett, 'vastly exceeded British strength.'[30]

In theory, France could have pre-empted the Blitzkrieg of 1940 with one of its own. But it had been clear since 1923 that this was out of the question unless Britain took part. Both countries inclined instead to diplomatic containment and accommodation of Germany's demands and grievances. 'When it was finally clear that diplomacy was not going to check Hitler,' as John Mearsheimer has written recently, 'it was too late for a military solution.'[31]

Blimps were hardly the German problem either. Nor, in contrast to Britain's situation, were force structure, strategic priority and economic resources necessarily inadequate to German responsibilities. But they were inadequate to the enormity of German purposes, irrespective of Hitler. It might be argued that when it was finally clear, or when the generals had persuaded themselves, that diplomacy was not going to make Germany a world power, it was too early for a military solution. But, as the generals realized themselves, it would be too early for years to come, and possibly for ever. 'The modern economy and its problems' might 'lead inexorably to a situation where peace would prevail,' Groener noted in a memo on 'The Significance of the Modern Economy for Strategy.'[32] As early as the 20s, only the United States and the Soviet

Union could fight the kind of war the Germans had in mind without recourse to foreign resources. It was no coincidence that the Reichswehr leadership had successively turned to both before turning both into implacable enemies.[33] Groener accepted the consequences of Germany's dependency. His successors did not. They rearmed despite them. Their exertions only made matters worse. The foreign threat, domestic obstacles and internal contradictions multiplied in proportion to the growing arsenal. The prodigies that followed in 1939-41, let alone thereafter, may testify to the courage and skill of German soldiers. But they can also be seen as the inspired, even desperate, improvisations of men quite literally fighting for their lives under circumstances different from any they imagined. Technical virtuosity was not merely a first condition. It was a last resort. German aspirations, to paraphrase Barnett, vastly exceeded German strength. The Germans started World War II because, ironically, they were unprepared for it after thinking for 20 years about little else.

For all that separates us from the 30s and distinguishes today's established American superpower from the monstrous dynamism of the Third Reich, two dimensions of the German experience might be of particular contemporary interest. The first is the nature of national security, and the relative utility of armaments. The German experience suggests that long before nuclear weapons, the classical calculus no longer worked. War might still be a usable instrument elsewhere. It was no longer usable in Europe, where the interdependencies of economics and diplomacy precluded meaningful limits. Hitler's fantasies acknowledged, even welcomed, unlimited war for unlimited objectives. But the generals' fantasies led in the same direction, despite their personal conservatism. As Groener showed, there were ways to conceive of German security that were adequately deterrent, economically feasible, even politically advantageous. His colleagues, and a majority of Germans, opted instead for an accelerated unilateral armament program that soon achieved a life of its own, and led to unambiguous military disaster.

The second relevant dimension is the nature of military professionalism. The German experience suggests that national security was indeed too serious to be left to the generals. This was not for any reasons intrinsic to the military or because civilians would necessarily have done better. It was because the Germans were so wrong about what they believed themselves to be right about. One need not make the German generals complicit in Auschwitz in order to find them wanting. Their original sin was an arrogant <u>Fachidiotie</u>, the blinkered professionalism of specialists indifferent to the context and consequence of their profession. It won battles, but lost wars. Conventionally admired for their scholarship, imagination, objectivity and analytical brilliance, the German generals proved in reality to be opportunists, <u>naifs</u> and Faustian romantics at their own profession and, as Clausewitz himself said, 'the man who sacrifices the possible in search of the impossible is a fool.'[34] Or worse.

Notes

1. Robert Lansing, The Peace Negotiations (Boston and New York: Houghton Mifflin, 1921), p. 197.

2. Michael Geyer, Aufrüstung oder Sicherheit: Die Reichswehr in der Krise der Machtpolitik 1924-36, (Wiesbaden: Franz Steiner Verlag, 1980), pp. 76 ff.

3. For an overview of the debate, see Manfred Funke (ed.), Hitler - Deutschland und die Mächte (Düsseldorf: Droste Verlag, 1977)

4. W.E. Suskind, Die Mächtigen vor Gericht (Munich: List Verlag, 1963), p. 182.

5. For an introduction to the huge literature, see Gordon Craig, The Politics of the Prussian Army (New York: Oxford University Press, 1955), Gerhard Ritter, Staatskunst und Kriegshandwerk (Munich, 4 vol., 1956-68), Matthew Cooper, The German Army (New York: Stein and Day, 1978), K.J. Müller, Armee, Politik und Gesellschaft in Deutschland 1933-1945 (Paderborn: 1979).

6. The interested reader might begin again with Ritter, op. cit., Herbert Rosinski, The German Army (New York: 1966), Karl Demeter, Das deutsche Offizierkorps in Gesellschaft und Staat (Frankfurt, 1965), Larry H. Addington, The Blitzkrieg Era and the German General Staff (New Brunswick, N.J.: Rutgers University Press, 1971).

7. Viz. Gerhard Ritter, Der Schlieffen Plan (Munich, 1955), and the relevant chapters in Martin Van Creveld, Supplying War (New York: Cambridge University Press, 1977) and Addington, op. cit.

8. Viz. Holger Herwig, The German Naval Officer Corps (New York: Oxford University Press, 1973) and Politics of Frustration (Boston and Toronto: Little Brown, 1976), Volker R. Berghahn, Der Tirpitz Plan (Düsseldorf: Droste Verlag, 1971), Jost Dulffder, Weimar, Hitler und die Marine (Düsseldorf: Droste Verlag, 1973).

9. Viz. E.L. Homze, Arming the Luftwaffe (Lincoln: University of Nebraska Press, 1976), David Irving, The Rise and Fall of the Luftwaffe (London, 1973), K.H. Völker, Die deutsche Luftwaffe 1933-39 (Stuttgart, 1967).

10. T.N. Dupuy, A Genius for War (Englewood Cliffs, N.J.: Prentice-Hall, 1977), p. 5.

11. For a few recent specimens, viz. Paul L. Savage and Richard A. Gabriel, Crisis in Command (New York: Hill and Wang, 1978), Edward Luttwak, 'The Operational Level of War,' International Security, Winter 1980/81, Colin S. Grey, 'National Style in Strategy,' International Security, Fall 1981, p. 32.

12. Clausewitz, On War (Princeton: Princeton University Press, 1976), p. 97.

13. Ibid., p. 605.

14. Ibid., p. 702.

15. Michael Geyer, Aufrüstung oder Sicherheit (Wiesbaden: Franz Steiner Verlag, 1980); Wilhelm Deist, The Wehrmacht and German Rearmament (London and Basingstoke: Macmillan 1981).

16. Geyer, op. cit., pp. 98-99.

17. Cf. Stephen A. Schuker, The End of French Predominance (Chapel Hill, N.C.: University of North Carolina Press, 1976).

18. Geyer, op. cit., p. 206.
19. Ibid., p. 306.
20. Wilhelm Deist, The Wehrmacht and German Rearmament, p. 1.
21. Ibid., p. 45, 89.
22. Ibid., p. 84.
23. Cf. Alan S. Milward, War, Economy and Society 1939-45 (Berkeley and Los Angeles: University of California Press, 1977), T.W. Mason, 'Women in Nazi Germany', History Workshop, Spring 1976.
24. Cf. T.W. Mason, 'Innere Krise und Angriffskrieg 1938-39' in Friedrich Forstmeier and Hans-Erich Volkmann (eds.), Wirtschaft und Rüstung am Vorabend des Zweiten Weltkrieges (Düsseldorf: Droste Verlag, 1975).
25. Ibid., p. 170.
26. Deist, op. cit., p. 89.
27. Ibid., p. 112.
28. Ibid., p. 111.
29. Cf. John Bushnell, 'The Tsarist Officer Corps 1884-1914,' American Historical Review, October 1981.
30. Quoted by John Mearsheimer, 'The British Generals Talk,' International Security, Summer 1981, p. 169.
31. Ibid., p. 181.
32. Quoted in Deist, op. cit., p. 8.
33. Cf. Geyer, op. cit., pp. 178 ff.
34. Clausewitz, op. cit., p. 637.

INJUSTICE AND RESISTANCE : BARRINGTON MOORE

AND THE REACTION OF GERMAN WORKERS TO NAZISM

Tim Mason

'The human capacity to withstand suffering and abuse is impressive, tragically so.' The sense of injustice, Barrington Moore continues, 'can be an acquired taste: a learned response and an historically determined one, not an automatic and instinctive human reaction.'[1] Reflecting upon the passivity of the iron and steel workers in the Ruhr before 1914, men who were subjected to novel and arbitrary managerial authority and to intensely demanding forms of labour, Barrington Moore concludes that 'human beings may have to be taught what their rights are'.[2] The essential part of this learning process, he argues, is 'the conquest of the illusion of inevitability', the conquest of the sense that pain, suffering, poverty and sub-ordination are natural, necessary and therefore legitimate: 'The conquest of this sense of inevitability is essential to the development of politically effective moral outrage. For this to happen, people must perceive and define their situation as the consequence of human injustice: a situation that they need not, cannot, and ought not to endure.' And, 'Without strong moral feelings and indignation, human beings will not act against the social order'.[3]

These basic, deceptively commonsensical judgements inform the author's moral history of the German working class from 1848 to 1920; this moral history constitutes the core of his study, Injustice: The Social Bases of Obedience and Revolt. Barrington Moore's intentions in this book, as in his previous works, reach far beyond those of conventional historical writing. His ultimate concern, in the tradition of rational critical sociology, is with political action - with the social, economic and institutional conditions of those political choices which may reduce the sum of human misery.[4] The specification of such conditions and choices is, for Barrington Moore, a task which demands systematic and wide-ranging empirical study, and prescriptive reticence. Unlike professional historians, he believes that there are lessons to be learned from history, but these lessons are complex and uncertain. Faced with the record of centuries of violent oppression in the cause of projects for human society of which the costs and incompleteness are at least as evident as the enduring achievements, the scholar's first duty is to a constructive scepticism, but not to total abstinence. Theorizing in the social sciences, on the other hand, is all too often unsceptical, a literary usurpation of the role of the political subject, all of whose important decisions are, among other things, moral choices seldom of a simple kind. What is required is the detailed, sympathetic study of carefully selected periods of decisive change in such a manner as to make them yield their general significance for basic questions of the social and political order - here, that of injustice and the combating of injustice.

It is not my intention in this essay to engage directly in such arguments about the philosophy of history and the social sciences. Barrington Moore's intensely independent approach to these problems leads him to find all of the major conflicting schools of thought wanting: Injustice is, refreshingly, a sustained argument with the evidence and with the reader, rather than with other writers. However, the author leaves no doubt about his complete rejection both of Marxism and sociological positivism on account of their neglect of human perceptions, and of standard types of cultural history and moral philosophy on account of their distance from real questions of politics and power.[5] Most explicit and most comprehensive is Barrington Moore's rejection of Marxism. This is a matter both of politics and of scholarly method. His study of how the German working class perceived the injustice of the social and political order in Germany up to 1920 leads him to the conclusion that it never constituted a revolutionary force, and never could have done so even if its political leaders had been united in pursuing a revolutionary strategy. If the largest and most fully organised proletariat in Europe was unable to generate sufficient moral anger over its exploitation and subordination to mount a revolutionary challenge to capitalism and autocracy, so the argument runs, then the very idea of the possibility of working-class revolution has to be abandoned.[6]

While it is not fully comprehensive - little attention is paid to the franchise question or to the wartime measures for the mobilisation of labour - Barrington Moore's examination of the historical evidence for his conclusion is so subtle and so discursive that it does not lend itself to summary. His central propositions can perhaps be re-stated in the following terms:

Before 1914 many groups of workers, like those in the Ruhr iron and steel industry, were unable to articulate a sense of their own oppression in the form of effective collective protests; coal-miners, who were able to do so, drew for their sense of corporate identity and rights upon a system of representation which pre-dated trade unionism, and their demands were local, peculiar to the mining industry, devoid of a generalised consciousness of the injustices of industrial capitalism; the evidence of autobiographies and questionnaires suggests that the strongest and most persistent form of a general sense of injustice was formulated by workers as a desire for 'decent human treatment' by those in power, not as a desire for a quite different system of power and authority; moments of mass anger and mobilization did occur, but they were not informed by a socialist class consciousness and did not generate those forms of organisation or tactics which might have given a degree of permanence to radical class antagonism - repression, collapse and suffering-as-usual soon followed. The mass revolutionary movements of 1918-1920 were basically defensive in character, and the fundamental reason why a socialist revolution did not take place in Germany was that an insufficient number of people was actually struggling for such new forms of social justice. Wanting a radically different public order which rests upon new moral standards is not a sufficient condition for attaining it, but it is, Barrington Moore insists, the necessary condition. His central concern in Injustice is to explore the difficulties which the oppressed have in formulating such a desire at all, and then in translating it into effective political action.

Although this interpretation is, arguably, over-stated at almost every step,[9] the range and depth of the book are such that it should become a new focus for the study of modern social history.[8] While the early history of capitalism has been widely understood as the history of moral conceptions of the public order, most work on the 19th and 20th centuries buries such questions under an accumulation of technical knowledge about the development of social and political relations. That class conflict in industrial capitalism has been, among other things, the conflict of different, evolving conceptions of a just social order is not obvious to the reader of most of the many monographs and articles on trade union growth, political mobilization, state intervention and welfare reforms, economic development, living and working conditions, etc. etc. In the work of Marxists and non-Marxists alike, the emphasis falls (though for different reasons) either upon the evolution of social and economic structures, or upon the ways in which various social groups attempted to achieve their specific goals. Debates over why certain things happened, or the elucidation of the complexities surrounding how they happened, all too often take precedence over the identification of their general historical significance. The historiography of working-class movements is perhaps especially prone to an emphasis upon the particular achievements of activists and organisations, and upon moments of open conflict. Injustice is an attempt to elucidate the limits and the political meaning of normal subjection, which is much less well documented.

Barrington Moore's overall conception of history is certainly not evolutionist in character - his thinking is too much dialectical and his temperament too cautious. However, both in his historical account of German workers' perceptions of the public order and in his general analysis of resistance to injustice there is a strong evolutionist undertone. Almost against the author's will, progress can be discerned. The workers who responded to Adolf Levenstein's questionnaires (1907-1911) may have had a very unclear notion of Socialism, and many of them may have accorded a low priority to the struggle for this goal in the conduct of their lives, but steadily increasing numbers of them were joining and voting for the Social Democratic Party before 1914. Faced with the powerful Imperial state on the one hand and such an uncertain base of mass support on the other, party and trade union leaders alike may well have concluded that there was room for little more than shrewd and persistent organisational work, but they had conquered a substantial area of 'social and cultural space' by 1914 and this was, as Barrington Moore himself argues, the crucial pre-condition for any contest over the political and economic system.[9] Even if the pre-war development of the German labour movement can be summarised in terms of the Imperial government having 'allowed large-scale mediating organizations with a considerable interest in the status quo to grow up against its will',[10] the protagonists on the working-class side had derived some measure of expertise and of corporate self-confidence from the conduct of the limited struggle. Finally, the insurgent movements of 1918-1920 may not have been predominantly socialist, but they were both novel and large-scale, and they were not ephemeral. They were not the actions of people whose suffering and subjection appeared to them, in the last analysis, to be pre-ordained, beyond constructive and militant challenge. Thus the 'implicit social contract' which defined the terms of the subjection of the working class in Imperial Germany was being continually renegotiated in an incremental manner.[11]

Like his history, Barrington Moore's general analysis of the ways in which people begin to emancipate themselves from repression and self-repression - an analysis which draws critically upon an immense range of literature from anthropology, psychoanalysis, experimental psychology and political science, as well as social and political history - also suggests that such developments tend to be cumulative. At the most general level, the diffusion of literacy critically facilitates the formulation of new moral codes by which existing institutions stand condemned; markets help to subvert hereditary forms of authority and to deprive them of their immutable naturalness; advances in scientific understanding and in technology bring more and more causes of human suffering in principle within the control of human agency and thus deprive them of that aura of inevitability which commands acceptance of pain.[12] In political terms, conflicts over authority and the distribution of goods and services are often learning processes, and such practical social learning is the very backbone of resistance movements. And if, in psychoanalytical terms, 'the super-ego', which enjoins acquiescence, self-abnegation, 'is the internalization of the past', the past itself changes over time, and its injunctions may become less simple, less austere.[13] Once they have been conquered, those illusions of inevitability which make the bearing of injustice seem necessary and therefore right, are not easy to resurrect. However, 'new issues' emerge. . . . there is progress, but it is immensely slow and costly.

The whole burden of Injustice is to show how extremely difficult it is for the oppressed to rise up; to show how in most forms of social organisation suffering and injustice are endowed with a moral authority 'that stifles the impulse to do anything';[14] to delineate the immense resources which are always at the disposal of the holders of wealth and power in any conflict over the principles of the public order, provided that they can defend their subjects from external aggression; to show 'why it is so terribly hard to believe that long-established authority is not essentially benevolent'.[15]

That the evolutionist thread in Barrington Moore's exposition is definitely secondary is made clear right at the outset, for Part One is systematic and transhistorical: discussion of three extreme cases, Asceticism, the Untouchables and the Concentration Camps, is designed to demonstrate that the human capacity for submission and suffering is indeed formidable, and to help to identify the principal 'social processes that serve to inhibit collective efforts' to resist injustice.[16] One of these 'processes', however, is qualitatively different from all the others, and raises a question which reaches beyond the main themes both of the historical exposition and of the concluding reflections: Barrington Moore insists that 'the complete destruction of existing institutions and habits of cooperation' is a real historical possibility, and that this 'may make resistance impossible, indeed unthinkable, by destroying the basis from which it can start'. Radical disruption 'may cause nothing more than apathy, confusion and despair'; it can make people 'malleable to new and oppressive forms of authority'.[17] There is clearly no room for a more than very temporary possibility of this kind in any evolutionist schema; and in general terms the point represents an important and much-overlooked truth: extremes of oppression do not automatically produce resistance.

However, the historical analysis in Injustice includes only a single, and ill-defined, instance of a destructive power which left people without the social support necessary to begin effective resistance: the iron and steel workers, who, from the 1880s on, were drawn from the most various occupations into an industry which was both tradition-less and complex, overwhelming in its technology and ruthless in its managerial procedures. The men, socially fragmented at the work-place, remained largely un-unionized and politically disoriented, taking 'an astonishing amount of abuse' until well into World War I.[18] The instance is ill-defined because the workers were not only victims of destructive social processes and managerial powers, but also in some measure subjects of a patriarchal entrepreneurial authority. This ambiguity is such that Barrington Moore can detect fundamental similarities between their condition on the one hand, and, on the other, both that of concentration camp prisoners and that of the Untouchables. These are the two groups which, in the author's transhistorical perspective, are identified as experiencing something like the maximum conceivable degradation and suffering without being able to sustain effective resistance. The iron and steel workers resemble concentration camp prisoners in that both were deprived of the possibility of group solidarity, which is a primary condition of resistance; and they resemble the Untouchables in so far as they acknowledged their subjection to possess the legitimacy of the inevitable and were in this sense accomplices in it.[19] Power relationships of the latter kind are, it is argued, characteristic components of patriarchal authority which does not assert itself through continual open violence.

Following this line of enquiry rather than that suggested by the concentration camps, Barrington Moore concludes, in a crucial passage of summary, that the difficulties which people have had in resisting oppression throughout human history can be read as 'responses to one of the oldest and commonest of human experiences, generalized patriarchal authority'.[20] And his analysis of the social processes and human choices which make resistance possible after all focuses upon conflicts with this kind of authority: that is, on conflicts in which it is the burden of the past which has to be overcome by the creation and enforcement of new moral criteria, and in which progress may be possible in small incremental steps.[21] Terroristic dictatorship presents a qualitatively different set of problems with respect to power and resistance. Although Injustice has much to say both directly and indirectly about some aspects of Nazism, the forms of Nazi power and of resistance to it are not addressed in an extended or systematic manner.

Barrington Moore places the concentration camps prior to and thus outside his history as a didactic laboratory of domination and suffering; he confines his history to the period which demonstrates the impossibility of proletarian socialism, rightly judging that the Ruhr War of 1920 marked the end of an epoch in German labour history; and he discusses Nazism directly only to prove in a brilliant and extended excursus that moral outrage is not always politically progressive. That the historical realities of Nazi rule and of resistance to it do in fact lie beyond the (very generous) boundaries of Injustice is brought out sharply by a question which is both rhetorical in its mode and evolutionist in its implications: 'And what group of workers in modern capitalist industry would put up with the long hours, arbitrary discipline, lack of procedure for the expression and settling of differences... which were commonplace before the first World War?'[22] One possible answer is: the German working class after 1933.

To observe that Barrington Moore 'raises, even if he does not answer, the question of why there was in Germany so little resistance to Hitler',[23] is not to enter a criticism of the book, but to take up one of its many invitations to further enquiry. The injustice inflicted upon the German working class by the Nazi regime was in a variety of ways new. The fact that it included the comprehensive and violent abrogation of existing individual and collective rights marks it off from any of the class experiences discussed by Barrington Moore. In some important respects most German workers no longer needed to be taught in 1932 what their rights were: freedom of association, collective bargaining, shop-floor representation, labour courts, social insurance, representative access to state power had all become familiar under the Republican Constitution. By this time the problems of German workers were not, in the first instance, those of 'overcoming dependence', of developing 'a new diagnosis and remedy for their suffering', of 'overcoming the moral authority' of that suffering,[24] nor even, except perhaps in terms of political tactics, of establishing an appropriate 'new definition of friend and foe'.[25] They were rather the very different problems of the loss of their own organisations, and of other institutional safeguards of the rights which they had gained since 1918, to a novel and openly destructive attack. No illusion of inevitability required to be conquered after 1933, for the new subjection was manifestly a consequence of human injustice; and there was nothing patriarchal about the authority claimed by the Nazi regime. Attempts by rulers to impose additional burdens upon the oppressed, to make an unjust relationship even more unjust, are singled out by Barrington Moore as occasions when moral anger is most easily expressed and most effectively mobilized; workers' movements characteristically show greater self-confidence in struggles which are, or appear to be, defensive in origin. However, this was not the case in Germany after 1933.

While the Nazi regime was not sufficiently destructive to 'make resistance impossible, indeed unthinkable', it was able successfully to contain all forms of working-class opposition and resistance. This is a complex subject of which I want to try to identify here only a single part.[26] The sucess of Nazi repression suggests that there was one new dimension to the moral framework of social and political conflict after 1933. To state the issue as an oversimplified hypothesis: the terroristic nature of Nazi rule deprived the oppressed of the capacity to resist in a politically effective manner not only through intimidation, but also by defining the terms of the conflict between the regime and its opponents in such a way that the latter felt morally superior in their suffering. Just as before 1933 the Social Democratic Party did not debase the coinage of electoral campaigns by challenging the Nazi movement on its own ground of demagoguery and hooliganism, and defined itself up to its destruction as the party of reason, so after 1933 the working-class resistance was unable to challenge dictatorial terrorism on its own terms. This relationship was quite different from what Barrington Moore calls 'the moral authority of suffering' which is characteristic of patriarchal power. Social democrats and communists who were persecuted did not generally acknowledge that the Nazi regime had any moral authority to treat them in this manner. Rather they were inhibited by practical moral restraints which were inherent in the confrontation between their politics and the politics of the Gestapo from meeting violence with violence, terror with terror.

To pose the question in this manner does not entail asserting that only those activities which aimed directly at the overthrow of the Nazi regime can be classified as resistance.[27] However, it may offer one avenue for understanding why working-class resistance was so large in scale, and yet had so little political impact. The forms and methods of resistance which communists, social democrats and trade unionists selected or invented were highly specific: the underground press, leaflets, fly-posters; the maintenance of illegal underground organisations in being, and contacts with exiled leadership groups; propaganda by word of mouth based upon news from foreign radio stations; assistance to the families of those imprisoned for political reasons, etc.[28] The principal characteristic of these resistance activities was party and group solidarity. Nothing in the following analysis should be taken as implying that more effective forms of resistance lay to hand, but were not adopted by underground groups: there was no such thing as an optimal or adequate set of resistance practices, for all such activities carried the risk of terrible costs, both to the resistance fighters themselves and to other persons who were not directly involved. This was one part of the moral dilemma of resistance 'from below'. The historical problem is to understand why the resistance of the Left took the specific forms which it did take, and not others. In this context it is the exceptional cases which shed light upon the rest.

The practical possibility of successful counter-violence was certainly slight, but it was not nil. Any prudential assessment of the balance of physical force in the Third Reich showed it to be massively weighted in the regime's favour, but it did not follow from this that every act of violent resistance was automatically condemned in advance to be a mere gesture of suicidal defiance or protest. Some such acts were more likely to be detected than, for example, the distribution of subversive leaflets, but during the war the latter crime also normally carried the death penalty. It was only by chance that Georg Elser was arrested after his unsuccessful attempt to assassinate Hitler in November 1939;[29] and in the Cologne area during 1944 the insurgent gangs of Edelweisspiraten killed eighteen representatives of the regime (and eleven other persons) before their leaders were liquidated by the Gestapo.[30] Neither of these resistance efforts was successful, but neither of them was doomed to hopeless failure from the start. They raise the question: why did social democrats and communists not express their hatred of the Nazi regime in comparable ways?

This question is in fact several different questions, for the violence of the Edelweisspiraten had a quite different quality of ruthless immediacy from that of Elser's lonely long-term planning. The former acted like people who had been provoked and threatened by their rulers to an anger such that they cast prudence aside. As military defeat drew nearer and the repression became more terroristic, politics became for them a matter of kill or be killed; more precisely, kill before being killed. The distinctive characteristic of the Edelweisspiraten was their youth. Most of them were too young to have had any experience of organised working-class politics before 1933. The fact that the working-class as a whole desisted, despite extreme provocations, from such acts of spontaneous demonstrative violence may well reflect the success with which both of its political parties and the trade unions had instilled a sense of organisational discipline into their members and supporters before 1933. This style of class politics called for the deliberate selection of tactics and strategies appropriate to specific ends, and then disciplined adherence to them. Spontaneous rage and expressive violence were, by this canon, immature and dangerous to the movement, since they could launch struggles at the wrong moment, alienate potential supporters and provoke reprisals.[31] It was precisely the cadres of the working-class movement who constituted the local leadership of the underground resistance struggle who were most deeply imbued with the values of collective political discipline. They did not encourage street fights, demonstrations or desperate acts of insurrection after 1933. To have done so would have appeared the more irresponsible since, through its control of the media, the regime could prevent any one such rising from acting as a beacon or inspiration to workers throughout the country. In mid-1936 a woman communist compared the mood of the working class in her town with the glowing embers of a smouldering fire which could be set ablaze at any time by a stiffening of the wind.[32] Although the regime showed itself to be cautious, even uncertain, on the few occasions when it was faced with mass unrest,[33] no such political combustion in the form of an outbreak of popular working-class fury actually occurred.

Clandestine violence or counter-terrorism raised issues of a different kind. Political killings or arson were the acts of individuals or small groups, not of crowds, and such acts were likely to be premeditated and carefully planned. This was the kind of resistance which the Nazi regime expected of the Communist Party, and the police discouraged it by the most ruthless means: indiscriminate terror as a form of deterrent vengeance. Such was the Nazi response to the burning of the Reichstag, and it was repeated on a smaller scale on numerous occasions, especially in the years 1933-34. Thus the killing of a man who had acted as an undercover agent for the Gestapo was answered in February 1934 by the judicial murder of John Schehr and three other leaders of the communist party.[34] In Augsburg between July 1933 and May 1934 there were six instances of severe police reprisals against communists in which innocent people were made to pay for 'political crimes', such as the drowning of a Nazi official or the burning of an assembly hall, which the police chose to lay at the door of undetected communist underground groups.[35] Yet more drastic, in May 1942 a communist resistance organisation with many Jewish members set fire to the 'Soviet Paradise' exhibition in Berlin: not content with the arrest and execution of the activists, the SS rounded up 500 Berlin Jews, shot half of them on sight and sent the rest to their deaths in Sachsenhausen.[36] While it cannot be demonstrated in any one case exactly how an awareness of the likelihood of such retaliations influenced the choice of methods in the underground, the readiness of the police to exact vengeance of this kind (which was extended during the war to include the arrest of the families of suspected resisters) placed an awesome burden of moral responsibility upon those who set out to attack the Nazi regime directly.

The choices which they made at the end of the war, however, indicate that moral considerations of a more basic kind inhibited most communists and social democrats from meeting terror with terror after 1933. The fact that murder, arson and the like did not come easily to them was one of the reasons why they were anti-Nazis in the first place; in this respect, the communist underground appears to have been only slightly, not qualitatively, more ruthless than that of social democracy. People who suffered and witnessed the worst brutalities and persecution at the hands of the Nazis stuck to their own codes of decent behaviour. Thus in Buchenwald the international camp committee of the prisoners was headed by a German communist; on 11 April 1945 the prisoners staged a successful armed uprising, seized control of the camp and interned 220 of their SS guards; they did not harm these guards at all, but handed them over to the US Army.[37] In the small Bavarian mining town of Penzberg a group of the pre-1933 miners' leaders, which included both communists and social democrats, took power on 28 April 1945. They believed, with good reason but mistakenly, that the German forces in Munich had surrendered, and they wanted to prevent the destruction of the mine in accordance with Hitler's scorched earth orders. On taking control they gave the Nazi mayor a safe conduct, and left the senior police officer at his post, but under their orders. This was not the reason why the rising failed, but later in the day these two men helped to organise a massacre of politically suspect citizens of the town a matter of hours before it was occupied by the US Army. If the miners' leaders had killed the mayor and the police officer, the Nazi retribution might well have been even more terrible, but it is clear beyond doubt that they did not make calculations of this kind: at the time when the two men were in their power, the miners' leaders had no reason to believe that their rising would be crushed. In their brief exercise of authority they simply did what they thought was right, acting with decency and civic responsibility.[38] To take just one further example, shortly after the end of the war a leading social democrat in Berlin publicly recalled that he had often vowed to himself before May 1945 to settle accounts in a personal and arbitrary ('unordentlich') manner with Nazi criminals the moment that the chance to do so should come; in fact he did not carry out his vow, but directed his energies towards clearing up the shattered city.[39]

Persons of this cast of mind were unlikely to have been drawn after 1933 to industrial sabotage or espionage as methods of damaging the Nazi regime. In one form or another actions of this kind were open to resisters of the political left - they called for less exceptional leaps of the technical and political imagination than Elser's attempt to assassinate Hitler, and they were also not especially easy for the authorities to detect. These are highly obscure topics, and one can only note fragments of evidence which indicate the dilemmas which people experienced in making choices of this kind. Nothing suggests that such tactics enjoyed an easy or broad appeal among class conscious, anti-Nazi workers. Thus in 1936 a communist building foreman accepted from a Russian intelligence officer the task of leading a group which would engage, among other things, in industrial espionage and subversion; he found it difficult to recruit active assistants, although he worked in an area where the Communist Party had been very strong before 1933.[40] The new communist underground organisations of the years after 1941 set high store by industrial sabotage as a tactic in the resistance struggle, and the Uhrig group issued detailed and sophisticated instructions about the most effective procedures, but it is not clear that these suggestions were widely implemented.[41] When the leader of an independent socialist resistance group in Bavaria proposed in 1941/42 that the group begin to take offensive action against the Nazi regime in the form of derailing trains, a heated debate broke out among the members on the propriety of such methods.[42] For similar reasons of elementary patriotism Schulze-Boysen and Harnack were not able to convince all of their associates in the 'Red Orchestra' that treason, in the form of intelligence work for the Soviet Union, was a proper form of resistance to Nazism.[43] We do not know for sure whether the patriotism of those resisters on the Left who were opposed to sabotage and espionage had a specific social (and thus moral) content, but it is evident that the price for successful actions of this kind was paid in the first instance not by the leaders of the regime but by ordinary soldiers, who as a result lacked equipment or found their movements betrayed. The moral dilemmas of patriotic army officers of the conservative resistance have been documented in detail; those of the Left underground were more complex, since, unlike officers, socialists and communists did not have such positions of power that they could choose their targets precisely or control the consequences of their actions.

The Nazi regime succeeded in oppressing and exploiting the German working class and in destroying its resistance until the military defeat of 1945. To attribute this fact to the unique power of the modern totalitarian state is to employ a sort of shorthand rather than to offer an explanation. One small part of such an explanation may lie in the circumstance that the victims of this particular kind of terroristic injustice had, formally speaking, to descend to the moral level of their oppressors in order to try to obtain redress or relief, and were unlikely to obtain it even then. But this may in turn be an extreme case of a more general dilemma: the rectification of all injustice requires power struggles, in the course of which the necessary means of waging the struggle may seem to discredit, devalue or undermine the end itself, while not certainly bringing that end any nearer.

Notes

1. Barrington Moore, Jr., Injustice. The Social Bases of Obedience & Revolt, London 1978, pp. 13, 188.
2. Ibid., p. 492.
3. Ibid., pp. 462, 459, 469.
4. The continuity of Barrington Moore's ultimate concern through all of his writing is very marked. It is well summarized in the review edsays of Guenther Roth, American Journal of Sociology, vol. 86, no. 6; and James Sheehan, Theory and Society, vol. 9, no. 5.
5. On these basic questions of method, the political theorist John Dunn finds Injustice to be an original and successful achievement, Times Higher Education Supplement, 29 Sept. 1979, while Sheehan, loc. cit., p. 732, argues that the subject of the book is 'too amorphous', and that 'the analysis does not cohere'. While I am not convinced that Barrington Moore achieves his own intellectual goals in Injustice, it is at the very least a powerful critique of all other approaches.
6. This is typical of the uncompromisingly radical quality of many of the judgements in Injustice. Although the tone of his argument remains conversational, Barrington Moore follows the logic of his scepticism to extreme and general conclusions.
7. Thus, to take only three examples, he underestimates the role of working-class intellectuals in the trade union movement, exaggerates the provincial, small-town character of German industrialization, and disregards evidence that organised resistance activities were possible in the concentration camps: see the reviews by Klaus Tenfelde, Theory and Society, vol. 9, no. 5; Sheehan, ibid.; James Joll, New York Review of Books, 28 Sept. 1978; Peter Gay, New York Times Book Review, 30 July 1978. These are all over-statements rather than basically distorted judgements.
8. Such is also the assessment of Reginald Zelnik in his excellent review essay, Journal of Social History, vol. 15, no. 3.
9. Injustice, p. 483.
10. Ibid., p. 364. The author frequently expresses his scepticism in the form of a sharp irony.
11. Cf. Injustice, pp. 17-25, 489-496. Zelnik, loc. cit., pp. 486f, rightly criticizes the looseness with which Barrington Moore uses the concept of the social contract.
12. See the explicit evolutionist formulations, Injustice, pp. 462, 476f.
13. Ibid., p. 497.
14. Ibid., p. 78.
15. Ibid., p. 463.

16. Ibid., p. 79.
17. Ibid., pp. 79, 470f. Barrington Moore does not develop fully his argument that such destruction may result either from the deliberate use of dictatorial power or from 'diffuse social processes that bring about the disappearance of traditional ways of gaining a livelihood' (p. 79).
18. Ibid., pp. 260, 272f.
19. Ibid., pp. 461, 471. Sheehan, loc. cit., p. 728, is wrong to assert that concentration camp prisoners and the Untouchables represent 'an exceedingly eccentric choice of cases'. While Barrington Moore does not explain the reasons for his choices, it is obvious, I think, that he regards each as the most extreme available example of two quite different types of degradation and suffering.
20. Injustice, p. 461; see also p. 463, and the introductory working hypothesis, pp. 23f.
21. It is difficult to condense this argument without conveying a misleading impression that it is cast in idealistic or psychological terms; the argument is in fact always historically and sociologically specific.
22. Injustice, p. 477.
23. Joll, loc. cit. It was rather that the resistance was not effective.
24. The capacity of the unemployed to blame themselves for their own lack of work in the years 1930-33 is one important exception to this generalization.
25. Injustice, pp. 87f, 462. The quotations represent what Barrington Moore calls the basic processes of emancipation.
26. I have attempted a broader discussion in the introduction to Carola Sachse et al., Angst, Belohnung, Zucht und Ordnung, Opladen 1982.
27. This point is strongly argued by Martin Broszat in 'Resistenz und Widerstand. Eine Zwischenbilanz des Forschungsprojekts', in Martin Broszat, Elke Fröhlich, Anton Grossmann, eds., Bayern in der NS-Zeit, vol. IV, München/Wien 1981, p. 708. However, it does not follow from this that all acts of violent resistance were condemned from the start to be fruitless, or worse.
28. See the excellent study by Detlev Peukert, Die KPD im Widerstand, Wuppertal 1980.
29. See Anton Hoch & Lothar Gruchmann, Georg Elser: Der Attentäter aus dem Volke, Frankfurt a.M. 1980.
30. Detlev Peukert, Die Edelweisspiraten, Köln 1980, p.106.
31. Barrington Moore himself strongly emphasizes this theme in his interpretation of the pre-1914 labour movement, Injustice, pp. 219f.
32. Kuno Bludau, Gestapo geheim! Widerstand und Verfolgung in Duisburg 1933-1945, Bonn-Bad Godesberg 1973, pp. 147-151.
33. For mass demonstrations by Roman Catholics, see ibid., pp. 192-197, and Jeremy Noakes, 'The Oldenburg Crucifix Struggle of November 1936', in Peter D. Stachura, ed., The Shaping of the Nazi State, London 1978, p. 223. The size of some of the demonstrations by gangs of young people left the police in a quandary about what to do - cf. Lothar Gruchmann, 'Jugendopposition und Justiz im 3. Reich', in Wolfgang Benz, ed., Miscellanea. Festschrift für Helmut Krausnick, Stuttgart 1980, pp. 103-130.
34. Stefan Weber, 'Nach der Verhaftung Ernst Thälmanns leitete John Schehr die illegale KPD', Beiträge zur Geschichte der Arbeiterbewegung,

1982, no. 4.

35. Gerhard Hetzer, 'Die Industriestadt Augsburg. Eine Sozialgeschichte der Arbeiteropposition', in Martin Broszat, Elke Fröhlich, Anton Grossmann, eds., Bayern in der NS-Zeit, vol. III, München/Wien 1981, pp. 160-163. In only two of the cases was communist authorship of the offences clear.

36. Horst Duhnke, Die KPD von 1933 bis 1945, Köln 1971, pp. 479f.

37. See the report by the chairman of the prisoners' committee, Walter Bartel, in Christoph Klessmann & Falk Pingel, eds., Gegner des Nationalsozialismus, Frankfurt a.M./New York 1980, pp. 243-251.

38. Klaus Tenfelde, 'Proletarische Provinz. Radikalisierung und Widerstand in Penzberg/Oberbayern 1900-1945', in Broszat et al., eds., Bayern in der NS-Zeit, vol. IV, pp. 376-381.

39. Frank Moraw, Die Parole 'Einheit' und die Sozialdemokratie, Bonn-Bad Godesberg 1973, p. 66.

40. Bludau, Gestapo geheim!, pp. 151-155.

41. Duhnke, KPD, pp. 460f; cf. also Bludau, Gestapo geheim!, p. 165.

42. Hetzer, 'Augsburg', pp. 200-205. Some members seem to have drawn a distinction between derailing trains during the war, and preparing an armed uprising for the moment of Germany's military defeat.

43. Heinz Höhne, Codeword: Direktor, London 1973, pp. 119ff.

CHARLES MAURRAS AND THE TRUE FRANCE

H. R. Kedward

Among the theorists and leaders of political reaction since the mid-19th century, Charles Maurras (1868-1952) holds a place no less exalted than Pobedonostsev and Pius IX. For decades he was the most important intellectual figure on the French Right and eventually became the grand ideological master of Vichy France, at least in its first two years. He gained his original reputation as the most dynamic of the anti-Dreyfusards after his defence of the forger Colonel Henry,[1] and he came to the head of the Nationalist revival in the early years of the 20th century by the sheer force of his relentless polemic against the Third Republic, the systematic strength of his ideas, and the range and intensity of his anti-Germanism. He even persuaded his colleagues at the start of the new movement, Action Française, that they too, like himself, should be monarchists, and his arguments for a Classical model for the True France eclipsed the Romanticism of Déroulède and Barrès, though he never quite usurped the position of Barrès as the foremost Nationalist personality of the years before and during World War I. In his own circle he was the 'Maître', but for the public outside he was an aloof, unapproachable person, handicapped by his deafness and lacking the charisma felt to be necessary for a political leader bent on the overthrow of the existing system, which he had christened the Anti-France.

True France and Anti-France, known in Nationalist language as pays réel and pays légal, were not his creations, but he made them household words on the French Right. Obsessive anti-Germanism was not his invention, but he gave it a dimension in historical and cultural terms which few could rival. Where he was original was in his monarchism, which does not concern us here, and in his positivism, on which this essay is centred. There are many 20th century Nationalists who look back to Herder, Fichte, Hugo, Byron, Walter Scott, Mazzini and Mickiewicz, but very few who claim descent from the classical writers and still fewer who start with Auguste Comte. Charles Maurras was both a classicist and a Comtean.

In over fifty years of political writing he claimed an unswerving consistency of ideas, and in every book and newspaper article he claimed to argue from the concrete facts of the situation and not from abstract principles. These facts were not economic and rarely social, except in its most cultural sense: they were political, literary and intellectual, with politics always at the forefront. People who traded in economic arguments were dismissed either as Marxists or crude laissez-faire capitalists, both seen as Anglo-German products of the 19th century and of total irrelevance to the True France. Indeed almost the whole of the 19th century was seen by Maurras as a foreign import, and his aim was to link the 20th to the 18th in the way that someone might welcome back and restore a perfect machine which had been stolen and abused by intruders. The problem was to recover it, and Maurras was at his weakest when it came to the issue of how he proposed to rescue his True France from the Third Republic. His movement was frequently dubbed 'in-action française' mostly by young disciples who moved away in the 1930s to more fascist alternatives. It was not seen as so ineffective by opponents, who held it responsible for the attempted coup of 6 February 1934, the assassination attempt on Léon Blum, the politics of Vichy, and incalculable damage to the Resistance. When he was tried and convicted early in 1945 for collaboration with the enemy, he saw it as one more malevolent act by the forces of Anti-France, and the irony of the most noted anti-Germanist of his generation being tried for assisting the German invader has been standard comment ever since.

His defence, embodied in a long autobiographical self-justification delivered over several hours, was characteristically a restatement of the conflict between his Nationalism and the Republic, and a repetition of his persistent hostility to Germany. Still more, everything was argued as incontrovertible fact, including his own identification with the True France. By such definitional arguments he presented himself as a victim of error, hatred and intrigue.[2] This was echoed by the first inside historian of Action Française, Robert Havard de la Montagne, shortly after the movement was officially banned; by Fabre-Luce, the independent right wing critic of the Liberation; and by Henri Massis of the Académie Française, one of the bodies from which Maurras was expelled after the verdict. Among Resistance writers there have been two major denunciations of the trial, by Jean Paulhan shortly afterwards and by Colonel Rémy more recently, while several historians have pointed to the vague interpretation of 'intelligence with the enemy' and have noted the skilful demolition by Maurras of the testimony brought against him by Paul Claudel.[3] But there has been no serious attempt by anyone other than his followers to rehabilitate him, not least because there appears to be no mystery or challenge in his life or ideas for new researchers to explain. His claim to consistency is widely accepted, and it can easily be shown that he was the kind of nationalist for whom the ideological pull of fascism was irresistible, leading inevitably to admiration for Mussolini and finally to compromise with the Nazi presence in Europe.[4]

But although there may be little left to add to the general picture, there is one feature of his ideas and politics which needs constant re-emphasis. If there was a seamless weave in Maurrassian thought it was not the anti-Germanism claimed by himself and his supporters, but his highly subjective form of positivism, and it was this as much as his fascist potential which led to his downfall and a not unjustified conviction. In his own terms it was even a reasonable one, though he failed entirely to see it.

Maurras started his career as a literary critic with a marked preference for all things classical, and as a philosophical writer looking for something to replace the Catholic certainties of his boyhood. This strong classical preference and the vigour of his philosophical search led him first into an evaluation of classical France as the True, Eternal

France, and secondly into a discovery of Comte, whose positivist system had offered the rationalists and humanists of the early 19th century a set of certainties based on science and reason and not on religion, belief or abstract principle. In Comtean reason Maurras saw a defence against the individualism of the Romantics and the disorders of Revolution, and in Comtean method he saw a way of establishing Truth which did not depend on theological speculation.[5] Furthermore Comte had argued that there was a collective, corporate human reason established over time which should exercise authority over the anarchical tendencies of individual opinion, and in this Maurras saw an equivalent of the collective authority of classical and renaissance values which he wished to establish over the anarchy of Revolutionary France. In L'Avenir de l'Intelligence (1905) Maurras explained to the intellectuals of the nationalist revival how Comte could be seen as a forerunner of nationalist reason, in the sense that he had raised the collective reason of humanity above the dissonant voices of individuals in the way that the nationalists had raised the collective authority of the Nation over warring parties and divisive factions.[6] Humanity, as a grand concept placed at the head of the Comtean system, was too abstract for Maurras, but in replacing it with the Nation, or more specifically France, he believed he was utterly consistent with Comtean method, in so far as the facts and existence of a Nation were more concrete than the attributes of Humanity.[7] What exactly the facts of a Nation were, or are, might be thought to be a subject of endless debate, increasingly open-ended as a nation evolved through historical events, but Maurras at this point exercised his political opinion and made a flagrantly individual choice which he paraded throughout the rest of his life as rational observation of the facts, objective and scientific. His Nation, the True France, was, he decided, exclusively composed of classical elements; absolute monarchy, a permanent hierarchy, ancient provincial liberties and rural values, classical culture and the humanism of the Renaissance. In this pays réel you could not be truly French if you were a Jew, Protestant, revolutionary, democrat, socialist, laissez-faire liberal, or anarchist. Against these forces of the pays légal, Maurras believed he could mobilise not just the force of argument but the force of fact. With positivist methods he set out to demonstrate that classical France had been, and still was, the perfection of French civilisation. Anything else was alien to the collective and corporate French tradition.

But did he need the term 'alien'? Why should not the error and discord of the Republic be as much the internal product of French history as the reason and truth of classical France? In many ways his constant polarisation of True and Anti-France, presented as an almost Manichaean struggle, seemed to acknowledge this. But his system was never really Manichaean: it was far too essentialist for that. He never lost his respect for Aristotle and Aquinas. His True France, located historically in the period before the Revolution of 1789, preceded the Anti-France of the 19th century. He therefore had to face the problem of how the True France, if it had been so perfect, had managed to produce its opposite. Nietzsche, his older contemporary, had a similar problem in the Genealogy of Morals of how the noble gave way to the ascetic. It is the problem of anyone maintaining a Paradise lost. But unlike Nietzsche, Maurras refused to accept the idea of dialectical change, and whereas Nietzsche, for all his hatred of the ascetic, allowed it to have rivalled the noble in sheer force of will, as well as having outmanoeuvred it by cunning, Maurras could not accept that the Anti-France incorporated any of the qualities of the True France or had derived its strength from the same national energy. He therefore had to look to outside agents to explain the errors and evils with which he claimed France had been plagued since 1789, and he began with that very year, arguing that the Revolution had never been French.

This insistence on 'outside' agencies was not only the most irrational ingredient in his system; it was also the most important. It enabled nationalists to claim that their hostility to internal enemies was not a question of political choice but a question of patriotism. Unmasking internal enemies was seen as protecting France from the external agencies which nurtured them. Nor was it sufficient to argue that the internal enemies were dangerous for France: Maurras went further and claimed that they were not even part of what was truly French. This could only be argued if there was enough evidence to show that it was a fact and not an opinion, and this was the aim of Maurrassian positivism. Having disguised a naked political preference in patriotic clothes he set out to provide it with the overcoat of Truth. His positivist insistence on the facts gave his followers that necessary illusion of reality to make their fantasies look like explanations,[8] and the process of constantly pointing to fact and claiming reality gave to Maurras himself the illusion of being consistent, even when he changed the facts quite dramatically. By persistently stressing his positivist method Maurras arrived at the point where this process by which he named facts as real and true became more important than the substance of the facts themselves. This allowed him to minimise, or even deny, the discrepancy between his anti-Germanism, expressed incessantly from the Dreyfus Affair into the 1930s, and his anti-English polemic which grew steadily from the late 1930s until his death.

In his early period, which is also the best known, he arraigned Germany and German culture for imposing the Revolution of 1789 on France, and for all the subsequent revolutionary movements and upheavals of the 19th century. It was Germany and German culture which were poisoning the French educational system: Kant was replacing Descartes and a German Protestantism invading the academic hierarchy. True to his positivism Maurras remained opposed to all religious explanations of phenomena, whether Catholic, Protestant or Judaic, but he valued the Catholic church as an institution of traditional authority and as a fact of classical France. Protestantism, no less than Romantic ideas of liberty and individualism, was yet another German import to be exposed, not just theoretically but factually, by pointing to Protestants with positions of influence in French society. The Monod family took the brunt of this hostility in the way that Léon Blum was later to be exposed as the supreme fact of Jewish infiltration.[9] Right through to the 1930s Maurras pounced on any German connection in France, notably the subservience he presumed of Jean Jaurès to the German socialists and Aristide Briand to the German foreign office.[10] His public prestige was enhanced when Germany declared war in 1914, but the other side of his equation, the Anti-France, did not dissolve under the impact as he had predicted, and his campaign against the Republic lost much of its credibility. It revived with his plausible attacks on Briand for betraying the victory of 1918, but during the 1930s the evidence linking Germany with the ideas and politics of the Republic became even more fanciful than it had been in the decade before World War I, and, in order to save his system, he adapted himself to making a major shift in the facts. By 1940 he had convinced himself that England had always been the principal enemy.

Had he remained true to the bigoted anti-Germanism for which he had become internationally known, it is difficult to see how he could have become a supporter of peace with Hitler's Germany at almost any price, a protagonist of Munich, and a violent opponent of the Resistance. Some Action Française members, like Jacques Renouvin and Guillain de Bénouville, were so conditioned by their movement's anti-Germanism that there was never a moment's doubt over who was still the major enemy when it came to Munich in 1938, to the declaration of war in 1939 or to the Occupation of 1940.[11] Other members wrote to Maurras to express their dismay at his attitudes, but the leader of Action Française stood firm by his new analysis of the facts. It was now England who had always been behind the history and politics of the pays légal. The Anti-France was English in its inspiration.

He had criticised England for its departure from absolute monarchy and its colonial ruthlessness in the face of French competition, but the emphasis on England as the enemy in his last two major books and in his journalism throughout the Occupation was not the development of latent anti-Englishness to the level of his anti-Germanism but a total substitution of England for Germany. In a remarkably unselfconscious rewriting of his chosen facts and history, Maurras now held England, not Germany, responsible for the French Revolution, for the Romantic and revolutionary movements of the 19th century which had brought about the collapse of monarchs in 1830 and 1848, for the democratic and socialist ideas which had fuelled French Republicanism and for the infiltration of Jews, Protestants and other aliens. To round off the century, England was also responsible for the Dreyfus Affair. In the 20th century he accused England of propping up the Third Republic in order to keep France weak and divided, of undermining the victory of 1918 by betrayals at the Paris peace conference, and in the 1920s and 1930s of leading France into the disastrous policy of Briandism and then into the opposite but equally disastrous war policy of 1939. Finally, not content with the defeat that France had suffered in 1940, England proceeded to harbour and finance the Gaullist conspiracy. Was it not a fact, he asked, that the first broadcast of de Gaulle was on 18 June 1940, the 125th anniversary of the Battle of Waterloo?[12]

The phobia in this gaggle of accusations was no more florid than that of his anti-German period. But the positivist confidence was greater, his system tighter and the facts more consistent in themselves. If Demos had always been one of the greatest enemies of the True France, then it made far more sense to indict the parliamentary democracy of England than a Germany which, from Frederick the Great to Hitler, had shown a marked predilection for autocracy. It is clear from La Seule France, written in 1941, that his identification of English interests with the interests of those who led the Anti-France made more positivist sense than the connections he had made between the Third Republic and Bismarckian or Wilhelmine Germany. Most satisfying of all for Maurras was the highly factual collapse of the Republic in the vote at the Vichy Casino on 10 July 1940, the collapse which he had always predicted but which had failed to materialise in 1914. Had Germany attempted to restore the politicians of the discredited Republic as a puppet government he might have returned to his anti-Germanism with renewed vigour. In 1940 and throughout the Occupation he denounced Pierre Laval as a Republican infiltrator, and he was coldly contemptuous of other Republican politicians originally from the Left, like Déat and Doriot, who became the pro-German vanguard of the fascist collaborators in Paris. But Germany did nothing to rescue the Republic from its humiliation, but rather accepted, with some residual doubts and a good deal of circumspection, the Vichy government of Marshal Pétain whose policies and attitudes read like any editorial from L'Action Française. By contrast England not only rejected Pétain but accepted the Gaullists, though both actions were a great deal more ambivalent than they seemed to the public at the time.[13] What had sealed the fact of English malevolence for Maurras, as for so many of the French, had been the English attack on the French fleet at Mers-el-Kébir on 3 July 1940. Most supporters of Maurras now felt he was talking more sense than ever. The facts of English treachery seemed all too apparent, and Maurras was given renewed credit for his grasp of the facts rather than criticised for his departure from an earlier set of facts which he had proclaimed as unalterable. Thus, despite a radical inconsistency in his factual analysis of the 'alien' presence in France since 1789, he survived into the period of the Occupation with his reputation as a consistent thinker still largely intact. In addition he appeared even closer to reality, for he now had a direct influence on those in power.

La Seule France was a triumphant celebration of this influence, couched in terms of unquestioning obedience to the leadership of Pétain. In advocating this obedience, the positivist assurance of Maurras is displayed just as imperiously as in his earlier insistence on a monarchy. Writing after Pétain had met Hitler at Montoire in October 1940 and had called for the French public to endorse the meeting and to accept a form of collaboration which meant more than mere coexistence, Maurras might have found words to express a guarded acceptance of the event, the mere suggestion of which would have provoked him to cries of treason in his earlier career. Instead he denied that the French should even discuss the Marshal's action, let alone criticise it, and he justified his attitude by quoting Bossuet, 'The heretic is the one who has an opinion'. Heresy is, by definition, a departure from what is deemed to be the truth. Having an opinion about Pétain's meeting with Hitler was, for Maurras, just such a departure from truth. But surely the belief that Pétain was right is also an opinion? No, is the answer implied by Maurras, it is neither a belief nor an opinion but a statement of fact. Does anyone have beliefs or opinions about established mathematical facts? You either accept them or you are in error. The same applies to the authority of Pétain, the embodiment of the True France.[14] And

Pétain was to say much the same in his message to the nation in support of Darlan's negotiations with Hitler in May 1941:

> Today it is no longer a question of allowing opinion to calculate our chances, to measure the risks or to judge our actions. Opinion is so often anxious because it is badly informed. No, it is a question of following me, without any reservations, on the paths of honour and national interest.[15]

Pétain was for Maurras what Clotilde de Vaux was for Comte, a turning point which made positivism into a religion of the heart as well as a certainty of the intellect. Comte's affair with his femme fatale led to his acceptance of the affective, emotional, factor in life.[16] Maurras had theoretically accepted this factor in his early writings, but his adulation of Pétain took him into an emotional world where a new language was necessary. In his chapter on the Marshal he ended with the words:

> Faust believed that in the beginning was action. What an error! Well before action there was thought, the directing idea which, alone, gives action its effective potential and its concrete effect . . . But is thought the first thing? Not any more. Before it there is the heart, that veritable king to which thought is 'the minister' but 'to which it must never be the slave'.[17]

La Seule France was, unsurprisingly, dedicated to Pétain, not in the name of Maurras himself but in the name of 'la patrie', and later in the book Maurras declares that he is not speaking about France but for France. This was hardly a new claim, but in this particular book, at this particular time in his career, Maurras brings together all his Truths and mixes them interchangeably, True France, the Truths of History and Politics, the Truths of his own arguments and the True Authority of Pétain. Phrase after phrase propounds the Truths of the situation: 'The defeat is. What is, is', 'certain reality', 'true realism', 'Pétainism is', 'Pétainism is a true power', and he linked every truth with action, ideas into politics through the Comtean formula, rephrased by Maurras as 'Know in order to foresee in order to provide'.[18] The sense of being close to realising the positivist dream of a society structured entirely on Truth allowed Maurras at least two years of personal exultation. At last the 18th century seemed likely to be united with the 20th.

The final, dehumanising result of such certainties was to deny not only truth but reality to the history and politics of the Anti-France. Looking back over 150 years since the Revolution, Maurras reached the point where he began to push the unacceptable events of history into a kind of fictional time and to replace them with events which he would have preferred to have happened. To this end he drew up what he called his 'Uchronie', an ideal account of time in the same way that Utopia is an ideal place. In this Uchronie there was no 21 January 1793, no 2 December 1804, no revolution of 1830 or 1848 and no Third Republic;

there were no invasions of 1792 or 1793, of 1814 or 1815, of 1870, 1914 or 1940; no Trafalgar, no Leipzig, no Waterloo, no Sedan, no Charleroi, no Dunkirk. It is a negative ideal tantamount to the elimination of all Republican history from the history of France.[19] It was also a theoretical version of the racial and political persecution carried out by Vichy with his full support. He claimed that he had no hatred against the Jews and that their elimination from the history of France and its citizenship was merely a necessity of fact, since the Jews could not 'factually' be part of the True France.[20] It was dehumanisation by intellectual definition.

Maurras never recovered from the damage he did to himself and others in this period of positivist exultation. Not content with removing reality or even existence from the forces of the Anti-France, he tried to free his truths from any conditioning context at all. Pétain was to be followed without any discussion, and the True France was to be preserved as la seule France, or la France seule, independent of all outside influences, cocooned in its own essential truthfulness. He not only believed that this was possible but that it was already in 1941 a reality to be protected at all cost. Because he had always defined the True France as independent of all outsiders, and because the True France had now arrived in Pétainism, there was no way in which Pétain or Maurras himself could be accused of serving outside interests. By his own logic Maurras could never be a traitor, a logic he argued as fact during his trial. What then of the all too concrete facts that by 1943 the public support for Pétain was ebbing fast, that Laval had been publicly endorsed by Pétain in his broadcasts, that the armistice by which Pétain claimed to have saved France was in ruins, that the Bourbon pretender to the throne had rejected Maurras, that the French monarchists were split into as many factions as any Republican party,[21] that the peasants were refusing to play the role of contented children of the pays réel, and that Vichy France was more subservient to an outside, enemy power than any French government in modern history? What did all this mean to Maurras? It meant only that anyone arguing these points was accused of mistaking the truth of the situation.

This was the theme of his attack on the Resistance as the high-point of Republican, and English, treachery in his book written from prison with its title and tone savagely mocking the hopes of liberated France. Votre Bel Aujourd'hui appears to be a final justification of his long career, but it is heavily weighted by the events of the Vichy period and is more an embittered sequel to his Occupation writings than an attempt to put them into a long-term perspective. It is full of the same anti-English accusations, updated to take in the Normandy landings which he treats as an enemy invasion, and the internal triumphs of the Resistance and the Maquis which he treats as a criminal conspiracy engineered by England and carried out by the dregs of the international underworld. As for the trials and executions which accompanied and followed the Liberation, he calls them the worst terror in two thousand years, and calculates the victims in astronomical figures.[22]

It would not be a book giving further insight into Maurras if it were not for the testament he leaves of himself and Pétain as the true liberators of France. Rejecting the euphoria of the Liberation he claims that a false liberty has triumphed, an abstract principle which can only enslave the true liberties which are factual and not abstract. These liberties were those enshrined in the ancient communal pride and autonomy of villages and small towns such as his Provençal birthplace, Martigues, liberties which he claimed had been destroyed by the Jacobinism of the Revolution. It was a claim he had made countless times in his first adoption of the cause of Provençal and Languedoc revivalism through the literary movement of the Félibrige. At a time of Republican centralism this had given his polemic an appearance of being rooted in local realities, and it was the nearest he came to any sociological content. In La Seule France he suggests that the money confiscated from Jewish business should be put into a peasant fund, and he applauded enthusiastically the Vichy ideal of a return to the land. Provincial liberties, community traditions and a peasant economy - it sounded like a practical programme linking Action Française directly with the rural majority of France. Maurras undoubtedly believed it was. But although he mocked Republicans for paying only lip-service to local liberties and Jaurès for quoting Mistral's Mirèio but saying not a word in favour of the teaching of Occitan, his own contacts with the peasant realities of the Pays d'Oc were no more impressive, and in the rebirth of Occitanism in the last twenty years his name and ideas have been conspicuously absent.[23]

When he moved from Martigues to Paris at the start of his career he was appalled by the capital's cosmopolitanism, but in effect he became as Paris-based as most other leading intellectuals. He claimed that his regionalism was a movement from below, but when the villages and countryside of the South began to lose all faith in Vichy during the last two years of the Occupation, when Occitan-speaking peasants and artisans began to join or supply the Maquis in the hills, when the declining Félibrige was rivalled by young Occitan poets steeped both in ancient local traditions and in the recent local pride of the Resistance, Maurras could only reiterate his positivist logic that all such manifestations were false and that the Resisters were criminals and enemies of the True France. But if the True France of Maurras ever consisted of real people and not just abstract ideas, then Maurras had abandoned and betrayed thousands of True French people when he called for the arrest and execution of Resisters. To use his own categories he was guilty of betraying the True France of those Occitan villages and countryside long before a court in Lyons is convicted him of intelligence with the enemy.

But it is all too apparent that people were ultimately an irrelevance to Charles Maurras, whose mental constructs were designed to protect him from human realities rather than to explain and understand them. It is therefore tempting, as a form of retributive justice, to declare Maurras an irrelevance to the humanity he so rigorously ignored. But in a century in which dogmatic and inhuman ideologies have thrived as ideas and as politics this would, unfortunately, be a distortion of fact.

Notes

1. Charles Maurras, 'Le premier sang', La Gazette de France, 7 Sept. 1898.
2. For his trial see: Le procès de Charles Maurras et Maurice Pujo devant la Cour de Justice du Rhône. Vérités françaises, 1945.
   José Agustin Martinez, Les procès criminels de l'Après-Guerre. Albin Michel, 1958.
   Dominique Pado, Maurras, Béraud, Brasillach, Odile Pathé, 1945.
   Geo London, Le procès de Charles Maurras, Bonnefon, Lyon 1945.
3. Robert Havard de la Montagne, Histoire de l'Action Française, Amiot-Dumont, 1950.
   A. Fabre-Luce, Au nom des Silencieux, Fabre-Luce, 1945.
   Henri Massis, Maurras et Notre Temps, Plon, 1961.
   Jean Paulhan, Lettre aux Directeurs de la Résistance, Editions de Minuit, 1952.
   Colonel Rémy, Interview with author, Paris 1980.
   See also the special number of Aspects de la France, the post-war newspaper which continues the ideas of Action Française, entitled 'Justice pour Charles Maurras', 25 April 1948.
4. Ernst Nolte, Three Faces of Fascism, Weidenfeld and Nicolson, 1965, examines Action Française as Fascist, but for a more thorough history and analysis of the movement and its leader see Eugen Weber Action Française, Stanford U.P., 1962. Note also Victor Nguyen, 'Esquisse d'une posture historique de l'Action Française', Etudes Maurrassiennes, No 3, 1974, pp. 7-16 and Auguste Rivet, 'Maurras et la politique extérieure de la France 1938-1944', Etudes Maurrassiennes, No 4, 1980, pp. 251-267.
5. Well before the foundation of Action Française Maurras was interpreting Comte as a forerunner of his ideas. See, for example his article 'Auguste Comte méconnu, Auguste Comte conservateur' in La Gazette de France, 21 Novembre 1898.
6. Charles Maurras, L'Avenir de l'Intelligence, Albert Fontemoing, 1905.
7. See the very interesting essay by Michael Sutton, 'La souveraineté de la collectivité: nationalisme maurrassien et pensée de Comte', Etudes Maurrassiennes, No 3, 1974, pp. 199-209.
8. Much of the Maurrassian evidence advanced to justify his use of the word alien was designed to make a simple, instant impact on his readers. For example, he stated during the Dreyfus period that the names of Jewish shopkeepers in Paris contained letters of the alphabet which were never used in the French language. The shops could therefore never be French.
9. For his attacks on Gabriel Monod see Charles Maurras, Quand les Français ne s'aimaient pas, Nouvelle Librairie Nationale, 1916, and on Blum see for example, L'Action française, 3 July 1936 where Blum is described as 'Ce juif allemand...n'est pas à traiter comme une personne naturelle. C'est un monstre de la République démocratique...Détritus humain, à traiter comme tel...'
10. For his anti-Germanism see articles collected in the following:
    Charles Maurras, Romantisme et Révolution, Nouvelle Librairie

Nationale, 1922; Quand les Français ne s'aimaient pas, Nouvelle Librairie Nationale, 1916; Au signe de Flore, Collection Hier, 1931; Le mauvais traité, Editions du Capitole 1928; Devant l'Allemagne éternelle, Editions à l'Etoile, 1937.

11. Guillain de Bénouville Le Sacrifice du Matin, Laffont, 1946. See also H.R. Kedward, Resistance in Vichy France, O.U.P., 1978 pp. 67-9 and 263-265.

12. Charles Maurras, La Seule France, Lardanchet, Lyon, 1941 pp. 119-123, and Votre Bel Aujourd'hui, Fayard, 1953 p. 248. Note the similarities of his anti-English polemic to the pro-Nazi propaganda of Jean Luchaire Les Anglais et Nous, Editions du livre moderne, 1941, and the speeches of the Nazi cultural envoy in France, Dr Friedrich Grimm e.g. 'Faisons la Paix Franco-Allemande' circulated by the Cahiers de l'Institut Allemand in a collection called Regards sur l'Histoire, Sorlot, 1941

13. cf. R.T. Thomas, Britain and Vichy. The dilemma of Anglo-French Relations 1940-42, Macmillan 1979.

14. Charles Maurras, La Seule France, pp. 283-290.

15. Maréchal Pétain, 'Message du 15 mai 1941', La France Nouvelle, Fasquelle, 1941 p. 153.

16. Comte met Clotilde de Vaux in 1844 and fell passionately in love. She died two years later and was celebrated in Comte's last writings as 'Sainte Clotilde, la Patronne de l'Humanité'.

17. Charles Maurras, La Seule France, pp. 291-2. The last line is from Comte.

18. The original Comtean formula was 'Science d'où prévoyance, prévoyance d'où action'.

19. Charles Maurras, La Seule France, pp. 234-5.

20. Charles Maurras, La Seule France, ch. 'Juifs et francs-maçons'. For an authoritative account of the antisemitism of Vichy France, Pétain and Maurras see R. Paxton and M. Marrus, Vichy France and the Jews, Basic Books, New York, 1981.

21. cf. Archives départementales du Gard CA 1512 in which at least 5 different monarchist pressure groups are listed for the département in 1943.

22. Charles Maurras, Votre Bel Aujourd'hui, pp. 250-357. The figures he gives of 100,000 murders by the Resistance, and hundreds of thousands of other trials and executions of 'True Frenchmen', can also be found in certain histories of the period. But the most recent detailed research into missing persons, mounted by the Comité d'histoire de la Deuxième Guerre mondiale puts the figure of those executed for collaboration at about 12,000 for the whole of France.

23. Charles Maurras, La Seule France, pp. 179-81, 198-9; Votre Bel Aujourd'hui, pp. 281-94. cf. Michael Bergès, 'Le provincialisme pétainiste' Amiras/Repères (Revue Occitano-française), No 3., September 1982, pp. 27-51.

ROMAN DMOWSKI AND ITALIAN FASCISM

Antony Polonsky

Roman Dmowski was the principal ideologist of the Polish Right. Before the First World War it was he who, together with Jan Poplawski and Zygmunt Balicki, provided the intellectual underpinning for a new movement, National Democracy, which, in its various forms, dominated right-wing politics in Poland until the end of the Second World War. Indeed, there has been tendency in certain circles to see Dmowski as one of the intellectual founding-fathers of the present-day Polish state since the Poland he favoured - ethnically homogeneous, industrialized, allied with Russia, anti-German and Catholic - bears a close resemblance to the Polish People's Republic.[1] However, attempts to portray Dmowski as an early exponent of Russo-Polish understanding have diverted attention away from some of the most crucial aspects of his view of the world and have obscured the extent to which he derived his ideas from the reaction against liberalism and democracy which was such a characteristic feature of the 1890s. In this article, I will attempt to show that Dmowski's ideas should be seen, above all, as a Polish variant of the intellectual current represented in Western Europe by people like Enrico Corradini, Vilfredo Pareto and Gustave Le Bon. Accordingly, his decision in the 1920s to espouse the virtues of Italian fascism, far from being an aberration, constituted a natural progression from his earlier beliefs and an adaptation of them to the new conditions of post-war Europe.

Dmowski was a biologist by training and his political ideas were deeply influenced by Social Darwinism, which began to have an impact in Poland in the last decades of the nineteenth century.[2] He believed that modern political life was characterized by a new phenomenon, the emergence of nations in which all classes of society would have a role to play:

> The interest of the nation has recently emerged in political life to replace the interests of dynasties and of lay and clerical hierarchies. This development is the inevitable consequence of the democratization of the political system and the democratization of culture, or in other words, its extension to all strata of society. . . As a result, patriotism, which formerly was made up on the one hand of a partly physiological link with the land and conditions into which one was born and partly of loyalty to a king and allegiance to a given state organization, is becoming ever more an exclusive bond linking one with one's own society, its spirit, its traditions, a union with its interests, which

goes far beyond political unity or difference or even territorial separateness.[3]

As a Social Darwinist, Dmowski accepted the view, common in western Europe at the end of the nineteenth century, that nations were bound by natural laws to struggle with each other for survival. Talk of international peace and brotherhood was so much hot air used to cloak national ambitions. The struggle for survival was however a positive force and, like Lord Salisbury, Dmowski had a clear vision of dying and decaying nations which had lost their historical mission:

> The surface of the globe is not a museum to preserve ethnographic displays in order, unities, each in its place. Humanity is going forward swiftly, and in the contest of the nations, each is bound to do as much as it can for progress, for civilization, to raise the value of man. . .[Yet] the fact is that continual improvement and progress are not natural characteristics of man – the majority of today's population of the earth is standing still and not advancing at all. And the greatest factor in progress is competition, the need continually to improve the weapons which enable one to defend one's own existence.
>
> . . .Is this a philosophy of struggle and oppression? . . .Perhaps. But what if this struggle and this oppression are a reality and universal peace and universal freedom are a fiction?. . . One must have the courage to look truth in the face.[4]

Dmowski's aim was to equip the Poles for this national struggle. In his view there were many aspects of Polish political culture which placed the Poles at a disadvantage in conflict with other nations. Their bid for independence had led them to see themselves as the embodiment of all struggles for freedom and had led them uncritically to adopt the values of western liberalism. This altruism, best exemplified in the Polish insurrectionary slogan, 'We fight for your freedom and for our own', had impeded the pursuit of a healthy national egoism. The very phrase 'national egoism', first used in the Polish context by Dmowski's intellectual mentor, Zygmunt Balicki, calls to mind similar ideas in western Europe. It was the Italian nationalist Alfredo Rocco who had affirmed in 1914 that 'nationalism, especially in Italy is . . . above all an exclusive and exclusivist attitude. Nationalism puts the nation first, relates every activity to the national interest and subordinates everything to the prosperity and power of our race.' As a result, 'nationalism wants to prepare for war because it considers that the expansion of the Italian race will inevitably lead to armed emigration, that is to say, to war, and it intends that such unavoidable wars shall be crowned by victory.'[5]

As models for the sort of national movement which he believed the Poles should create, Dmowski adduced in the first place the Czechs and the Irish who, in his view, had both succeeded in creating a coherent national community capable of resisting oppression. More significantly, he called on the Poles to emulate the two most successful nations of his time, the English and the Germans. Unlike most of Polish opinion, he supported the British in their struggle with the Boers and wrote with approval of Britain as a society in which patriotism was deeply embedded in the political culture and sustained the social order:

> Modern patriotism, or rather nationalism in the noblest meaning of this word, has reached its highest stage of development in that country where political self-government by society has been longest established, namely in England. Its basis - attachment to the English language, to English customs and traditions, to English institutions and expressions of the English spirit. Its main manifestation has been the defence of English institutions always and everywhere and the taking with oneself of England throughout the whole world. This has been possible because the English have such a strongly marked national identity and are so firmly attached to it that even in small groups they are able to create life on the English pattern and resist the assimilatory influence of their environment.[6]

He saw the Germans as irreconcilable enemies of the Poles. Yet he could not withhold his admiration for the success with which the German nation ruthlessly advanced its own interests. In his words:

> The German who, having seen that it is in the interest of the Prussian state to subdue Poznan for German culture, settles there and devotes all his energy to strengthening in our country all that is German, who will gather in Polish children and teach them in German, who organizes his possession in the German manner and alters his environment by cultural influence into a part of Germany - shall arouse in me nothing but esteem, notwithstanding that I shall regard him as a more dangerous enemy for that and shall attempt before all to combat his endeavours.[7]

Dmowski called himself a democrat and certainly wanted all sectors of society to be involved in the movement for national regeneration which he hoped to foster. But he was opposed to the introduction of western liberal institutions in Poland, which he felt did not correspond to the level of social consciousness and would lead to the emergence of sectional and class interests among large sections of the population who were not yet mature enough to be conscious of their obligations as citizens, so that the national interest would at best be obscured or at worst destroyed by sectional conflict. As he put it:

> Social life depends on the principle that individuals sacrifice a part of their private interests in a different form to the general interest ... Where the force of public opinion is stronger, moral pressure from society to fulfil

one's obligations as a citizen will be more powerful and the need for physical coercion will be less. As a result the role of the state will be smaller and the area of state power can be more restricted. On the other hand - and this applies in particular to our nation - where the state does not concern itself with the interests of society and indeed adopts a hostile attitude towards it, the whole future of our nation depends on the strong development of moral coercion, in the establishment of a healthy and steadfast public opinion imposing the obligations of citizenship on those who are not yet mature enough to be conscious of their obligations as citizens.[8]

Himself of petit-bourgeois origins, Dmowski energetically favoured the rapid industrialization of Poland, which he believed was being impeded by the gentry values which still dominated Polish social life. He was also strongly hostile to the large Jewish community in Poland, arguing that the presence of the Jews had prevented the emergence of a Polish middle-class.

Thanks to the Jews Poland remained a nation of nobles down to the middle of the nineteenth century and even longer as it is such in certain degree today. If they had not existed, a part of the Polish people would have organized itself to perform the social functions which they fulfilled and would have emerged as a rival political force to the nobility as a third estate which has played such an important role in the development of European societies and has become the principal force in modern social life.[9]

In addition, though he believed that a nation demonstrated its health by assimilating other groups and called on the Poles to absorb Byelorussians and Ukrainians, he felt that the Jews were too numerous and had too strongly marked a national character for this process to take place successfully.

The national organism must aim to absorb only that which it can assimilate and use to increase the growth and collective strength of the body.

The Jews are not such an element. They have an individual character too distinct, too crystallized by thousands of years of civilised life to allow themselves to be assimilated by a young national character such as ours, which is only now being created. Rather they would be capable of assimilating our majority spiritually and in part physically. On the other hand, in the character of this race which has never lived the life of societies of our type so many distinctive characteristics have been accumulated and established themselves which are alien to our moral code and are in fact harmful to our life that the pouring in of the bulk of this element would destroy us, replacing with disruptive elements those young creative forces on which we are building our future.[10]

In spite of his admiration for German institutions, Dmowski regarded Germany as Poland's principal enemy. In his view, Prussia had played the principal role in the partitions of Poland and, unlike Austria and Russia, had acquired territories which she believed were essential to her national existence. To Prussia, he wrote, 'the lands she took from Poland were necessary for the territorial linking of her possessions.'[11] Without them, the German aim to dominate East-Central Europe could not be achieved. Prussia was bound to oppose the re-establishment of a Polish state, since this would call into question her hold on her own Polish lands. In this sense, whereas Russia could afford to reach a compromise with the Poles, Prussia-Germany could not. As he put it:

Prussia grew up from the fall of Poland. The revival of Poland . . . would be a brake on German eastward expansion and would undermine the leading role which Prussia plays in the German Reich. Thus Prussian politicians understand they can make no compromise with the Poles.[12]

From this essentially geo-political analysis he drew the seemingly paradoxical conclusion that a free Poland could only emerge from cooperation with Russia. Poland would be Russia's barrier against the eastward spread of Pan-Germanism. He was convinced that German ambitions in Eastern Europe would lead to a clash with Russia and he aimed to win the trust of the Russian government by his anti-German policies and his general political responsibility, so that the Russian authorities would seek an accommodation with the Poles.

Dmowski's ideas in the period before the First World War were written in clear, easily assimilated language and soon acquired wide currency and evident popularity. His originality lay not in his basic concepts, which were commonplaces of the nationalist reaction of the 1890s, but in his application of the anti-democratic theories which had grown up in Western Europe to a political environment in which the central problem was not how to counteract the negative features of liberalism and constitutionalism but rather how to achieve national independence. Partly because of the obvious need to reach an accord with Russia and partly because of the attractiveness of its ideas to wide sections of Polish society, the National Democrats, who quickly established themselves as the dominant political grouping in both the Russian and Prussian portions of Poland and during the First World War, emerged as the dominant group in the principal pro-Entente force, the Polish National Committee, set up in November 1914. As Russia became a less effective element in the coalition, National Democratic hopes became centred on the western allies, and as early as November 1915 Dmowski moved to western Europe, where he believed he could work more effectively to promote the Polish cause. In August 1917, he and his associates re-established the Polish National Committee, and by the end of the year it had been recognized by the Allies as an official organization representing Polish interests, particularly in relation to the Polish army then being established in the West. In late 1918, the Polish National Committee was recognized by the French, though not by the U.K. and the U.S. as a <u>gouvernement de fait</u> and Dmowski himself headed the Polish delegation at the Versailles peace conference.

Yet the creation of an independent Poland was to prove a disappointment to the group. Although it established itself as the largest single political force, it achieved office only for a short period in 1923. Political life in the new state was overshadowed by the charismatic ex-socialist and independence fighter Jozef Piłsudski, who eventually seized power in May 1926 and who had always been a bitter opponent of the National Democrats. The anti-Semitism of the National Democrats lost them much sympathy in western Europe while demagogic demands for a rigidly nationalist policy alienated the national minorities who made up nearly one-third of the population of the country. Above all, their social conservatism despite Dmowski's earlier hostility to the gentry and their rather mean-minded pursuit of narrow nationalist goals put them at odds with the prevailing mood in the new state.[13]

Dmowski himself, worn out by his exertions during the war, failed to find his appropriate place in political life and became increasingly dissatisfied with the democratic institutions which had been established in Poland. Always an anti-Semite, he now became convinced that the western democracies were dominated by Jewish influence. Writing of the settlement of the Polish-German border at the Versailles conference, he observed:

> Lloyd George prevented at the peace conference the incorporation into Poland of areas which it had already been agreed should be incorporated, the overwhelming majority of Upper Silesia, Malbork, Sztum and Kwidzyn, Danzig. In this matter, Lloyd George acted as the agent of the Jews and he would not have achieved his goal had Wilson been more independent of them. The Jews, for their part, acted in accordance with a pact with German freemasonry, according to which, in return for help on the border question at the peace conference, they were offered a series of leading positions in the German republic.[14]

Dmowski was convinced that the Jewish domination of European political life would inevitably provoke a violent reaction, telling the National Democratic politician Julian Zdanowski on 4 April 1922 that 'just as he had predicted the war, so he now predicted a great anti-Jewish revolution in a few years and that society should be organized and prepared for this outside the parliamentary and strictly political sphere.'[15]

He also began to manifest growing sympathies for Italian fascism. In December 1925, for instance, he asserted:

> ... the idea of dictatorship is not at all revolting to me ... If
> we had a man who had even half the worth of Mussolini, if
> we could create even half an organization like the fascists
> ... I would willingly agree to a dictatorship in Poland.[16]

In early 1926, Dmowski paid a visit to Italy, where his principal host was the Italian nationalist leader Enrico Corradini, who had long been a fervent advocate of Italian colonial expansion and who had also been one of the principal supporters of Italy's intervention in the First World War. His Nationalist Party had supported the march on Rome and had merged with the fascists in 1923, Corradini himself becoming a Senator. The two men had first met in Rome in late 1916. They were linked not only by their support for the Allied cause but by their hostility to parliamentary government. According to Dmowski, at that first meeting Corradini had observed that 'only mediocrities can pass through the parliamentary net; there is no place for strong men in this system.'[17]

Dmowski seems to have gained a favourable impression from his visit to Italy and his disillusionment with liberal democracy and growing interest in fascism were intensified by the coup of May 1926 which brought Piłsudski back to power and seemed likely to consign the National Democrats to a long period in the political wilderness. Dmowski set out his views in a long private letter (written in French) to Corradini, which, because of his fears that his post was being opened, he sent by a private courier. After explaining to Corradini that during his recent visit to France he had attempted to persuade influential circles in that country to adopt a more pro-Italian and less pro-British foreign policy, he continued:

> It is my opinion that we are witnessing the beginning of a
> great crisis in European history. The Germanic, Protestant
> nations - and this means also the materialistic nations -
> which have in recent times represented the highest level of
> economic well-being, material culture and political power -
> are entering a period of decadence. This is the result of the
> fact that, in present economic conditions, the material
> requirements of the mass of workers in these countries
> have been raised far too high and cannot be satisfied. In
> addition, among the intelligent classes there are no
> disinterested individuals capable of making personal
> sacrifices for their country and finally these countries have
> been so corroded by parliamentarian freemasonry that they
> cannot liberate themselves from these forces.
>
> The turn is again coming of those nations brought up by the
> Catholic Church, the Latin nations, the turn of Rome. And
> it is your role, the role of Italy to stand at the head of the
> new Europe or rather the old Europe which is moving to
> establish its supremacy.
>
> The Germanic and Protestant world, even in its decadence,
> will long constitute a major power, since it is strengthened

by the existence of new Anglo-Saxon societies across the seas. Thus, in order to counterbalance this force you will have to unite the whole Latin world without exception, and supplement this power with younger nations, like my own, which have not been corroded by the Germanic, Protestant, materialist spirit and which sooner or later will emancipate themselves and follow you.

France constitutes a serious problem. It is Latin, but it is permeated by the materialist spirit of the Protestants. It is necessary to balance the strength of the other side. A rapprochement between Italy and France will transform France and accelerate the beginning of the new era and the establishment of a new order in Europe.

I am sure that my country will be one of the first which in its internal organization will follow your example. The May events in Poland are only the beginning of a crisis which will end well for us. We will end with the establishment of a constitution based on a limited representative system controlled by an organization of national forces. Freemasonry which could see the rapid evolution of the country in this direction carried out the coup to save its position and guarantee its power. But it is too weak to hold on to power for long and you may be sure that, having begun the work for us, it will be superseded by a nationalist organization of fascist type.[18]

He concluded by explaining to Corradini that he was about to write two series of articles for Polish newspapers on fascism and nationalism and that he hoped these would have a major impact on public opinion in Poland and would also accelerate a Franco-Italian rapprochement. The letter was sent by Corradini with a covering note to Mussolini explaining that 'you certainly know its author R.D. . . . He has long been linked to us by bonds of friendship. I am convinced that his action, whether in the direction he suggests or in any other way, will prove helpful to us.' The letter was seen both by Mussolini and by the undersecretary and later Minister for Foreign Affairs, Dino Grandi, but their comments have not been preserved. Given the nature of Italian foreign policy in the 1920s, though Mussolini may have been grateful for Dmowski's efforts to improve Franco-Italian relations, he cannot have taken him particularly seriously. The Italians were well aware that Piłsudski had securely established himself in power and Mussolini had gone out of his way to deny rumours that he had been prepared to respond to pleas from Stanislaw Kozicki, a long-standing associate of Dmowski and the Polish ambassador in Rome at the time of the coup, to intervene on behalf of the government Piłsudski had overthrown. Indeed the Italian ambassador in Warsaw, Cesare Majoni, in his reports in 1926 and 1927 stressed the similarities between Piłsudski's seizure of power and that of Mussolini, while the government even displayed some fitful interest in the small Polish groups which attempted to push Piłsudski in a more fascist direction and which underlined the parallels between the 'march on Rome' and the 'march on Warsaw'. The Italians were quickly disillusioned however and soon came to the conclusion that although Piłsudski was there to stay, he was no fascist in the making. Rather he was an anachronistic survival, 'a liberal-democrat in the clothes of an old-world knight', whose regime resembled that 'of the government commissioners established in some Italian provinces after their union with Piedmont'.[19]

As he had promised, Dmowski duly published a series of five articles on fascism in the main National Democratic newspaper <u>Gazeta Warszawska Poranna</u> between 22 June and 1 July 1926. In these, he set out at greater length his observations on the decline of Britain and the rise of Italy in the post-war world. These phenomena, he claimed, were the result of a very deep-rooted crisis of European civilization. The principles of liberalism and representative democracy as they had developed in the nineteenth century were on the brink of collapse. The democratic idea had always had, at its heart, a fatal flaw. It was based on the principle that the people should rule. Yet the fact was that the 'people' as such were incapable of ruling themselves:

> In every nation, the overwhelming majority is made up of people lacking any understanding of the needs and tasks of the state, people incapable even of assessing who can better understand these needs and tasks. Always under any system of government an oligarchical minority has ruled; under autocratic governments this was made up of those who knew how to acquire the confidence of the monarch; under democratic governments, it comprises those who know how to acquire the confidence of the masses.[20]

Dmowski now gave vent to his obsession with the power of the freemasons, which was to be a feature of his work throughout the inter-war period. In every European democracy, he claimed a political elite had emerged which had realized that for government, to function effectively a machinery had to be provided to guide and control the 'unconscious masses'. This was provided by 'a secret organization made up of masonic lodges. In all countries with a democratic constitution, it was they who ruled and who understood well how to ensure that their will was expressed by the voice of the people'.[21] Yet although masonic control of democratic institutions worked reasonably for a while, it carried within it the seeds of its own destruction. The masonic lodges recruited their followers from the most cosmopolitan and least nationalist elements of the population and they worked sedulously to weaken national bonds. The result had been to destroy the social instinct in many countries and undermine national cohesion. In addition, Dmowski argued, freemasonry had worked to diminish the influence of religious ties and had thus been one of the main factors which had caused the increase in materialism and the pursuit of individual self-interest. As a quasi-religion, with strongly Jewish characteristics, freemasonry had always been extremely hostile to the influence of the Catholic Church, while in Protestant countries it had rather worked from within the Protestant churches in order to take them over and subordinate them to its interests. In addition, the masons also incited class antagonisms to weaken national sentiment and strengthen their own influence.

The consequence of these developments had been that democratic governments had become less and less effective and that the First World War, which at first seemed a major triumph for the freemasons, was in fact the first stage in their inevitable downfall. Indeed, the post-war world had seen a major split within masonic ranks, since one group saw the use of the slogans of class warfare merely as a means to advance their own interests while another genuinely wished to establish the dictatorship of a small group of individuals ostensibly acting for the proletariat.

The post-war crisis of democracy had come to a head first in Italy, where the rule of the masons had proved particularly ineffective and where class divisions during the war had done a great deal to undermine the Italian war effort. However, the Italian nation possessed a number of characteristics which had enabled it to resist the masons and eventually drive them from government. The continued influence of Catholicism meant that a large section of the population was untainted by materialism. This meant not only that they were prepared to work for lower wages than their counterparts elsewhere, but also that they had an idealistic streak which emerged in the courage they showed in the bitter social conflicts of the post-war years.

These had ended in the victory of fascism -'the greatest revolution of our times . . . For the fascist revolution, from a fundamental political point of view is more profound than the Bolshevik revolution.'[22]

This revolution should not be seen primarily as the replacement of parliamentary government by the dictatorship of an outstanding individual. It is true that Mussolini was such an individual, combining 'youthful energy, iron will, the capacity to rule over individuals and over the masses and in addition to all this an uncommon intellect capable of dealing with the entirety of state problems and of choosing the correct path in every area'. But his role had been above all to organize and direct the forces of which fascism was made up:

> Mussolini is not solely an ambitious individual seeking power and the fascist organization is not solely his bodyguard . . . Fascism is a great idea which has created around itself a great political camp. It is a great school of political thinking, the elevation of a new great principle in the life of the nation and indeed of the whole civilized world. The essence of the fascist revolution is that in the place of a secret international organization there now stands an open national organization.[23]

The masons and their followers had accused the fascists of abolishing democracy in Italy. But this was not what had occurred. What had taken place was that a secret organization acting against the interests of the nation had been ousted as the controlling force of the democratic constitution by a national elite acting for the broad interest of the nation. 'It is only under the direction of such an organization that the nation will be truly free in the deepest, most important meaning of the word. Individuals and groups which attempt to act to the detriment of the collectivity have less freedom, but the nation as a whole has complete freedom in expressing its collective will and in acting in accordance with the spirit of its great ambitions.'[24]

The fascist revolution would be widely imitated. Not all countries would be able to follow the Italian example. Some were too deeply set in their old ways and were condemned to inevitable decline. Others would be able to make the break. Already this had begun to occur in Spain, but here since conditions were not as favourable as in Italy the process had not gone as far.

In his second series of articles, 'Nationalism and Fascism', published in Gazeta Warszawska Poranna between 12 and 20 July 1926, Dmowski traced the intellectual origins of fascism to the Italian nationalist movement which had developed under Corradini's influence at the end of the nineteenth century.

> The nationalist camp, although the number of its members was not impressive, because of its high intellectual and moral values and because of its energy, in a few years acquired an enormous influence over public opinion in Italy. Its pressure forced Italy into the Libyan war which gave her Tripoli, and it was thanks to its strong influence in the country that Italy decided to take part in the world war. Finally they prepared the ground in Italian thinking for the fascist revolution, and after the seizure of power gave to Mussolini a whole range of first-rate people.[25]

The emergence of a new form of nationalism had not been a solely Italian phenomenon. It had occurred in France under the leadership of Charles Maurras and also in Poland where it had given rise to the National Democratic movement. This development was above all the result of the growing weakness of liberal democracy. Whereas in the first half of the nineteenth century liberalism had been a healthy force and had worked together with nationalism to overthrow an unjust order, in the period after 1848 it became corrupted. Two opposing forces, international socialism and the 'liberal financial international', had come to dominate it, in both of which a primary role was played by the Jewish element.

Inevitably this had led to a national reaction against liberal democracy, which had occurred first in Catholic countries. Partly this was because Protestantism as a religion had encouraged the pursuit of individual self-interest which had favoured the growth of capitalism and led to the economic and political dominance of the Protestant and Germanic countries. In addition the division between Protestant and Catholic Europe ran along an older rift between that part of Europe which was most deeply influenced by the Roman Empire and that area where Roman civilization had not struck very deep roots. It had thus been in Catholic countries that the hollowness of liberal-democratic phraseology and the inadequacies of parliamentary government had first been clearly perceived.

In the pre-war world, the nationalist movement had been on the defensive. Now with the crisis of the Protestant and Germanic world far more advanced, it was going on to the offensive. Mussolini was right to talk of the 'historical initiative which Italy was undertaking' which would 'give her leadership in the world'. Fascism was destined soon to become the dominant political ideology in Europe and would rescue it from decline. A new fascist internationalism - a true universalism based on Roman principles - would supersede the doomed and sterile internationalism of the League of Nations.

Although predominantly Catholic and linked with the Latin world, Poland had inevitably been affected by the general crisis. A symptom of this was the May coup which had brought Piłsudski to power. The government he had established could not provide a lasting solution. What was needed was thus a new political group which could play the role in Poland that the nationalists had in Italy. It was true that the Polish and Italian nationalist movements had emerged at the same time, but they had followed divergent courses. Instead of remaining a tightly knit and coherent elite, the National Democrats had been compelled by circumstances to concentrate on practical politics and had also attracted more followers than they could really absorb. As a result ideological work had been neglected and the original cohesiveness of the party had been lost.

The new group should be a small elite with a clear ideology derived basically from Italy.

> From the beginning of our history we would have turned our eyes to the west: there we have sought models and imitated them uncritically. In our own times we have taken much thoughtlessly from the north west, from the German and Protestant world. This has diverted us from the true path of our historic mission. Today we must turn our eyes to the south - to the Latin countries from whom Poland, over the heads of the Germanic world which stands between, received the bonds of civilization, to whom we are linked spiritually by being brought up in a common church and a common religion which, as is being demonstrated today, constitutes a stronger foundation than anything else for civilized life. Then we will more easily find ourselves and build the future which belongs to us.[26]

What Dmowski had in mind very quickly became apparent. On 4 December 1926, a number of the principal younger activists in the National Democratic movement met in the western Polish town of Poznan and founded the Camp for a Greater Poland (OWP).[27] Its aim was not to supersede the Popular National Union, the principal National Democratic grouping in parliament, but rather to transform the ideological scene in Poland and create a basis for a broader nationalist coalition which would unite all healthy right-wing forces.

This was made quite clear by Dmowski in his inaugural speech at the founding of the OWP:

> Our organization at the present, initial stage in its
> organization does not intend to concern itself with current
> political issues. These will be left to the representatives of
> the country in the legislative bodies. It will devote its
> attention to organizational work, to the formulation and
> consolidation of its governing principles above all within its
> own ranks, to the disciplining of those ranks so that they
> will be capable most effectively to serve the great goal to
> which we are devoting ourselves.[28]

This task was an urgent one since, in Dmowski's view, the Piłsudski
government was likely shortly to collapse and might be succeeded by a
radical regime of the left. A disciplined nationalist organization was the
only way to prevent this:

> It is not yet clear how far off that moment is when action
> by us will be necessary, when the one salvation of the
> fatherland will be a powerful organization of the nation.
> We therefore differ from all other political camps above
> all by nature of our organization, which is based on the
> principles of hierarchy, discipline and the responsibility of
> the person assigned the task of leadership in every branch
> of our work.[29]

This was an accurate description of the way the OWP was organized.
All positions within it were filled by nomination from above and every
branch was headed by a camp commander so that the principle of one-
man leadership was established at all levels. At the head of the
organization stood Dmowski, the 'Great Camp Commander'. In fact,
however, disillusioned as he was by his experience of practical politics,
Dmowski saw himself as a remote ideological theorist, rather as he
thought of Corradini, who would not concern himself with the day-to-day
running of the organization. 'Only disinterested individuals free from
lesser ambitions', he had written of his Italian friend, 'people who are not
concerned with dignities and honours, are able to undertake that hard
work in the soul of the nation which can pave the way for epochal
changes in its history'.[30]

In order to acquire the widest possible support, the programme of
the OWP was vague and general. But its ideological affinities with
fascism were clear. National life was to be based on faith, Polish
civilization and statehood. A privileged position was to be granted to
the Catholic church and the movement would derive its ideals from the
principles of 'Polish civilization', which were defined as 'attachment to
tradition, a feeling of responsibility towards the nation, a feeling of
hierarchy and discipline and the acceptance of the need to struggle
against those forces which act to weaken or decompose the nation.' A
strong state was needed to contain social conflicts and defend national
interests abroad.[31]

Dmowski himself defined the relationship of his movement to Italian
fascism as follows:

Fantasies of imitating the methods of fascism will also lead nowhere. Fascism is a great creative movement but its greatness and its creativity are derived from the fact that it is a national movement, the Italian reaction to the ideas of the nineteenth century, and that it also involves a revival of religious life. Although in general we can derive encouragement and a strengthening of our own belief in the future of our national aspirations from the victory of fascism we have no need to imitate this last aspect. We can also learn much from its creators to enable us to deepen our own political thought and to give a proper political expression to our national aspirations. Yet the political methods of fascism are specifically Italian and are well adapted to Italian conditions and to the Italian national character. They constitute that side of fascism which we should not imitate. To imitate the methods of fascism without its spirit is something which stands at the completely opposite pole, it is near to Bolshevism.[32]

The OWP quickly established itself as a significant force on the right, and when in October 1928 the Popular National Union was reorganized as the National Party, it retained its independence as a pressure group, hoping to push the party in a more authoritarian direction. The rise to power of Hitler and the speed with which he was able to disenfranchise one of the wealthiest and most influential Jewish communities in Europe came as a great encouragement to the OWP. It stepped up its agitation not only among students but also among workers and the lower middle class, increasing its membership from 35,000 in January 1930 to 120,000 in May 1932. By early 1933, when it was banned by the government, it could claim a membership of nearly a quarter million. Its dissolution led to a disagreement among its leaders, who wished to continue their activity underground, and the more conservative older leadership of the National Party who opposed conspiracies and who wanted the members of the OWP merely to join the youth section of the party. This course was followed but it increased the belief among some young activists that the party leadership was 'weak and legalistic' and 'filled with opportunism'. One group even decided to seek an understanding with the government, while a second group founded in April 1934 the openly violent and fascist National Radical Camp (ONR). It was duly banned and most of its members were imprisoned. After Piłsudski's death, one section of its members continued to operate underground, while another reached agreement with the authorities to form a pro-government youth group.

Even among the former OWP leadership who remained in the National Party there was considerable dissatisfaction. In April 1934, a number of the young extremists were able to force their cooption on to the party executive. By February 1935, with the support of Dmowski, they had consolidated their power and as a result the party as a whole drew increasingly close to fascism, though it rejected the Führerprinzip and the anti-religious character of Nazism. Though a number of people in the party continued to uphold liberal views, its evolution in a generally fascist and anti-parliamentarian direction was a phenomenon pregnant with danger for the future.

This evolution was actively supported by Dmowski until his death in January 1939. Illness somewhat diminished his output, but he continued in the late twenties and thirties to argue that liberal democracy was merely a shield for 'Jewish-masonic dominance' and that a national revolution on the Italian pattern was necessary. The real enemy in his view was not the government but the reviving left, the Popular Front, generally called the 'Folks Front' to underline its allegedly Jewish character.[33] Dmowski's continued belief that the German-Protestant world was in a state of terminal collapse had a great deal to do with his failure to recognize that the dynamic and aggressive character of Nazism posed a real threat to Poland, in contrast to his earlier opposition to German ambitions. His political acumen was widely respected on the Polish right, even among those who refused to go along with all his views and there seems little doubt that his underestimation of the German danger was one of the factors which created that fatal overconfidence in Poland which paved the way to the disaster of September 1939.

Notes

1. On this see A. Bromke, Poland's Politics: Idealism vs. Realism (Cambridge, Mass. 1967) and idem, Romantyzm czy Realizm? Polskaw latach 80-ych (Romanticism or Realism? Poland in the eighties, Hamilton, 1982).

2. On this, see A.M. Fountain II, Roman Dmowski: Party, Tactics, Ideology 1895-1907 (Columbia, 1980) pp. 103-6; S. Kozicki, Historia Ligi Narodowej: okres 1887-1907 (The History of the National League, the period 1887-1907, London, 1964) p. 450. Sections of Darwin's Origin of Species had been published in Warsaw in 1873 and a complete edition appeared in 1884-5.

3. Mysli nowoczesnego Polaka (The Thoughts of a modern Pole, first published Lwow, 1903. Page references are to the London edition of 1953) p. 72.

4. Ibid, p. 87.

5. Quoted in ed. Adrian Lyttelton, Italian Fascisms from Pareto to Gentile (London, 1973) p. 245.

6. Mysli nowoczesnego Polaka pp. 72-3.

7. Ibid, pp. 88-9.

8. Ibid, p. 79.

9. Ibid, p. 40.

10. Ibid, p. 01.

11. Niemcy, Rosja i kwestja polska (Germany, Russia and the Polish question), p. 30.

12. Ibid, p. 151.

13. On the National Democrats see R. Wapinski, Narodowa Demokracja 1893-1939 (The National Democrats 1893-1939, Warsaw, 1980) A. Micewski Z geografii politycznej II Rzeczypospolitej (On the political geography of the Second Republic, Warsaw, 1964), and Roman Dmowski

(Warsaw 1971); R. Wapinski, 'Niektóre problemy ewolucji ideowo-politycznej Endecji w latach 1919-1939 (Some problems of the ideological political development of the Endecja in the years 1919-1939) Kwartalnik Historyczny LXXIII (1966) No 4, pp. 861-77; 'Miejsce Narodowej Demokracj w życiu politycznym II Rzeczypospolitej, Dzieje Najnowsze, I (1969) pp. 47-62.
14. Quoted in Micewski, Roman Dmowski, p. 354.
15. Julian Zdanowski, Dziennik (Diary, unpublished) quoted in Micewski, Roman Dmowski, p. 302.
16. 'Sny a rzeczywistosc' (Dream and reality) in Od Obozu Wielkiej Polski do Stronnictwa Narodowego (From the OWP to the National Party, (Częstochowa, 1939) p. 34.
17. Nacjonalism i faszyzm' (Nationalism and fascism) Gazeta Warszawska Poranna 22 July 1926.
18. Ministero degli Affari Esteri, Rome, deposit Ministero della Cultura Populare, vol. 724. I am grateful to Jerzy Borejsza for drawing my attention to this material, which he has also discussed in Mussolini byl pierwszy (Mussolini was the first, Warsaw, 1979).
19. On this see Mussolini byl pierwszy, pp. 114-36. The quotations come from a report of the Italian ambassador Guiseppe Bastianini dated June 1934 and quoted in Mussolini byl pierwszy pp. 134-5.
20. Gazeta Warszawska Poranna, 29 June 1926.
21. Ibid.
22. Ibid.
23. Ibid.
24. Ibid. 1 July 1926.
25. Ibid, 22 July 1926
26. Ibid, 29 July 1926
27. Obóz Wielkiej Polski. On its development see J. Holzer, Mozaika polityczna Drugiej Rzeczypospolitej (The Political Mosaic of the Second Republic, Warsaw 1934) pp. 351-373; Wapinski, Narodowa Demokracja, p.. 253-298; S. Rudnicki, 'Narodowa Demokraja po przewrocie majowym. Zmiany organizacyjne i ideologiczne (1926-1930) (The National Democrats after the May coup. Organizational and adminstrative changes 1926-30) Najnowsze Dzieje Polski 1914-1939, Vol II, 1907.
28. Od Obozu Wielkiej Polski do Stronnictwa Narodowego 'Przemowienie inauguracyjne wygloszone przy zalozeniu OWP w Poznaniu 7.XII 1921 r. (Inaugural address at the founding of the OWP, Poznan, 1 December 1926) p. 106.
29. Ibid.
30. Gazeta Warszawaka Poranna 22 July 1926
31. Czem jest Obóz Wielkiej Polski. Deklaracja ideowa odczytana najezdzie w Poznaniu grudnia 1926 r. i przemowienie wygloszone na zebraniu OWP w Warzawie w styczniu 1927 (Warsaw, 1927)
32. 'Zagadnienia rzadu' (The problem of government) in Polityka narodowa w odbudowanym panstwie (National politics and the reborn state, (Częstochowa, 1939) p. 152.
33. 'Folks Front' was intended to draw attention to the fact that its adherents were Yiddish speaking. Many of Dmowski's speeches and articles in these years are reprinted in Od Obozu Wielkiej Polski do Stronnicwa Narodowego, in Polityka narodowa w odbudowanym Panstwie

(National Politics in the reborn state, Częstochowa, 1938) and in Przewrot (Upheaval, Warsaw, 1934) See also T. Bielecki, W szkole Dmowskiego (In Dmowski's school, London 1968).

THE FACTORY AS SOCIETY

IDEOLOGIES OF INDUSTRIAL MANAGEMENT IN THE TWENTIETH CENTURY

Charles S. Maier

'For a theoretical inquiry into the course of civilized life as
it runs in the immediate present, therefore, and as it is
running into the proximate future, no single factor in the
cultural situation has an importance equal to that of the
business man and his work.'

Thorstein Veblen, 1904.[1]

Theories of management are to the practice of business as theories
of architecture are to building. Few buildings follow the canons of design
announced by leading architects, even if they may incorporate individual
elements. Still, architectural manifestos are crucial for orienting the
profession to what might be their solutions if clients, money, and site
constraints allowed. So, too, few industrial plants incorporate the
doctrines of management experts as coherent ensembles. Very few
factories, for example, were actually organized as Taylorite institutions
before and after World War I, even in the United States. Nonetheless,
Taylorism or scientific management dominated the discourse of
industrial relations.

Taylorism and successive ideologies of management in this century
repay close study, for they have become imperial statements. Imperial,
in the sense that increasingly the task of ordering the factory has
seemed impossible unless the encompassing political and economic milieu
was also to be transformed. This essay will examine three important
stages in the development of management ideologies as an index to
broader concepts for organizing capitalist society. In the first stage,
during which notions of Taylorism and scientific management dominated
the rhetoric of industrial leadership (1910-1930), the manager was
supposedly to serve as engineer. In the second stage, from the Depression
through the 1940s and into the 1950s, the manager was to act as
psychologist. His task was to make employees happy and motivated, not
merely to harness men to machines. After World War II, a further
dimension was added: the ideal manager was called upon to help shape
national policies and values. He could best assure the future of his own
enterprise by influencing what happened outside its walls as well as
within; indeed those walls seemed to dissolve conceptually.

Thus the arenas for managerial intervention became ever wider.
Managers had first to govern the shop floor, then win their employees'
hearts and minds and finally shape economic and social priorities. The
continuing premise was that if the social environment influenced the
factory and its workers, then managerial activists had eventually to alter
society itself. The line between enterprise and capitalist environment
became increasingly hazy. Managing the factory and managing society

would be envisaged as tasks of the same order and would draw upon the same talents.

Finally, at the end of these developments one can discern an additional concept: the manager as strategist, the business leader directing corporate acquisitions in a global economic milieu. In this essay we can only allude to this most recent mission, increasingly in vogue since the 1960s. It differs from the three stages under examination here, for they tended to envisage the manager's role as a homeostatic one designed to preserve or restore the equilibrium of the enterprise. The assumption that a given productive unit should tend toward equilibrium, however, suggested a confidence in Western economic capacity that after a decade of inflation and stagnation has largely dissipated. In different ways each of the three management ideologies discussed here reflects an economic confidence we have lost.

Managerial ideologies did not evolve just under the pressure of cultural and economic trends outside the firm. They changed as well in response to organizational developments within business. Engineer, psychologist, and policy activist were managerial personae suggested by technological advances and internal evolution. The enterprise grew from a factory that simply aggregated related workshops to the site of continuous-process manufacture, then to multiple-divisional firm, and finally to a holding company conglomerate. Managerial concepts changed their nature with the broad phases of this evolution. This brief essay must vastly simplify the succession of ideas: for despite our referring to stages, earlier managerial ideas did not simply give way to new ones, but often remained in circulation even as the newer prescriptions captured the business imagination. This essay can propose only a skeletal argument for a phased development of management doctrines, stimulated on one side by changing techniques of production and, on the other side, by broader trends in capitalist society. Fully to understand that society we need to know its factories, those real and those imagined.

1. The Manager as Engineer

Before the twentieth century a self-conscious vocation of management hardly existed in its own right. Nonetheless, the business skills that later flowed into modern management were becoming professionalized. Late nineteenth-century American society sought to train its industrialists and financiers: the Wharton School of Finance and Economy opened in 1881, to be followed by similiar establishments at Chicago and the University of California -- each adding instruction in commerce to augment the engineering curricula that had earlier been viewed as the academic preparation for industrialists in-so-far as one had been required at all. If Veblen argued that the modern businessman too often worked for the 'derangement' and corruption of the industrial process, he remained a dissenter. By the time Schumpeter wrote his treatise on economic development he placed the entrepreneur, who combined all needed business skills 'for the joy of creating, of getting things done,' at the heart of innovation and progress.[2]

Management, however, also entailed concern for the enterprise as a social organization and not merely as a productive unit. It drew upon legacies of paternalism derived from social Catholicism on the continent, from evangelical reform in Protestant cultures, and from the liberals' search for rehabilitative institutions in the late eighteenth and early nineteenth century. The theme of concern for the moral and material welfare of employees was to linger in management doctrines even during the heyday of Taylorism. It motivated not only conservatives but settlement-house reformers, Fabians, and those preoccupied with the human costs of industrialism. B. Seebohm Rowntree pioneered in the ethnography of poverty in York, then ran a cocoa factory as a model plant. As his director insisted, 'The aim of management must be to render industry more effectively human, more truly a corporate effort of human beings, united for a common object and moved by a common motive.' Edward Cadbury of the Bourneville chocolate firm insisted that his worker was 'an intelligent and capable citizen'; he organized company teams, leisure activities and a large dining canteen, but also segregated male and female workers to preserve good morals.[3]

It was not just chocolate manufacture that encouraged such benevolent paternalism (recall, however, Roald Dahl's Willy Wonka for an apt fable!). Sometimes a nonconformist religious background contributed to a reformist stance. Similarly Jewish entrepreneurs were often receptive to collaborationist models of labour relations (Filene in Boston, Olivetti of Ivrea, Alfred Mond of ICI) or to corporatist schemes for national economic planning (Rathenau of AEG and Swope of General Electric). Occasionally a utopian patriarch could institute the most modern experiments, as in the Bat'a factory community of Zlin, Moravia. One common factor tended to be a negative one: the absence of representatives from heavy industry. Instead, those entrepreneurs identified with benevolent labour relations often headed firms that depended upon light manufacture, where the plant still remained a conglomeration of ateliers (e.g. the famous mica room at Hawthorne) and workers might assemble small motors, or packaged sweets, or, in the case of Bat'a, shoes. Conversely, this style of labour relations was also compatible with the less labour-intensive, continuous flow production of the chemical industry, or with far-flung electrical concerns that owned factories to assemble motors and insulators as well as generating plants that needed minimal supervision. Rarely, however, did the heavy iron and steel manufacturing industries that employed masses of men at large-scale semi-skilled production provide the incentive for the paternalism of a Rowntree or others. That sort of standardized large-output plant suggested a more rationalized and often combative style of management. It was also the key sector of industry from 1890 to 1930.

It was Taylorism and scientific management that seemed to fit the iron and steel model of manufacture. Taylor's own background was as an engineer in metallurgical work; the workers he used as the models for his incentive schemes were stolid, semi-skilled providers of heavy labour. Similarly, when Frank Gilbreth proselytized his chronometric analyses of efficiency, he chose brick-laying as a prime example. Taylorism proposed central allocation of tasks, suitable for a factory that could draw upon standardized labour and routines and Taylor applied his incentives to raw labour. Europeans tended to interpret Taylorism as mass production pure and simple, and much of their enthusiasm or criticism after the war focused with misplaced specificity on Taylor.[4] By the mid-1920', moreover, Henry Ford's idea of combining high wages, assembly-line output, and an affordable machine product had also evoked enthusiasm (if not imitation) abroad, and 'Fordist' notions were often conflated with Taylorism. They were hardly identical and, as I have argued earlier, Fordism could be assimilated with fewer utopian implications than Taylorism. Nonetheless, together they stood for scientific management, for the most efficient (and rewarding) way to exploit large-scale standardized manufacture.

The pay-off for labour unions, for management, and for society in general was to be a high level of material reward. Taylorism and Fordism promised more efficient output and corresponding bonuses for workers. Taylor stressed that labour as well as management would share the surplus his methods created. Nonetheless, his plans assumed a continuing rigid division between managerial expertise and manual labour. Employers could apply his ideas to centralize control of the work process, standardize factory tasks, and weaken the shop-floor power that skilled workers still retained.[5] Taylorism allowed management to purchase control of labour by incentives and task division that were supposedly costless because they mobilized time formerly wasted. And just as the methods could overcome conflict in the factory, Taylor and his disciples felt they might enrich and reconcile industrial society as a whole.

Taylorite and Fordist visions of industrial society postulated a centralized factory where workers toiled as adjuncts of machines and the assembly line. After World War I assembly-line methods spread from the United States to European slaughter houses, auto factories, biscuit producers, clothing manufacturers, and other industries. By the late 1920s scientific management still encountered the skepticism of businessmen imbued with older concepts of paternalist responsibility. Nonetheless, the enthusiasts of scientific management were dominating the reviews, tracts, and professional congresses as they urged rationalization of factories, offices, and even the Taylorization of leisure, the home and the city. Trade union spokesmen could also endorse scientific management providing they could retain a voice in its application.[6]

Meanwhile, as Taylorite concepts were winning adherents throughout Europe, industrial organization was going beyond the centralized assembly-line plant that formed their archetypal image of the factory. The giant autoworks at River Rouge or Turin-Lingotto might capture publicists' imagination, but innovations in the organization of corporate empires were as crucial as spectacular factories. The image of the factory remained compelling (and the stylized social-realist murals of the Depression only made it more pervasive) but new paradigms of management would be needed.

2. The Manager as Psychologist

The forgotten premise of Taylorism and Fordism was Say's Law: incentive systems and mass production could reward workers only if their output could be sold. The world economic crisis shattered this assumption and with it the belief that efficiency and engineering could resolve industrial conflict. The Depression sharpened ideological divisions between capital and labour. Workers might not possess the collective strength to wrest control of the plant; still, it was harder to exorcize politics from the factory. Appeals to a rational technocratic consensus were eclipsed. Instead the new influential ideologies reflected a growing belief in the propensity to non-rational behaviour. Whether deriving from once-socialist theorists (e.g. Hendrik de Man's 1926 Psychology of Socialism), or from right wing images of crowd behaviour, the postulates of managerial ideologies became far darker. In the new discussion of the 1930s, industrial man followed murky mass instincts. He had to be controlled not with rational incentives, but with appeals to collective drives and sentiments. Even at its crudest, Taylorism had addressed the incentives of individual workers, proposing a manipulated calculus of rewards for the man, not the mass. Now, however, the factory appeared as a social whole, a beehive or organism that had to be organized as a system.

The connection between management and psychology had already been forged in several different countries. The German psychologist, Hugo Munsterberg, recruited to Harvard by William James, sought to overcome Taylor's 'helpless dilettantism' through the application of Psychotechnik in industry, especially by means of vocational selection. The study of psychological adjustment was coopted for frankly conservative ends of indoctrination by the right wing politicians and businessmen of the German DINTA, who sought to mould nationalist and anti-Marxist cadres among the proletariat. In Great Britain and the United States the issue of industrial 'fatigue,' with its ramifications of monotony and moräle, provided the starting point for a vast elaboration of psychological approaches. From the 1915 Health of Munitions Workers Committee in Britain emerged the Industrial Fatigue Research Board, to be extended in 1921 by the National Institute of Industrial Psychology, uniting academics and industrialists, and supported by the Carnegie Trustees. The Board's avowed concern with the 'reduction of waste' along with 'selection of the most suitable workers' and the psychological aspects of labour was typical of the widespread post-war conviction that industrial society need only reduce its wasteful use of human and capital resources to assure prosperity for all.[7]

Still, these early studies did not originate in any presuppositions about the irrationality of workers. Rather psychology was intended to help employers deal with the normal process of discovering aptitudes, overcoming the physical tensions and stress that led to accidents, and smoothing unnecessary conflict. But once psychology had claimed a role it promised a far broader appeal than fatigue studies alone permitted. By the 1930s industrial psychologists ascribed to the manager the redefined mission of yoking non-rational employees together in a common enterprise. No longer was the starting point the single individual, but the factory community with its own collective laws. Goetz Briefs' writings in the German-speaking world, (later translated), described the proletariat as a psychological entity. And rather than designing a structure of material rewards the manager had to evoke trust, community, joy in work.[8] In the modern era these seemed especially hard to ensure. The factory was no longer an isolated community, and the influences emanating from outside were not conducive to nurturing these values within the plant. German industrialists had already declared that labour relations within a business could not partake of democracy: 'The large factory without authority is an absurdity.'[9] The difficulty was, as one industrial relations expert wrote in 1932, the worker was also a trade unionist, party adherent, and perhaps church goer:

> More than ever before we can talk today of a front hostile to the factory, determined to narrow the sphere of factory life and subject it to the influence of the state and the collective right to work. All these influences of an internal and external sort increase the alienation of the worker. The factory, therefore, must exclude social disturbances as far as possible for the sake of its self-preservation.[10]

Such ideas became popular as part of a growing acceptance of irrationalist concepts of human nature -- and not merely in the fascist regimes. A certain Paretan chic made inroads even in the United States where the Treatise on Sociology was translated in 1933, and the notion of the circulation of elites became a staple of historical and social analysis. In Europe, former socialist adherents as well as conservatives accepted the darker interpretation of collective behaviour. One revealing indication was the analytic reliance on the concept of 'masses' in the new treatises. Another, of course, was the left-to-right trajectory of many of the 'front generation' who became convinced that doctrinaire socialism neglected man's vitalist drives, his hunger for communal loyalties and for obedience. From Michels to de Man and thence to Emil Lederer and even into the 1940s and 1950s the disillusion with social democracy dominated sociological discourse. Politically, of course, the passage from left to right marked the New Conservatism in Weimar (not to claim National Socialism), the French Neo-Socialists or the rebellion of the frustrated and arrogant Oswald Mosley.

In this climate of opinion could it be any surprise that the task of the manager should also be redefined? Even before the Nazis reorganized German labour relations, commentators suggested that the provisions of Weimar legislation, conceived of as a social-democratic advance, permitted 'extensive dictatorial power' on the part of the employer. 'Employer and employee are united in one organism into a community of labour in which the latter subordinates himself freely to the command of the former for the sake of a commonly sought goal of productivity.'[11] In the perspective of the 1930s the engineer himself no longer appeared just as an efficiency expert, but as a more occult arranger, a potential ally of the new rulers in Germany or of, say, the proto-Vichyite groups in France. Jean Coutrot, polytechnicien, Teilhardiste Catholic, and organizer of the planning enthusiasts in the X-Crise, sought to perfect industrial administration through the application of both engineering and psychology. In the wake of 1936's labour upheavals, he urged separation of ownership and managerial administration, the latter to become a board-certified profession. And he speculated on the analogy of treating 'the psychological equilibrium within a business' as a sort of 'concentration camp conceived of as a sanatorium: provisional, with teachers and nurses, where one isolates until the end of their cure those whom one has not been able to convince so that they do not disturb others or hurt themselves.'[12]

With a less polarized political system than the Europeans, Americans could share the new management ideology with fewer authoritarian overtones. Elton Mayo began from the observations at Western Electric's light manufacturing plant at Hawthorne, Illinois, that workers responded positively to special attention. The approach to emerge would be called 'human relations.' Summarizing his work, Mayo began with the analyses of fatigue during and after the First World War, then presented the Hawthorne studies of the late 1920s and early 1930s, then turned to the difficulties of the wider society. The problem for management did not lie in any irreducible individual irrationalism; Mayo explicitly rejected Freudian ideas for an eclectic behaviourism. Nor did the problem lie in the factory alone. The disintegration of the wider society, a Durkheimian <u>anomie</u>, afflicted industrial civilization, but the same techniques might remedy the difficulties whether 'for a factory on the Volga or for another on the banks of the river Charles.' Mayo appealed to Malinowski, Piaget and Pareto among other to stress that selection of an administrative elite was the crucial need. Only the administrator could restore human collaboration within the factory and in society as a whole.[13] As Mayo's disciple, F.J. Roethlisberger, wrote at the end of the 1930's: 'The function of management, stated in its most general terms, can be described as that of maintaining a social system of the industrial plant in a state of equilibrium such that the purposes of the enterprises are realized.' The task was to align wills: Hawthorne workers had demonstrated 'neither logical nor irrational behavior. It was essentially social behavior.'[14]

Entrenched at the Harvard Business School, human relations could remain a dominant managerial theme throughout the 1950s. Outside the United States the Tavistock Institute of Human Relations and publicists such as Georges Friedmann in Paris continued the emphasis on integration. Its implications were sometimes contradictory. On the one hand, spokesmen for integration sometimes implied that the industrial system should obey its own frictionless logic, safely insulated from the surrounding social and political environment. On the other hand, it was suggested, only the transformation of political society itself, its subjection to administrative and managerial skills, might assure the harmony of the factory. Happily for the writers of the post-war decade, this seemed to be taking place. Just as a confrontational style of labour relations was disappearing within the factory, so ideological conflict was also slipping into the past: macrocosm and microcosm were converging in the benign process of modernization. The manager, as Roethlisberger suggested in 1948, in effect spanned both: 'the manager is neither managing men nor managing work ... he is administering a social system.[15]

Thus a reorientation of managerial ideas that took root under the impact of depression found apparent confirmation because of post-World War II prosperity. The Depression had undermined the notion that the managerial task was to harness men to machines. It fostered the conviction that the real challenge was to nurture a community of producers. Under the stress of inter-war social and political conflict, the plant could no longer be treated as the safe domain of the machine and engineer. The response could be the harsh psychological leadership inculcated by the DINTA and then legislated by the Nazi Labour Front (with the factory envisaged as a band of workers under a chief who was always obeyed, but still observed a primitive egalitarian consultation among his production team). Or it might be the planiste transformation suggested by X-Crise, or the collaborative evangelical paternalism advocated in Britain, or even the environmental behaviourism suggested by the Americans. In each case, though, the new emphasis required dealing with the collective mentality of employees. Harmony became as crucial as efficiency.

Just as the Depression created a new social and economic context for management ideas, so too did developments in industry itself. The auto industry, with its assembly-line production, was no longer so exclusively the archetype of an industrial plant. Now chemicals and oil and electrical generation captured the public imagination alongside iron and steel based manufacture. So, too, the idealized vision of the manager now transcended the mastery of assembly-line production. It came to involve organizing the multi-divisional firm. Even in the auto industry the change was evident in the eclipse of engineer-managers such as Charles Sorensen of Ford or William Knudsen of GM (who proved inadequate at the Office of War Production in the 1940s) as contrasted with the new eminence of Alfred Sloan. Industrial organization became far more than a Fordist concept.

The political orientations of industry also encouraged the new concepts of management. The electrical and chemical industries often became identified as special supporters of National Socialist and Italian fascist policies in the 1930s. Directors of the traditional iron and steel firms and the heads of the manufacturing concerns based on steel certainly proved happy enough to benefit from government contracts and autarkic protection, but they lost political influence. The German iron and steel industrialists had been close to the Nationalist Right in Weimar, but I.G. Farben became more central to the war-planning combinations sponsored after 1936. Likewise Giovanni Agnelli of FIAT had maintained liberal connections and the Italian steel producers had supported the pre-fascist Right, while the fascist regime turned more to chemicals and electricity.[16] Interestingly enough, however, these industries had earlier been more affiliated with liberal politics than heavy industry. In Weimar Germany, Siemens and Rathenau, both electrical magnates, had counted as politically progressive; in Britain, Alfred Mond of ICI had sought collaborative labour relations, and Elton Mayo's Hawthorne experiments were taking place within the subsidiary of an electrical firm that he described as 'definitely committed to justice and humanity in its dealings with workers.'[17] The more consistent political stance over time, in fact, emerged from the classical industries of nineteenth-century development -- coal, iron and steel, and their manufacturing affiliates -- which did not vault from liberal to fascist identifications but stuck with a traditional conservatism. One reason was that they remained more labour intensive and often faced strongly organized work-forces, and they relied on a style of labour relations that was patriarchal at best and often brutally anti-union. In contrast, the more process-oriented, less labour-intensive newer industries of the twentieth century tended to be either more politically reformist or else authoritarian in a new and manipulative mode. For those thinking in terms of the needs of the newer industries, the theme of organization became crucial, whether authoritarian or behaviourist and psychological.

The managerial literature that emerged under these new economic and political conditions of the 1930s through the 1950s could become naively extravagant. At the apex of the factory or the society had to be men who combined broad training and intuitive gifts. Editors demanded an expertise based upon psychological insight, but one, interestingly enough, that they did not compare with literary insight. The manager was to master a world in microcosm but no comparisons were made with Tolstoy or Flaubert or Shakespeare (not even with Prospero, who in name and role might have seemed apt) -- perhaps because the writers understood that collective life often foundered on stubborn passions, on rancour, sexuality, jealousy, and ennui. Irreducible passion did not appear in the managerial discourse; contumaciousness, accidie could all be removed. At worst a diffuse crowd mentality clouded the creatures who needed attention and care and guidance. Implicitly the managerial function became the highest that might exist. As one British spokesman wrote, recapitulating the themes of the previous quarter century:

> A real philosophy of productivity should give us the right vision of a future state where the world of productive work will draw people into it, not primarily for the purpose of earning a living, but <u>where in fellowship as members of a team rendering a worthwhile service, they can unfold their personalities in work happily and successfully done, thereby serving their neighbours and their God.</u> A distant vision, it is true, and one we may never attain. Nonetheless, a vision worth striving for and one capable of drawing the best from the national team.[18]

3. The Manager as Policy Activist

The notion of the manager as a psychological organizer became most pervasive after the war. Nonetheless, it had to make room for other concepts as well. The 1930s had demonstrated that the manager must consider his firm as a social system often at odds with the larger environment. As Chester Barnard had written in an authoritative statement: 'The survival of an organization depends upon the maintenance of an equilibrium of complex character in a continuously fluctuating environment of physical, biological, and social materials, elements, and forces, which calls for readjustment of processes internal to the organization.[19] The task of a manager, in other words, was to navigate in the changing political and economic conditions of the wider world.

But might not management finally extend its purview into that wider world? Increasingly after World War II business spokesmen would call less for the responsiveness of their enterprises than for the shaping of the economic milieu. Nor did this mean just the traditional objective of securing favourable particularist policies, such as tariffs or tax relief, but rather a steady intervention on behalf of buoyant economic management. Forced to become a psychologist during the Depression, the manager was now to become a policy activist as well. 'We must participate in the formation of public policy even though the specific issues may not have an immediate influence on our individual businesses,' one writer argued by 1951. 'We must aim to tear down the psychological walls that have been built around group interests. We must realize that in these matters the whole is greater than the sum of its parts.'[20]

Business leaders had to reconquer territory earlier thought outside their control. Perhaps the major group effort was the Committee for Economic Development, organized by the chairman of the Studebaker Corporation, Paul Hoffman, and designed to lobby for an active and steady interventionist role on the part of government. The CED recognized that the Keynesian 'revolution' had come to stay and feared that a return to pre-New Deal attitudes could bring a relapse into depression. In effect the Committee proposed a government-business partnership to chart out an intelligent fiscal activism, to plan a beneficial mix of government spending and tax policies to spur continued high investment. To this end the CED orchestrated a succession of meetings, the establishment of local committees, and a series of publications on such economic issues as price-wage relations, problems of small business, and proper fiscal policy. CED economists especially urged acceptance of the idea of a full-employment budget, that is, one that yielded a balance when employment was high and business prospering, but that simultaneously allowed for a counter-cyclical deficit if economic activity flagged. In some ways the CED represented an American analogue of the industrial peak associations that had long been a feature of European business organization. But it defined its task in a more upbeat and less defensive way; it presupposed, not that business was a special interest, but that, in good American fashion, business was the general interest.

In the perspective of the CED, the factory became almost an archaic concept. While the firm remained the unit of private activity, government policy was a crucial formative influence; hence businessmen had to engage in an ongoing benevolent collaboration with the state. By 1947-48 the organization of the Marshall Plan -- with Hoffman becoming the head of the Washington executive agency, the Economic Cooperation Administration -- became paradigmatic of the new arrangement, that is, of a public policy designed to encourage and teach economic growth abroad and at home, entrusted to a partnership of political leaders, business executives, trade union spokesmen and academics. Justifying this broad collaboration, the concept of productivity played some of the same role in political economy discourse after the second war as did efficiency after the First. Productivity was an objective that every business and labour leader could seek to maximize within his own company and it provided a national objective as well. 'Productivity', declared the CED's research director at a meeting of its trustees in October 1947, 'is a vitally needed lubricant to reduce class and group frictions. As long as we can get more by increasing the size of the pie there is not nearly so much temptation to try to get a bigger slice at the expense of others. That applies particularly to the common and conflicting interests of labour and capital. If it weren't for possibilities of increased productivity the struggle between capital and labour would be more severe and dangerous than it is.'[21]

Productivity allowed the old management concepts to be combined in a new synthesis. It recapitulated the engineer's emphasis on efficiency of the 1920s, which like productivity was the measure of a ratio: usually physical output divided by labour time. Appeals to productivity and efficiency could stress both the role of growth, the effective increase of the numerator, and the need for rationalization (as in the late 1920s), which focused on lowering the costs expressed by the denominator. But invoking productivity also suggested concern with the psychological integration that the 1930s managerial ethos had highlighted. Productivity themes also played a political role; they rallied European business leaders and the representatives of the non-communist trade unions who participated in the productivity missions and productivity councils that proliferated in Western Europe under the auspices of the Marshall Plan. The Anglo-American Council on Productivity formed one transatlantic network; in France the Commissariat du Plan created a working group on productivity that organized 450 missions to the United States. What they stressed in their reports on return was not the technological backwardness of French industry, but the lag in terms of industrial and personal relations.[22] Productivity thus served as a business strategy, as slogan for an international political coalition, and as a managerial theme that revalidated the older approaches of the inter-war period.

What code of behaviour did American business leaders suggest to European counterparts and to their own colleagues by the years of the Marshall Plan? Intelligent political activism on behalf of a progressive fiscal policy comprised only part of a broader thematic of social responsibility. As the alumni association of the Harvard Business School was told in June 1948, 'Today most managements operate as trustee in recognition of the claims of employees, investors, consumers and government.'[23] Social responsibility as a managerial ideal often demanded, so friendly observers as well as critics pointed out, almost total immersion in business. The corporation claimed community participation on the part of its employees as well as the selfless loyalty of their wives. Enfolded in business as a total institution, corporate leaders could claim to serve the totality of institutions. As one of the more perceptive articulators of business aspirations, Peter Drucker, claimed in a 1951 symposium sponsored by the Advertising Council: 'We have gone a very long way in the direction of solving the basic ethical and basic political problem of an industrial society, the social and ethical harmony between the self-interest of our economic institutions and the social interests of society.' For Paul Hoffman, who chaired the symposium, America had triumphed by finding a decentralized way to collective action. 'The realization that through free non-governmental collective action in business you can not only have a better life business-wise, but also a more profitable individual business, is a comparatively modern development.'[24]

With the participation of the businessman in a fabric of social responsibility and national policy making, management ideology claimed a new inclusiveness. No longer could the managerial function be conceived in terms of the firm alone. In the era of the Cold War it involved a national mission: 'There is no higher responsibility, there is no higher duty, of professional management than to gain the respect of the general public through objective participation in, and consideration of, national questions, even though these questions in many cases do not relate directly to their business problems.'[25] In effect this attitude represented the socialization of management: the tendency to fuse factory and society. Indeed, one aspect of the new managerial claims was that the role of the manager was losing its specificity or becoming ambivalent in its meanings. 'Manager' now often implied more the concept of middle-management, the supervisor of a unit within a larger enterprise. 'Executive' was increasingly reserved as the concept for those at the top, and this role was described as almost a super-human calling:

> In many respects the role of the policy-forming executive in a business enterprise is unenviable. It is a perpetually demanding role; its rewards, both economically and socially, are rarely commensurate with the sacrifices it entails. Perhaps because of this, policy-making is an activity for which, like advanced medical research, only the exceptional and dedicated individual is truly fitted.

But top management had abdicated its leadership role to unions and government; its task was to reclaim them: 'to play, once again, the part of a leader -- the kind of leader who can capture the loyalty of the employees, represent and personify the company in the public eye, and present a point of view effectively at a Congressional hearing.'[26]

By the 1950s the tone of self-satisfaction could be almost suffocating. Still, there were difficulties. Management had resolved the problem of its enterprises by integrating them within the larger socio-economic consensus of post-war productivity and growth. But within the factory alone old problems remained, including those presented by the assembly line and by Fordist production. As one critic argued, assembly-line technology perniciously influenced the assumptions about human motivation held at all levels of management, which had to learn to deal with small group production teams and not individual cogs.[27] Peter Drucker argued that management too often merely claimed its 'prerogatives'. It still had to fulfil a function, but the function required transcended the firm: how to think about plant location so cities did not become hostage to vulnerable industries, how to provide for the employment of older workers, how to encourage small business.[28] In short, management still had not solved the issues that either its earlier mission from the inter-war period or its post-war social activism had laid upon it. And in a way managerial celebrants turned towards the wider world, towards the gospel of policy activism, because only by seeking to bring in broader resources of hegemony -- national mission, Keynesian macroeconomic policies, the ideological mobilization of the Cold War -- might the persistent conflicts inherent in the business enterprise be constrained and, indeed, made manageable.

The half-century trajectory of managerial ideologies thus involved a progressive claim to subject ever broader areas of economic and cultural life, of personality and public policy to the jurisdiction of business leadership. This expansiveness was not planned from the outset. But two processes impelled the efforts at more profound stabilization within the firm and wider circles of intervention beyond its traditional boundaries. One was the search for an adequate concept of the managerial function as the enterprise developed from simple factory into a financially linked network of multiple production or service units. The other was the increasing awareness that economic possibilities, social conflicts, and ideological dispositions were determined within the overall political economy. Ultimately the manager or executive was the man fitted to run society as a whole; indeed, he could hardly forbear from making the attempt.

To be sure, this broad thrust of management ideology remained peculiarly American and probably emerged most fully during the Eisenhower administration. Europeans remained more reserved: in Britain businessmen did not possess the cultural hegemony they had acquired in America; in France the state still claimed a major share of technocratic leadership; even in West Germany, where the American model might be received most congenially, the existence of a Social Democratic Party provided some counterweight. In Italy the dominant Christian Democratic Party responded to patronage networks in small towns and southern cities that allowed only a limited voice to spokesmen for entrepreneurship and modernization, who might dominate Confindustria or ENI, but not the regime. Nonetheless, in all these countries, engaging in the discourse of productivity meant accepting a good deal of American managerial ideals. In the United States, Charles E. Wilson, Eisenhower's Secretary of Defense designate, did not actually say that what was good for General Motors was good for the United States; he said that he always presumed that what was good for the United States was also good for GM. But the force of this patriotic productivism was the same: it affirmed the congruency of the managerial sphere within factory and society.

Still, this vision, too, was subject to erosion. By the mid 1950s there were critiques of the corporate thinking that it encouraged. Following upon David Riesman's critique of the other-directed personality, Theodore Levitt argued that the economy of abundance would produce stagnant management, a critique that echoed Schumpeter.[29] Whether the prediction was justified or not, by the late 1960s and 1970s management ideology would change again and this time towards a less celebratory mode. In this most recent phase business leadership has been cast less in terms of administration (management seems faintly derogatory) than strategy. Strategy implies the combining and re-combining of portfolio assets in a somewhat Hobbesian economic environment: it implies long-term objectives, the constant presence of uncertainty, and the existence of constraints. Whether as engineer, as psychologist, or as policy activist, the twentieth-century manager entertained an implicitly homeostatic vision. His task was to preserve or restore a high-level equilibrium, within a firm buffeted by its wider environment, or within the firm and economic environment simultaneously. By the 1970s the assurance of equilibrium faded, and a new doctrine of business in constant cyclical evolution became persuasive. Despite their occasional prayer breakfasts business leaders did not evoke the Biblical imagery of Jacob's ladder; instead consultants told them to acquire 'sunrise' industries that would flourish for a while as 'milk cows', then decline as 'sunset' industries, and be cast off as 'dogs'. In the world of Japanese video recorders, Korean steel, of bleak structural unemployment in Detroit, Nancy, and Charleroi, the benign assumptions of the 1950s no longer held.

Would managerial ideologies expand once again to claim and order the international economic milieu that now impinged upon the individual enterprise; that is, could the multinationals impose a new Fordist or productivist ebullience? Or would managerial claims retreat to more mercantilist doctrines? In either case, ideologies of management could no longer presuppose entrepreneurial equilibria without concepts of development, of change not just as a random variable or a beneficial unfolding of technological potential, but change as a historic succession of economic ascendancies and decline. After a half century of relying on engineering, human relations, and growth, entrepreneurial ideologies confronted the historicity of capitalism.

Notes

1.   Thorstein Veblen, The Theory of Business Enterprise (New York: Mentor ed., n.d.), 8. Since this essay is dedicated to James Joll, it is fitting to place its themes in relation to his work. Joll, of course, has written most often on politicians and thinkers at odds with capitalist managers. The significant exception was Walther Rathenau, who, as Joll pointed out, was a major publicist of some of the themes brought up here. (See Three Intellectuals in Politics, London: Weidenfeld & Nicolson, 1960). More generally, James Joll's work has always pointed to the problematic juncture of ideology with actual politics. Here we venture to explore a similar juncture, although for the range of economic activity that Joll has left relatively unexplored.
2.   On business education, Edward Chase Kirkland, Dream and Thought in the Business Community, 1860-1900 (Chicago: Quadrangle, 1964), 89-100; for Veblen's quote, Theory of Business Enterprise, 22, and chapter 3 for the general theme; for Joseph Schumpeter's view: The Theory of Economic Development [1911], Redvers Opie, trans. (New York: Oxford University Press, 1961), 93. On entrepreneurship, most recently see Alfred D. Chandler, Jr., The Visible Hand (Cambridge, Mass., Howard University Press 1977); Leslie Hannah, ed., Management Strategy and

Business Development (London: Macmillan, 1976); and the essay by Jürgen Kocka on Germany in The Cambridge Economic History of Europe, vol. VII, part 1, (Cambridge, 1977), chap. 10; also Alfred Chandler and Herman Daems, eds., Managerial Hierarchies (Cambridge, Mass.: Harvard University Press, 1980).
3.   For the Rowntree approach see Oliver Sheldon, The Philosophy of Management (New York: Prentice-Hall, 1924), 8. Also Rowntree, The Human Factor in Business (London: Longmans Green, 1921). For Edward Cadbury see Experiments in Industrial Organization (London; Longmans Green, 1912); also the papers collected in Alfred D. Chandler, Jr., Management Thought in Great Britain (New York: Arno Press, 1979); and Eugene A. Miao, 'British Managerial Thought, 1910-1930,' Harvard University honors thesis, 1983.
4.   See Charles S. Maier, 'Between Taylorism and Technocracy: European Ideologies and the Vision of Industrial Productivity in the 1920's,' Journal of Contemporary History, vol. V, no. 2 (April 1970): 27-61. Further citations can be found there and in Maier, 'The Two Postwar Eras and the Conditions for Stability in Twentieth-Century Western Europe,' American Historical Review, vol. 86, no. 2 (April 1981): 336-339. See also Judith A. Merkle, Management and Ideology (Berkeley and Los Angeles: University of California Press, 1980).
5.   On the issue of control see David Montgomery, 'The "New Unionism" and the Transformation of Workers' Consciousness in America, 1909-1922,' Journal of Social History, 7 (1974): 509-529. For Taylor's own evangelism: Scientific Management, Comprising Shop Management, The Principles of Scientific Management, Testimony before the Special House Committee (New York, Harper & Bros., 1911).
6.   For the spread of industrial methods, Aimée Moutet, 'Introduction à la production à la chaine en France du début du XXe Siècle à la grande crise en 1930,' Histoire, Economie, Société (1983:1) 63-82; Olivier Christen 'Les enjeux de la rationalisation industrielle (1901-1929),' Mémoire de maîtrise, Paris, 1982; Patrick Fridenson,'The Coming of the Assembly Line to Europe,' in The Dynamics of Science and Technology. Sociology of the Sciences, vol. II (Dordrecht, 1978). For a bibliography on conferences, etc., see Paul Devinat, Scientific Management in Europe, ILO Studies and Reports, series B, no. 17 (Geneva, 1927). For labour relations: M.J. Nadworny, Scientific Management and the Unions, 1900-1932 (Cambridge, Mass.: Harvard University Press, 1955); Bernard Doray, La Folie taylorienne (Paris: Dunod, 1981), 132-157.
7.   On the DINTA (Deutsche Institut für technische Arbeitsschulung) see Robert Brady, The Rationalization Movement in German Industry (Berkeley and Los Angeles: University of California Press, 1933), and the material in Peter Hinrichs and Lothar Peters, Industrieller Friede? Arbeitswissenschaft und Rationalisierung in der Weimarer Republik (Cologne: Pahl-Rugenstein, 1976). For Great Britain and the United States see George H. Miles, 'The Extent and Application of Psychology and Psychological Methods in English Industrial Life', Harvard Business Review, (henceforth: HBR) IV, 1 (1925-26): 138-144; Walter Bingham 'Management's Concern with Research in Industrial Psychology', HBR, X, 1 (1931-32) 40-53; also Elton Mayo, The Human Problems of an Industrial Civilization [1933] (New York, Viking: 1960), chaps. 1-2. For the theme

of waste see the Committee on Elimination of Waste in Industry of the Federated American Engineering Societies, Waste in Industry (New York, MacGraw-Hill, 1921) and Stuart Chase, The Tragedy of Waste (New York: Macmillan Co., 1925).

8.   Goetz Briefs, The Proletariat: A Challenge to Western Civilization (London and New York, MacGraw-Hill, 1937); also Briefs, ed., Probleme der sozialen Werkspolitik 3 vols. (Munich and Leipzig, 1930-1935).

9.   Reported Berliner Börsenzeitung, March 26, 1924.

10.   Rudolf   Schwenger,   'Die   Betriebliche   Sozialpolitik   im Ruhrkohlenbergbau', Schriften des Vereins für Sozialpolitik, 186/I (1932): 4; cited in T.W. Mason, 'Zur Entstehung des Gesetzes zur Ordnung der nationalen Arbeit vom Januar 1934,' in Hans Mommsen, D. Petzina, B. Weisbrod, Industrielles System und politische Entwicklung in der Weimarer Republik (Düsseldorf: Droste Verlag, 1974), 342-343.

11.   Otto Kahn-Freund, 'Das soziale Ideal des Reichsarbeitsgerichts,' cited by Mason, loc. cit., 344.

12.   Jean Coutrot, Les leçons de juin 1936, l'humanisme économique (Paris, 1936), cited in Luc Boltanski, Les Cadres (Paris: Editions de Minuit, 1982), 118-119. For German parallels see Gerd Hortleder, Das Gesellschaftbild   des   Ingenieurs.   Zum   politischen   Verhalten   des technischen Intelligenz in Deutschland (Frankfurt/M: Suhrkamp, 1974), 93-123.

13.   Mayo, Human Problems of an Industrial Civilization, 125-129, 161-180 (quotation, p.139).

14.   F. J. Roethlisberger and William J. Dickson, Management and the Worker (Cambridge, Mass.: Harvard University Press, 1939), 569, 575.

15.   Roethlisberger, 'Human Relations: Rare, Medium, or Well-Done?' HBR, vol. 26, 1 (1948): 94. For the Tavistock Institute see the work of Elliot Jacques, The Changing Culture of a Factory (London: Tavistock, 1951); and for Georges Friedmann, see the sophisticated study, with copious references: Industrial Society; The Emergence of the Human Problems of Automation (New York: the Free Press, 1955).

16.   For the trends sketched in these paragraphs see: Chandler, Visible Hand, chaps. 14; also Alfred D. Chandler, Jr., Strategy and Structure (Cambridge, Mass: Harvard University Press, 1962); Alfred P. Sloan, Jr., My Years with General Motors (New York: Doubleday, 1964); Valerio Castronova, Giovanni Agnelli (Turin: UTET, 1971), chap. V; Giulio Sapelli, Organizzazione, lavoro e innovazione industriale nell'Italia tra le due   guerre   (Turin: Rosenberg   &   Sellier,   1978);   Dieter   Petzina, Autarkiepolitik im Dritten Reich (Stuttgart: Deutsche Verlags-Anstalt, 1968), Alfred Sohn-Rethel, Economy and Class Structure of German Fascism (London: CSE Books, 1978).

17.   Mayo, Human Problems of an Industrial Civilization, 96.

18.   A.P. Young, American Management Techniques and Practices and their Bearing on Productivity in British Industry (London, 1948?), 65.

19.   Chester Barnard, The Functions of the Executive (Cambridge, Mass., Harvard University Press, 1938), 6.

20.   Frank W. Abrams, 'Management's Responsibilities in a Complex World,' HBR, XXIX, 3 (1951): 33-34.

21.   Ted Yntema at CED Board of Trustees, October 16, 1947. 'Minutes of Meeting,' in Paul Hoffman papers, Harry S. Truman Presidential

Library, Independence, Mo., box 40.
22. Boltanski, Les Cadres, 158-59 and chap. 2 in general: 'La fascination de l'amérique et l'importation du management.' Also Charles S. Maier, 'The Politics of Productivity. Foundations of American International Economic Policy after World War II,' in Peter Katzenstein, ed., Between Power and Plenty: Foreign Economic Policies of Advanced Industrial States (Madison, Wisc.: University of Wisconsin Press, 1978).
23. Clarence Francis address, cited in Roy Lewis and Rosemary Stewart, The Managers: A New Examination of the English, German and American Executive (New York: Mentor, 1961), 194.
24. 'Basic Elements of a Free, Dynamic Society - Part I, A Round-Table Discussion Sponsored by the Advertising Council, Inc.' (April 16, 1951) HBR, XXIX, 6 (1951): 57, 67.
25. Abrams, loc. cit., 34.
26. Robert N. McMurry, 'Man-Hunt for Top Executives,' HBR, XXXII, 1 (1954): 61-62.
27. Arthur N. Turner, 'Management and the Assembly Line,' HBR, XXXIII, 5 (1955): 40-48.
28. Peter F. Drucker, 'Management Must Manage,' HBR, XXVIII, 2 (1950): 80-86; also Drucker, The New Society: the Anatomy of Industrial Order (New York: Harper & Brothers, 1950).
29. Theodore Levitt, 'The Changing Character of Capitalism,' HBR, XXXIV, 4 (1956): 37-47.

THE OTHER GERMANY - THE 'NEO-LIBERALS'[1]

Anthony Nicholls

The failure of the conservative German opposition to overthrow Hitler in July 1944 marked the end of an era which had opened with the appointment of Bismarck as Prussian prime minister in 1862. The Prussian-German state, which had earlier survived defeat and revolution, was now irretrievably doomed. All the allies ranged against Germany were committed to its destruction. Within the Reich its moral foundations had been eaten away. The vicious purge conducted by Hitler's henchmen in the summer and autumn of 1944 liquidated many of its most distinguished surviving protagonists. The formal dissolution of Prussia - promulgated by the occupying powers on 25 February 1946 - set the final seal on a disastrous epoch.

It is a commonplace to remark that the circumstances of German unification helped to create a climate of opinion conducive to nationalism, and that the character of Wilhelmine Germany made its citizens vulnerable to the attractions of National Socialism. Professor Wilhelm Röpke wrote in 1945, 'Hitlers are to be found everywhere and at all times, but it is Germany's shame that such a wretched creature could become its leader.'[2] On the other hand it should not be thought that German intellectuals had all given themselves up to the worship of state power, nationalist self-assertion and international Darwinism. The disasters of the First World War and its aftermath, reinforced by the horrors of the Third Reich, caused an important minority to look back towards quite other traditions in Germany's past than those espoused by Bismarck or Wilhelm II. They saw as truly German the humane principles of the 18th century enlightenment and the liberal values which had come to the fore - albeit with confusion - in the revolutionary movement of 1848. They drew comfort from the Christian community of small states, thriving towns and peasant farms which had characterized most of the German nation before massive industrialization had given Prussia its economic preponderance. They saw the causes of the German catastrophe in the betrayal of liberal values, both in the political and economic sphere. In this sense they were opposed to both the conservative nationalist and the Marxist alternatives to Hitler. Both these tendencies would want to supplant one powerful, centralized, interventionist form of state with another. Ultimately their solutions would lead, whether intentionally or not, to a form of collectivism. By 1945 insistent voices, few in numbers but increasingly influential, began to be heard demanding a return to those liberal values which the Realpolitiker of Prussia-Germany had spurned.

The irrationality of vainglorious nationalism had been particularly apparent in the economic sphere, and it was from the ranks of German economists that the most important theoretical proposals for the rejuvenation of post-war Germany were to come. These were men whose ideas had been shaped during the inter-war period by the experience of two traumatic disasters; the hyper-inflation which destroyed Germany's currency in 1923 and the great depression which destroyed German democracy in the early 1930s. Both these catastrophes had been of immense importance in facilitating the rise of Hitler to power. Both were the result of government policies which had shown either an ignorance of, or a capacity to ignore, the principles upon which sound economies should be based.

Why had German economists been unable to foresee these disasters and propose measures to prevent them? This indeed was a question put by the former Prussian finance minister in the Weimar Republic, Hermann Höpker-Aschoff, to the Professor of Economics in Münster, Alfred Müller-Armack, when they used to walk through the war-damaged Westphalian city in the grey austerity of 1946.[3] Höpker-Aschoff complained that German social science had let the politicians down during the slump and that 'if only we had had a Keynes at that time everything would have been different'. Müller-Armack felt such charges to be unjust because there were indeed German economists who had seen the wrong-headedness of government policies. Yet he had himself experienced the frustration of seeing sound economic practice overridden by 'experts' whose views smacked more of political expediency than scientific principle. In particular, his generation of young economists in the 1920s had 'regarded it as a wretched failure on the part of our profession that, influenced by the historicist school of thought, it showed so little capacity to analyse correctly the phenomenon of galloping inflation after 1918'.[4]

Among that generation had been Walter Eucken, who had in 1923 published a critique of current apologetics for Germany's dangerous monetary policy, and who later became Professor of Economics at Freiburg. Then there was Wilhelm Röpke, a Professor of Economics at Marburg and a specialist in trade cycle theory. In January 1931 Röpke served on a government-initiated commission of enquiry into measures which might be taken to alleviate unemployment. Something had to be done to get the economy moving again and in particular two steps were necessary: the first was to attract long-term loans to Germany from abroad; the second was for the government to intervene on its own account so as to set the ball rolling and stimulate an upward cycle of investment. Röpke and the commission recommended a number of infrastructural public investment targets, such as improvements to the road network (though not Autobahns), agricultural improvement schemes, investment in power stations and support for the building industry in the construction of private dwellings.[5]

To his great annoyance the Brüning government showed very little interest in these suggestions. For the rest of his life Röpke remained highly critical of Brüning, describing him as 'a stubborn Westphalian imbued with reserve-officer and front-soldier complexes which often produced a comic effect'.[6]

Röpke's liberal views made him an early victim of the Nazi purge of Germany's universities. He carried on his work in exile - first in Istanbul and then later in Switzerland. In the summer of 1933 he set up an informal action committee to help German academics forced to leave their homeland, and he managed to persuade the Turkish authorities to make room for other intellectual figures threatened by the Third Reich.

From our point of view, the most important of these was Alexander Rüstow, a logician and philologist who had been drawn into socialist politics by the revolution of November 1918. He took up a post in the Reich Economics Ministry where he was involved in abortive plans to nationalize the Ruhr coal mines. This experience disillusioned him with socialism. In 1924 he became economic adviser to the machine tool industry, as head of the Economics Section of the Verband deutscher Maschinenbauanstalten.[7] His task was to defend the interests of small firms against the larger coal and steel producers. Such was his reputation as a liberal economist that he attracted the venom of nationalist groups in Germany. By 1934, however, he was safe in Turkey, occupying a chair of Economic Geography and Social History at Istanbul University. There he conducted investigations into the sociological causes of liberalism's decline in the twentieth century.[8]

Other critical minds remained in Germany, unobtrusively observing the establishment of a political tyranny and the directed command economy which went with it. One such was Alfred Müller-Armack himself. Of the four main architects of the Social Market Economy - Erhard, Müller-Armack, Röpke and Rüstow - only Müller-Armack actually became a member of the Nazi Party.[9] He was also, however, a committed protestant Christian. The incompatibility of Hitler's behaviour with Christian principles became glaringly obvious at the time of the so-called Röhm purge in June 1934. After the inception of the Four-Year Plan in 1936 Müller-Armack was confronted with dirigiste policies incompatible with his own commitment to the market economy. He turned somewhat aside from economic theory and began researching into the connexions between religious denominations and economic development in various parts of Europe. He concluded that religious beliefs were more important influences on the economic activity of man than cultural traditions or racial characteristics. The lack of a clear concept of social organization in German religious - and especially Lutheran - thought had, he believed, left Germany vulnerable to despotic systems, whereas in England Christian ideology had been able to resist it. Although 'Marxism' was the bogey referred to in a book published during the Second World War, it is clear that his message was equally inimical to Nazi racialism.[10]

In 1941 Müller-Armack had founded an institute specializing in marketing problems with particular reference to the textile industry. As a result of this activity he got to know and like Ludwig Erhard, who was working in a consumer research institute in Nuremberg.[11]

Erhard had also been trained in the dark days of the German inflation. He worked for his doctorate under Franz Oppenheimer, an academic figure with an original turn of mind. Oppenheimer was Professor of Sociology and Theoretical Economics at Frankfurt University. The combination of disciplines is not without interest, for it illustrates a tendency among neo-liberal thinkers to combine concern for healthy social relationships with their interest in the workings of the free market. In fact Oppenheimer developed his own rather idiosyncratic views into a concept of what he called 'liberal socialism'. This involved a rejection of both laissez-faire capitalism and Marxism and the establishment of a just social order within which free competition would be protected by the state. Before that could be done, however, there would have to be an assault on the unjust distribution of landed property, which Oppenheimer saw as the main cause of economic distress.

Erhard certainly did not swallow all of Oppenheimer's ideas, but he did regard him as the most influential of all his teachers. He took from him his commitment to free competition, the need to attack monopolies and cartels, and the belief that social responsibility was an essential aspect of the economist's profession.[12] The inflation had influenced Erhard's own interests; he became fascinated with the problem of currency stability and wrote his doctoral thesis on the nature of money.[13]

In 1928 he took up employment in an Institute founded at the Nuremberg Commercial College by Wilhelm Vershofen, a German pioneer in the field of market research. Vershofen strengthened Erhard's existing inclination to stress the importance of the consumer in the economic process. He was also a strong believer in open international trade and flexible exchange rates - a position which was to become very unfashionable in the years which followed.[14] During his early years at the Institute Erhard visited the headquarters of the Verband Deutscher Maschinenbauanstalten, where the head of the economics department was, of course, Alexander Rüstow. Rüstow had a soft spot for Vershofen, despite differences of opinion, and he evidently got on well with his new assistant.[15] It is also clear that Erhard was aware of Professor Röpke and admired his work.[16]

In his early years with the Institute Erhard had observed the collapse of the Weimar Republic. Later on he was to attribute it, not just to a lack of enthusiasm for democracy, but also to the Republic's 'impossible economic system, which was a fateful mixture of socialism, cartelization and old-fashioned capitalism'.[17] This observation illustrates the most important characteristics of the new socio-economic theory which was to challenge the entrenched orthodoxies of economic nationalism and Marxist socialism in Germany. The principles underlying this theory deserve explanation, since they have not always been clearly understood. First of all, there was a complete rejection of what was described as 'collectivism'. In particular this meant a commitment to the workings of the market and to the benevolent effects of competition. Such views are commonplace today. They were less prominent during an era which saw the Third Reich established in Germany, the collapse of political liberalism in Central and Southern Europe, and the 'achievements' of the Five-Year Plans in Soviet Russia. Even in Anglo-Saxon countries, British Imperial Preference had replaced the old commitment to Free Trade, and the American 'New Deal' implied an interventionist philosophy on the part of the government. In salons and universities Marxist and Fascist intellectuals agreed with each other on one point at least: economic liberalism was 'dead' and could not solve the problems of a mass age.

Röpke, Eucken, Rüstow and other protagonists of what came to be given the inelegant title of the 'neo-liberal' school of economic theory, never tired of defending competition and the free market against its collectivist enemies, whether they were to be found in the Fascist or the Marxist camp. Röpke believed that, with all its imperfections, only the market could ensure the effective working of a modern economic system, because only the market was a self-operating mechanism. It provided hundreds of millions of consumers all over the world with their individual needs. Yet who supervised it? Who ensured the ordered functioning of the market process? Nobody. 'There is no dictator who, surveying the entire scene, orders people to their various tasks...'.[18] The free market worked as the result of a constant series of choices made by individuals about their own needs and priorities - the 'plebiscite de tous les jours'. No planner could replace this, and if he did, who would control him?[19]

All this was, of course, very much in the spirit of Adam Smith - a forerunner whose wisdom the neo-liberals gladly acknowledged, and who had exercised a great impact on German economic thought more than a century earlier. But whereas Smith had been concerned to combat the evils of mercantilism and colonial monopoly, Röpke, Müller-Armack and their colleagues had to face more sinister foes in the collectivist tyrannies of the twentieth century. It was indeed a central principle of 'neo-liberalism' that economic control went hand in hand with political tyranny.

Müller-Armack approvingly quoted Montesquieu's dictum that freedom can only be secure where power is divided, and drew a parallel between the competitive free market - which prevented an overmighty concentration of economic power - and Montesquieu's balanced political system.[20]

If competition was one essential condition for both a healthy economy and a free society, another necessary prerequisite was sound money. Here the overwhelming impact of the German inflation after the First World War could be detected in the works of all neo-liberal economists, whatever other issues might divide them. This was one of the central premisses of Walter Eucken's teaching in his discourses on the theory of economic organization. Inflation was the most serious social evil, because it robbed the individual of his capacity to provide for his own security by own efforts.[21]

At first glance such views might seem to be merely reactionary. They could be identified with business interests in Germany eager to free themselves from government controls and social responsibility. Industrialists and entrepreneurs never like to be other than 'free' in the sense of being left to their own devices. But here one must observe that the new liberalism was of a very different stamp from that which had informed Germany's most powerful business interests under the Wilhelmine Empire and the Weimar Republic. They had succumbed to a form of 'national' liberalism which certainly left the industrialist free to dominate his work force, or to make his business arrangements as he wished. But this did not involve enthusiastic commitment to the benefits of open competition. On the contrary, German heavy industry had been protectionist in its trade policies abroad and had done everything it could to obliterate effective competition at home.

The neo-liberals were determined that the free market should be really free, undistorted by cartels or monopolies, and that tariff policies should be liberalized to encourage free trade. They believed that a fundamentally healthy system had been perverted in Wilhelmine Germany.[22] To prevent this happening again, stringent measures would have to be taken to ensure the transparency of the market and the elimination of restraints on competitive enterprise.

Walter Eucken and other associates at the University of Freiburg, such as Franz Böhm, were particularly concerned with the need to create an economic order in which competition would be protected from distortions created by laissez-faire. Eucken dedicated himself to working out a theoretical basis for what he described as 'complete competition' (vollständige Konkurrenz) which would prevent the establishment of cartels, price-fixing, or the elimination of business rivals by the abuse of economic power.[23] Franz Böhm had been a young civil servant in the Reich Economics Ministry during the Weimar Republic, and had worked for seven years in the section dealing with the cartelization of German industry. He had been involved in enquiries about the legality of different price-fixing arrangements and had become highly critical of the economic distortions created by cartels. He qualified as a university teacher at Freiburg in 1933, and worked as a lecturer with Walter Eucken. His first major book, Wettbewerb und Monopolkampf (Competition and resistance to Monopoly) was published in 1933 and became an important work of neo-liberal literature.[24]

It was a central feature of thinking of the 'Freiburg School' around Eucken that a properly functioning market could not simply be left alone; it had to be protected by an enlightened state. Businessmen could not be expected to control themselves, but would need a legislative framework to regulate their activity. That, of course, would be very different from a policy of state direction. To explain this Röpke used the well-known metaphor of the modern traffic system. Without rules of the road there would be chaos but, equally, traffic would soon cease its rapid flow if every vehicle had to have its route planned by a central authority. What was needed were clear rules, firmly and fairly enforced. The same was true of the economy.[25] Insistence on state action to protect the free market differentiates the architects of the German 'economic miracle' from the advocates of a return to laissez-faire in our own time. Nor was this the only major area of difference.

Even more important was their belief that free competition, though a necessary precondition for a decent society, was not an end in itself. Man did not live by bread alone. His happiness would depend on his social organization, his spiritual values and his prospects for a satisfying life at his work-place or with his family. The free market could not itself be expected to meet these requirements. Neo-liberals constantly reiterated their view that a mere return to the laissez-faire policies of the nineteenth century would only have disastrous consequences.

Nor did the neo-liberals shrink from the problem of the maldistribution of wealth. This was a burning issue which had obsessed man for centuries. They were quite prepared to advocate taxation policies which would militate against excessive concentration of wealth. The inequalities created by the inheritance of property might be a proper target for action by the state. Rüstow observed that the only justifiable inequalities were those arising from inequalities of accomplishment or the conditions of competition. 'Most unjust of all are those inequalities in the conditions existing at the start of economic life, derived in part from unequal inheritances, which depend on how carefully one chooses one's parents. This being the case we are led to demand equal opportunity and just initial conditions for all.'[26] Not all neo-liberals went as far as Rüstow, but the concept of evening out gross inequality of wealth remained an integral part of the Social Market Economy.[27]

All this is very different from the minimal state which was the ideal of the 19th century laissez-faire extremists like Herbert Spencer, and which has come to inform the minds of some Anglo-Saxon economists today.[28] It differed too from what passes as Conservative economic thought in contemporary Britain. The 'New Conservatism' has little time for co-determination in industry, the elimination of social evils connected with industrialization or state action to curb private monopolies.[29] In post-war Germany, on the other hand, the laissez-faire notion that the state should confine itself to external defence and internal policing was rejected by the neo-liberals as reactionary dogmatism. They rightly argued that such a policy would eventually lead to class war. Its ultimate outcome would be a collectivist dictatorship.

To sum up, the neo-liberals rejected both socialism and laissez-faire capitalism. They feared collectivist dictatorship but equally abhorred private monopoly or the injustices of feudal property relationships. They sought a 'Third Way'[30] which would ensure that the benefits of free competition should generate economic welfare for all, whilst at the same time preserving the dignity of the individual and offering him the chance to achieve spiritual fulfilment.

What did they do to realize these objectives? The old German Confederation destroyed by Bismarck had possessed its fair share of academic theorists committed to liberal idealism, but they had proved powerless in the face of military force and Realpolitik. It was to be the good fortune of the neo-liberals that Hitler's cataclysmic disaster discredited power politics in Germany. Yet it must also be recognized that those economists who advocated the 'Third Way' did not simply sit at their desks building castles in the air. They were ready to enter the political arena, however unfriendly the reception might be.

There did indeed seem little chance of making progress while Hitler's regime survived. Those neo-liberals abroad tried to do what they could. Röpke and Rüstow continued to champion the free market and the 'Third Way' from their exiles in Turkey and Switzerland. Inside the Third Reich criticism of government policy was a dangerous business. During the war muted discussions took place among German economists about the nature of the system which would follow the ending of hostilities.

On 3 November 1941 Walter Eucken told a meeting of a group called the 'Arbeitsgemeinschaft Preispolitik' that the current economic system could only be an interim phase, and urged a return to market prices and competition.[31] The aim of liberal-minded economists during the war years seems to have been to create a system within which the market could once again operate, although it was accepted that limits would have to be set by the state in its own interests.

This was very much the thrust of a memorandum drawn up by Ludwig Erhard himself. In August 1944 he circulated the document to various important industrialists and bankers, among whom were representatives of I.G. Farben, Flick, Siemens, the Dresdener Bank and the Deutsche Bank.[32] The wording of the document was cautious and obviously affected by the constraints of life in Nazi Germany. Its author also had to pay attention to limitations imposed on policy by an economy geared to war. Erhard could not, therefore, expound a blueprint for the Social Market Economy in the summer of 1944. Nevertheless, his memorandum is remarkable for its frankness, and for its restatement of several principles central to the neo-liberal viewpoint.[33]

'The most sought-after objective remains', he wrote, 'the free market economy based on true competition - with the inherent regulative mechanism which that system contains.'[34] Lest this should be misunderstood, however, he stressed that:

> Certainly the state will never again be pushed back into the role of a night watchman, because even the freest market economy, and especially this one, needs an instrument to draw up the rules and supervise their implementation.[35]

His aim was 'a peacetime economy serving human welfare'.

Erhard himself found a positive reception for his ideas, not only in industry but even in the Reich Economics Ministry, with which he maintained discreet contact in the last months of the war.[36] This did not, of course, mean that his views were compatible with those of the Nazis.

None of this activity was able to influence Nazi economic policy, nor did it lead to successful acts of resistance. It did mean, however, that both outside and within Germany a coherent form of economic alternative existed to the collectivist views which otherwise seemed dominant. As the Third Reich was destroyed the neo-liberals were presented with new problems and new opportunities.

Looking back from the prosperity and success of the 1960s Röpke remarked that until 1948 the proponents of the 'Third Way' could be likened to Henry V's army before Agincourt: 'We few, we happy few, we band of brothers'.[37] The difference was that, though few, their situation was anything but happy. For much of the time, indeed, they were not even sure that they had any brothers. Domestic tyranny and World War inhibited communication. Even after Hitler's death the circumstances in devastated Germany were such that mere exchange of ideas - let alone the mobilization of public opinion - was very difficult. Rigid control by Allied authorities, restrictions on travel, chronic shortages of newsprint and the lack of foreign currency were grave obstacles to those trying to enlighten both their countrymen and their occupiers about the true causes of Germany's economic distress. Müller-Armack, for example, found great physical difficulty in disseminating his views. Newsprint was almost impossible to obtain, and a licence was needed even to print a visiting card.[38] At the same time he was involved in discussions with Protestant churchmen who were trying - in collaboration with Dutch and Swiss co-religionists - to work out a Christian view of modern society.

171

Their aim was to create a social theory based on natural law. Meanwhile Ludwig Erhard was gaining experience of economic management at a more practical level. When the Americans liberated Fürth in April 1945 they asked him to take over the economic administration (Wirtschaftsamt) there. In September the new Social Democratic premier of Bavaria, Wilhelm Hoegner, was looking for a suitable person to fill the post of Economics Minister. The American authorities warmly recommended Erhard, who accepted the post. Hoegner later came to believe that Erhard had been pressed on him because the Americans were unhappy about the socialist characteristics of the draft constitution then being discussed by Bavarian political leaders. They hoped that Erhard would act as a brake on such tendencies.[39] Be that as it may, Erhard described himself in later years as 'an American invention' and his career owed much to this American patronage.[40] As Economics Minister he was faced with a multiplicity of problems, ranging from looting to demobilization, and he also had to develop Bavaria's export capacity.[41] Although he had to leave office the following summer when the Christian Social Union took over the government, his experience meant that he could not be written off as an unworldly academic, but could claim to be an expert with both practical and theoretical qualifications. After leaving this cabinet Erhard remained in Munich, teaching economics as a supernumerary professor. Erhard's practical abilities were not allowed to lie dormant for long. In September 1947 he was appointed head of the Bizonal special office for money and credit at Bad Homburg. From this there emerged the so-called Homburg Plan which was to be the basis of a draft law to stabilize the ruined German currency. In March 1948 he was appointed Director of Economics for Bizonia as the result of support in the Economic Council from Free Democrats, and with only the reluctant acquiescence of the CDU. From this time the principles of the Social Market Economy began to emerge as part of Germany's economic policy.

The miseries of the post-war economic situation in Germany, with an almost worthless currency, and with barter and the black market replacing normal trading conditions, helped to discredit state controls. However unjustified such an association may have been, 'planning' was held responsible for low production and shortages. The developing Cold War and the growing preponderance of American influence in Western Germany also aided the cause of free market economics.

The neo-liberals continued to promote their views with vigour as the political climate began to shift in favour of the relaxation of government controls over the economy. On 1st August 1947, Müller-Armack published an article beginning with the words 'The Social Market Economy has nothing to do with a return to outmoded Liberalism.'[42] There followed specific recommendations for creating the Social Market economy. The collapsing system of government controls should be replaced by the free market. This would encourage production and give consumer choice the power to establish real prices. Social security should be created by the following measures: the creation of a system of work which treated the worker as a human being and gave him what was described as the 'social right to participate' in the organization of his work (ein soziales Mitgestaltungsrecht) without, however, reducing managerial initiative and the responsibility of the employer. There should be a legally based system of competition designed to ensure that the energies of ambitious individuals would be channeled in a fashion beneficial to the common good. There should be a conscious policy of resistance to monopolies to prevent the abuse of economic power. There should be a policy of full employment achieved by regulating the business cycle through credit - and even limited state subventions if these seemed necessary. Unhealthy inequalities of wealth should be overcome by what was described as 'a market economy income equalization' (marktwirtschaftlicher Einkommensausgleich) achieved by taxation, family allowances and rent assistance for the needy. The state should encourage small businesses. Work structures should include chances for workers' advancement. Co-operative self-help - as in housing construction, for example - should be provided for in the rules of the market. Social security systems should be more widely developed. Town planning should be established. There should be minimum wages, and individual pay settlements should be secured as the result of freely negotiated contracts. The state should restrict itself to establishing the general principles of economic policy, leaving the individual entrepreneur, worker, farmer, merchant or housewife to operate within the framework so provided. Prices,[43] wages and the selection of one's place of work should be freed from state interference.

This was indeed the basic theory underlying Erhard's economic policy from March 1948 when he became Director of Economic Affairs in Bizonia. Certainly it was not a socialist programme. The element of worker participation was far more limited than that proposed by German trade unions, for example, but it was sincerely meant, as the intellectual background of the neo-liberals set out above has demonstrated.

The determination that economic freedom should not imply a laissez-faire attitude to social problems was implemented in the fields of social security and housing. Above all there was the belief that the market had to be established within certain ground rules so that it would operate in the interests of society as a whole. As Müller-Armack himself wrote in 1946, the market was not a natural phenomenon but a man-made one.[44] The manner in which it was organised - the 'traffic regulations' as Röpke had called them - were a legitimate and indeed vital concern for government.

The actual implementation of this policy was, of course, begun by Erhard as Economics Director in Bizonia and carried on under the first Adenauer government of the Federal Republic. Müller-Armack himself was summoned to the Ministry of Economics in 1952 and took over the department concerned with economic policy. Six years later he became state secretary responsible for European Affairs and was himself closely involved with Germany's integration into the E.E.C. Franz Böhm and other neo-liberals were closely involved in drawing up anti-cartel legislation which, despite the hostility of powerful industrial interests, became operative in 1957. Böhm had advised the Americans on cartel legislation and had been Kultusminister in Hesse. He and Walter Hallstein had drawn up a memorandum on workers' participation in industry.[45] Disciples of the Social Market Economy were also to be found advising the Economics Ministry through its academic think-tank.[46]

The practical successes of the Social Market Economy were formidable. They became enshrined in the journalistic phrase 'the economic miracle'. This was a description stoutly rejected by Müller-Armack himself because, he said, there had been no 'miracle' - simply the natural results of correctly applied economic theory.[47] He might have added that, without the concern for social welfare and labour relations shown by Federal and Land governments[48] in the early years of the German Federal Republic, the 'miracle' could easily have turned out to be a nightmare.[49] In the years 1949-53 the Federal Republic spent more of its national income on social welfare than any other comparable state. From 1950 to 1953 social security payments rose 60%, which represented a more rapid rise than that of the national income in the same period. In 1953 the largest item in the Federal Budget (32%) related to social welfare. The Federal Republic was very far from being a 'night watchman' state. This was one explanation for its success.

Notes

1. This chapter is part of a projected study of the origins and development of the Social Market Economy in the Federal Republic of Germany. I am particularly indebted to the Konrad Adenauer Foundation and the Ludwig-Erhard Foundation for their help and co-operation. I should also like to express my thanks to Professors Watrin and Willgerodt of the Department of Economics in the University of Cologne for their helpful comments on an earlier draft. All errors of fact or judgment remain, of course, entirely my responsibility.
2. Wilhelm Röpke, Die deutsche Frage (Erlenbach-Zurich 1945) 2nd Edn. p. 108.
3. A. Müller-Armack, Auf dem Weg nach Europa. Erinnerungen und Ausblicke. Hereafter cited as Europa (Tübingen 1971) pp. 14-16.
4. Idem, p. 12.
5. 'Gutachten zur Arbeitslosenfrage. Erstattet von der Gutachterkommission zur Arbeitslosenfrage' Sonderveröffentlichung des Reichsarbeitsblattes (Berlin 1931), Part II, pp. 4-5.
6. Letter from Röpke to Pechel, 7 Feb. 1947 in Eva Röpke (ed.), Wilhelm Röpke. Briefe. Der Innere Kompass 1934-1966 (Erlenbach-Zurich 1976) p. 93.
7. See the biographical sketch by his son, Dankwart A. Rustow, in A. Rüstow, Freedom and Domination. A Historical Critique of Civilization (Princeton U.P., 1980) p. xiii et seq.
8. Wirtschaft und Kultursystem. Festschrift für Alexander Rüstow. Ed. Gottfried Eisermann (Erlenbach-Zurich, 1955) pp. 15-17.
9. Correspondence relating to his denazification is in the Müller-Armack papers; Konrad Adenauer Stiftung (hereafter KA) I-236-030.
10. A. Müller-Armack, Genealogie der Wirtschaftsstile. Die geistesgeschichtlichen Ursprünge der Staats-und Wirtschaftsformen bis zum Ausgang des 18. Jahrhunderts. (3rd Edn., Münster, 1944) p. 268.
11. Müller-Armack, Europa, pp. 21-3. For further details of Erhard's career see V.R. Berghahn's chapter below, pp.000.
12. K. Hohmann. Fränkische Lebensbilder: Ludwig Erhard (Manuscript in

Ludwig Erhard Stiftung, Bonn) pp. 11-12. I am very grateful to Dr. Hohmann for allowing me access to his book while it was still in draft.
13. L. Erhard, Wesen und Inhalt der Werteinheit (Frankfurt 1924).
14. C. Heusgen, Ludwig Erhards Lehre von der Sozialen Marktwirtschaft. Ursprunge, Kerngehalt, Wandlungen. (Berne and Stuttgart 1981) pp 78-84.
15. T. Eschenburg. 'Aus Persönlichem Erleben: Zur Kurzfassung der Denkschrift 1943/4', in: L. Erhard. Kriegsfinanzierung und Schuldenkonsolidierung. Faksimiledruck der Denkschrift von 1943/44 (Frankfurt/M 1977) p. xv.
16. Ibidem.
17. J. M. Lukomski, Ludwig Erhard. Der Mensch und der Politiker (2nd Edn. Düsseldorf/Vienna 1965) p. 45.
18. W. Röpke, Die Lehre von der Wirtschaft (Vienna, 1937), pp. 3-4.
19. Idem, p. 13.
20. 'Die Markwirtschaft entspricht schon soziologisch dem Ideal Montesquieus', in A. Müller-Armack, Wirtschaftsordnung und Wirtschaftspolitik. Studien und Konzepte zur sozialen Marktwirtschaft und zur Europäischen Integration (Freiburg/Br., 1966), pp. 82-3.
21. W. Eucken, Grundsätze der Wirtschaftspolitik (Tübingen 1952, 4th Edn. Ed. W. Eucken and K.P. Hirsel). p. 319. This is based on notes by Eucken put into book form by Hirsel.
22. W. Röpke, German Commercial Policy, (London 1934). pp. 30-1.
23. See, for example, 'Was ist Wettbewerbsordnung?', in Eucken, Grundsätze der Wirtschaftspolitik, p. 245 et seq.
24. See Eucken, idem., p. 247 fn. For details of Böhm's career see Böhm papers, Konrad Adenauer Stiftung; introduction and 002/4.
25. W. Röpke, Die Gesellschaftskrise der Gegenwart (4th, revised edn. Erlenbach-Zurich 1942), p. 300.
26. A. Rüstow. Appendix to W. Röpke, International Economic Disintegration (London 1942), p. 281.
27. See the blueprint for the social market economy published on 1 August 1947 by Müller-Armack, section 19e, in R. Löwenthal and H.-P. Schwarz, Die Zweite Republik. 25 Jahre Deutschland - eine Bilanz (Stuttgart 1974), p. 147.
28. Herbert Spencer, The Man versus the State (London 1884, with numerous later editions).
29. To appreciate the significant distinction between the policies of men like Müller-Armack and contemporary British Conservatives, for example, one may contrast the account of neo-liberalism given in these pages with the views of Nigel Lawson, MP, as set out in The New Conservatism (Centre for Policy Studies) London, 1980. An obvious distaste for serious attempts to prevent monopolistic activity is to be found in Arthur Seldon's pamphlet, Corrigible Capitalism, Incorrigible Socialism. (Institute of Economic Affairs, London, 1980) p. 25. He is also dismissive of the problem of alienation and clearly dislikes 'industrial democracy'. Ibid., pp. 26-7.
30. A term Röpke had taken over from Franz Oppenheimer.
31. L. Herbst, 'Ludwig Erhards Beteiligung an den Nachkriegsplanungen am Ende des zweiten Weltkrieges' in Vierteljahreshefte für Zeitgeschichte, vol 25, no 3, July 1977, pp. 308-12.

32. Idem, pp. 321-30. See also Ludwig Erhard, Kriegsfinanzierung und Schuldenkonsolidierung. Faksimiledruck der Denkschrift von 1943/44. (Frankfurt/M. Berlin. Vienna 1977) with introductory comments by Erhard, T. Eschenburg and G. Schmölders.
33. L. Herbst stresses the extent to which Erhard seemed to accept the dirigisme of the Third Reich. He claims that the memorandum 'does not belong in the early history (Vorfeld) of the social market economy but is a typical document of the transition phase from war to peace economy...', Herbst, op.cit., p. 340. This does not seem to me entirely to do justice to the memorandum, especially when the circumstances under which it was written are taken into account.
34. Erhard, Denkschrift, p. 264.
35. Idem, p. 26.
36. Herbst, op.cit.,p. 335.
37. See Röpke's chapter in F. Greiss and F.W. Meyer (eds.) Wirtschaft Gesellschaft und Kultur (W. Berlin, 1961) p. 4.
38. Löwenthal and Schwarz, Die Zweite Republik, p. 124; Müller-Armack, Auf dem Weg nach Europa, pp. 50-1.
39. W. Hoegner, 'Erhard als bayerischer Wirtschaftsminister' in G. Schröder et al, Ludwig Erhard. Beiträge zu seiner politischen Biographie. Festschrift zum fünfundsiebzigsten Geburtstag (Frankfurt/M., 1971) p. 128.
40. Hohmann, Fränkische Lebensbilder, pp. 26-7.
41. Hoegner, op. cit., pp. 126-7.
42. Müller-Armack in Löwenthal and Schwarz, Die Zweite Republik, pp. 140-7.
43. With the temporary exception of bread, milk and fat prices and rents for the elderly.
44. Cf. Müller-Armack, Wirtschaftsordnung und Wirtschaftspolitik, p. 105.
45. G. Ambrosius, Die Durchsetzung der Sozialen Marktwirtschaft in Westdeutschland 1945-1949 (Stuttgart 1977), p. 108.
46. The Wissenschaftlicher Beirat beim Bundeswirtschaftsministerium was set up to advise the Bizonal economics directorate in January 1948. Among early members of the Beirat who could be classed as neo-liberals or at least sympathetic to the social market economy were Beckerath, Böhm, Eucken, Lampe (Freiburg), Liefmann Keil (Freiburg), Müller-Armack and Miksch. See Bundeswirtschaftsministerium: Der Wissenschaftliche Beirat bei der Verwaltung des Vereinigten Wirtschaftsgebiets. Gutachten 1948 bis Mai 1950 (Göttingen, n.d.) pp. 98-9. For an alternative view of the relationship between these ideas see V.R. Berghahn's chapter below, pp. 178-192.
47. Müller-Armack in Löwenthal and Schwarz, Die Zweite Republik, p. 123.
48. See H.G. Hockerts 'Sozialpolitische Reformstrebungen in der frühen Bundesrepublik' in Vierteljahreshefte für Zeitgeschichte, no. 25, heft 3, 1977, p. 351. Also H.G. Hockerts, Sozialpolitische Entscheidungen im Nackriegsdeutschland. Allierte und deutsche Sozialversicherungs politik 1945 bis 1957 (Stuttgart 1980) pp. 196, 430-1.
49. The extent to which the theories of the Social Market Economy were actually put into practice is a matter of controversy, and lies

beyond the scope of this chapter. From the early days of the Federal Republic there have been those who have sought to minimize or deny the causal connection between Erhard's policies and the economic recovery of Germany. See, for example, T. Balogh, Germany: An experiment in 'Planning' by the 'Free' Price Mechanism (Oxford 1950). For a more recent and scholarly critique see W. Abelshauser, 'Probleme des Wiederaufbaus der westdeutschen Wirtschaft, 1945-1953', in H.A. Winkler, (ed) Politische Weichenstellungen im Nachkriegsdeutschland 1945-1953 (Göttingen 1979), especially pp. 245-253. Attention is also drawn to Dr. Abelshauser's Wirtschaft in Westdeutschland, 1945 bis 1948. Rekonstruktion und Wachstumsbedingungen in der Amerikanischen und Britischen Zone (Stuttgart 1975). For a contrasting view see H.F. Wünsche 'Wirtschaft in Westdeutschland 1945-1948' in Orientierung (Bonn), No. 2, 1979, pp. 37-40.

IDEAS INTO POLITICS: THE CASE OF LUDWIG ERHARD

Volker Berghahn

This article is concerned with the ideas of the economist and politician Ludwig Erhard, who is generally considered to be the father of the West German 'Economic Miracle' after the Second World War and the main promoter of the Federal Republic's Soziale Marktwirtschaft during his term of office as Minister of Economics from 1949 to 1963. Scholars have, of course, been interested in Erhard's concepts of economic policy-making for a long time, and there are dozens of books and articles which attempt to analyse them. Sooner or later most of these analyses refer to the influence exerted upon Erhard by a number of prominent academic economists in the post-war period who, rather crudely perhaps, have been lumped together as members of the 'Freiburg School'. This has led to a widespread impression that he got his ideas from this quarter and in particular from men such as W. Eucken, W. Röpke, E. von Beckerath, A. Rüstow and F. Böhm whose writings have been scrutinized in order to distil from them the essentials of the type of capitalism which Erhard implemented in Germany in the late 1940s and early 1950s.[1] A. Hunold called Erhard 'the executor of the ideas' of Eucken and Röpke.[2] The problem with this approach is that it may have established all too direct a link between the 'Freiburg School' and the Minister of Economics to the exclusion of influences on his ideas which date back to the time prior to 1945 and of impulses which he received from elsewhere after the Second World War. Nor has it helped that, during the past fifteen years, the propagandist extolling of 'unsere soziale Marktwirtschaft', particularly by the Christian Democrats, has further blurred the issue.[3] Finally, the increased confusion was compounded by the fact that scholars have taken quite different views of what constituted the Freiburg essentials.[4]

Thus E.E. Nawroth came to the conclusion that the liberal German economists of the 1940s did not create anything new; rather they promoted a renaissance of the economic ideas current in Western Europe in the 18th and 19th centuries. Ultimately, he argues, they advocated no more than 'a conscious and persistent intellectual reorientation towards the prominent ideologues of the glorified English Enlightenment'.[5] It is not surprising that Nawroth's interpretation of the ideas of the 'Freiburg School' did not go down well with those who were loosely identified with it. Nor, in so far as they still had a chance to comment, did they like the other view which became more widely accepted on the political Left in West Germany from the mid-1960s and of which Harald Mey published one of the more measured summaries in 1971.[6] To him two features appeared to be crucial to an understanding of the essentials of Soziale Marktwirtschaft. The first one was that the economic model propounded by men such as Eucken represented 'in the final analysis a mildly authoritarian Ordnungsstaat'[7] which, by implication, could also be

178

detected in Erhard's programme. Secondly, Mey was struck by the emphasis on a capitalism which encouraged and supported the small and medium-sized business and was basically hostile to large-scale enterprise and trusts. Other authors have likewise regarded the mittelständische component as one of the most salient characteristics of Erhard's programme. Yet, unlike Mey who saw it as being intended to act as a counterweight to large concentrations of economic power in the hands of a few companies, some of them argued that it reflected Erhard's inclination towards a petit-bourgeois proto-fascism. And nothing else confirmed them more in this view than a speech which Erhard, by then Adenauer's successor as Federal Chancellor, made at the Party Congress of the Christian Democrats (CDU) at Düsseldorf in March 1965. It was in this speech that he put forward the notion of Formierte Gesellschaft.[8]

In trying to discover what he meant by this, it is important to remember that Düsseldorf was the same place where the CDU had published its Leitsätze some 16 years earlier which enunciated the Party's adherence to a free and competitive economic system. The Guidelines implied the shedding of its Christian Socialist ideas which had dominated the early post-war discussion and had been enshrined in the Ahlen Programme of February 1947. Now, in 1965, Erhard proclaimed the concept of a society which was not merely concerned to satisfy individual interests. The Formierte Gesellschaft, he postulated, 'represents a community (Gemeinschaft) which acts in solidarity as far as its vital problems are concerned, pursues joint objectives and does not allow itself to be guided exclusively by group interests'. The Formierte Gesellschaft is, he added, 'a society of Christian solidarity'. Erhard's speech unleashed an enormous public debate at the time and interpreters' views diverged widely over what kind of society the Chancellor had actually had in mind.[9] No doubt the term was hardly a fortunate one and lent itself to a large variety of interpretations. In view of this it is perhaps less surprising that some of Erhard's critics heard in it the ring of the much-vaunted Volksgemeinschaft of the 1930s.[10] The implication was that his statements of 1965 were considered reformulations of what he had, in essence, always believed in and what hence had also been underlying his programme in the late 1940s.

It is, of course, always possible to trace a person's fundamental assumptions and beliefs about the world back to influences and impressions earlier in his or her career. With reference to Erhard, the problem with this approach is that the concept of Formierte Gesellschaft purported to take account of perceived and real changes which the West German economy and society had undergone since the 1950s and which had in fact caused a crisis of Soziale Marktwirtschaft as originally conceived.[11] This implies that Erhard's ideas on socio-economic matters were not only more flexible, but also more eclectic, than both his protagonists and self-proclaimed mentors as well as his critics have made out. His critics, especially in West German industry and on the Right of the Christian Democrats as well as those on the political Left, have often portrayed him as a typical German professor with a mission turned politician.[12] In fact, he was much less a dogmatic academic than a pragmatic politician. This is not to deny that Erhard could be very stubborn if he was convinced that a particular programme was the only one available to deal with a particular situation. But the situations, he realised, would change and would hence require new remedies. In other words, his methods were adaptable over time, and so was the substance of his ideas. Nor did he fail to appreciate that the daily pressures of politics made a purist approach to economic problems impossible. This means, with regard to the influence of the 'Freiburg School', that even if he assimilated certain of its positions, he felt no inhibitions against responding to other ideas with which he came into contact both before 1945 and in the late 1940s and early 1950s.

Erhard's attitudes towards competition and economic concentration would appear to present a good testing-ground for the arguments which have been put forward in this article so far. At first glance this ground seems to be rather narrowly conceived. But it is hoped that the subsequent analysis will show it to be an arena which is central to his vision of <u>Soziale Marktwirtschaft</u>. It is also the field in which his links with the 'Freiburg School' are at their most tenuous. For it is true that Erhard was firmly in favour of competition in the market-place and opposed to monopoly. But it would be erroneous to deduce from this that he was an advocate of perfect competition as propounded by Eucken and others[13] and that he opposed large-scale enterprise, i.e. what the Americans call trusts and what is known in Germany as <u>Konzerne</u>. This was a misapprehension to which key figures of German heavy industry, for reasons to be discussed below, succumbed and, perhaps against their better wisdom, continued to adhere. It was to no small extent their noisy propaganda and in particular that of the <u>Bundesverband der Deutschen Industrie</u> (BDI), industry's principal association, which gave Erhard the reputation of being much closer to small business than was justified by his actual thinking on this point. Indeed, this propaganda appears to have contributed to casting him in the role of a petit-bourgeois economist and politician in which some critics have viewed him to this day. In reality, Erhard never had much interest in a search for principles and mechanisms which established, and permanently secured, a system of perfect competition. The explanation for why he, while rejecting monopoly, nevertheless leaned towards 'bigness' in industry is to be found partly in his gradually absorbing an increasingly heavy dose of American ideas on this subject and partly in his biography prior to 1945. Both aspects are now to be examined.

As far as his pre-1945 career is concerned it is important to remember that Erhard came from a family with liberal political views. His father had been an admirer of Eugen Richter before 1914.[14] Having participated in the First World War, Ludwig Erhard enrolled at the Nuremberg <u>Handelshochschule</u> where he received his first degree in economics in 1922. He moved to Frankfurt University in November of that year to start a doctoral dissertation under the supervision of Professor Franz Oppenheimer. The topic (<u>Wesen und Inhalt der Werteinheit</u>) was concerned with monetary and currency issues.[15] It appears that his work with Oppenheimer, who was then wrestling with producing a theoretical synthesis of liberalism and socialism and who held that social objectives could best be obtained by liberal means, had a profound formative influence on the 26-year-old Erhard. Having completed his doctorate, he took up a position as research fellow at the

Nuremberg Institut für Wirtschaftsforschung der deutschen Fertigware in 1928. But he kept in touch with Oppenheimer, and it may have been through him that he was given an opportunity to write a contribution to Leopold Schwarzschild's Tagebuch, a well-known left-liberal and pro-Republican weekly.[16] This article was a blunt and highly polemical attack on the ideas which no less a person than Hjalmar Schacht, the former Reichsbank President and prominent right-wing figure, had published that year in a pamphlet entitled Grundsätze der deutschen Weltpolitik.

The review character of Erhard's piece makes it somewhat difficult to reconstruct an exact picture of his own economic beliefs six months before the Nazi seizure of power. Nevertheless, two points emerge clearly from this review: 1) his opposition not merely to Schacht's ideas as presented in this booklet, but also to the 'rigid capitalism of the German Nationalists [i.e. Hugenberg's German National People's Party] and the vulgar socialism of the National Socialists'; 2) his support for an economic internationalism. As he put it, 'the trend towards autarky' must be rejected 'in all circumstances'. He added: 'We would behave like a bull in the china shop of the German national economy if we now proceeded to devalue further what productive capital the German national economy still has at its disposal. We would destroy more jobs for workers, and it is of little comfort if, by securing for the German people autarky in foodstuffs, agriculture and above all the big landowners reap great benefits, irrespective of the costs.' Finally Erhard also demonstrated a considerably greater sophistication in economic affairs than Schacht when he refused to blame the country's desolate economic state on its post-war governments. It is not clear whether Schacht ever saw this demolition job of his publication or whether others, with whom Schacht was in touch both after 1933 and after 1945, had private knowledge of Erhard's piece. However, the ideas reflected in this review would certainly help to explain why Erhard kept his distance from the Hitler regime and why he never occupied prominent positions in the Nazi economy.

On the other hand, he was able to continue his work for the Nuremberg Institute where he rose first to the position of departmental head and later of deputy director. Much of his activity there consisted of giving specialist advice to different branches of the finished goods industry and their industrial associations. Thus Roland Risse remembered after 1945, when he became one of Erhard's anti-cartel experts, that he had first met his future boss in 1932 during a meeting of the German porcelain manufacturers held in the building of the Reichsverband der deutschen Industrie at Berlin at which Erhard appeared as a consultant.[17] Between 1933 and 1940 he also acted as editor of the Wirtschaftspolitische Blätter der deutschen Fertigindustrie. His consultancy work frequently took him to Berlin. If he stayed in the capital overnight, he would do so at the house of his brother-in-law, Dr. Karl Guth, who worked for the powerful Reichsgruppe Industrie and indeed was to become its secretary general. There they would spend long evenings discussing politics, sometimes joined by Dr. Herbert Rohrer and Dr. Karl Blessing.[18] Two other members of the circle were Dr. Theodor Eschenburg and the above-mentioned Risse. Although Eschenburg recalled later that 'Erhard was reticent, but smoked a lot',[19] his views were apparently sufficiently outspoken and critical for his position at the Nuremberg Institute to become increasingly untenable. In 1942 Erhard finally seized the initiative and resigned to build up a private research institute of his own, the Institut für Industrieforschung. The title is significant in itself. But what is perhaps even more important in our context is that much of the financial support came via the Reichsgruppe Industrie of which Guth was now a top official and prominent leaders of industry like Wilhelm Zangen and Carl von Siemens.[20] What they hoped the new institute might do was to look at the position of German industry after the war by which was tacitly implied: after the defeat of the Third Reich. One of the most important think pieces to emerge from Erhard's new work was his Denkschrift of 1944, which Ludolf Herbst, in an important article, has recently put into the broader context of wartime industrial planning.[21] It was through this memorand̃um that Erhard succeeded in stimulating discussions among a circle of industrialists around Rudolf Stahl of the Salzdetfurth Trust. Some of the conclusions which this Stahl Circle reached were sent to influential people like H. Dinkelbach (Vereinigte Stahlwerke), F. Flick, H. Schmitz (I.G. Farben), Ph. F. Reemtsma and a number of bankers. Later Erhard was also in contact with O. Ohlendorf of the Reich Economics Ministry who, for his own reasons, had begun to collaborate with the Reichsgruppe Industrie. Although there is no space here to go into the details of this document, it is important to stress that, at a time when the Allies were debating the possibility of a de-industrialisation of post-war Germany, Erhard was putting forward proposals for the rebuilding of German industry. And it was also clear to him that this objective could not be achieved without quite large enterprises, at least not within the framework of a competitive and internationally-orientated capitalism which he had in mind.

What the various bits and pieces from Erhard's career and world of ideas prior to 1945 would appear to add up to is that he was anything but hostile to large-scale industry and economic concentration so long as it did not involve monopoly and in particular 'monopoly' of the kind which had established itself in Nazi Germany. He was concerned to build up the consumer goods industries, believing that production for ̬peaceful purposes would reduce the danger of nationalistic and autarkic armaments policies and of war as adopted by Hitler and would produce a prosperous and dynamic economy capable of paying high wages and of satisfying material expectations with, in turn, politically and socially stabilising results. The details of his programme may have been complex, but its basic principles were much less so and were in outline largely derived from his experiences and insights of the period prior to 1945. One of the lessons of the past which was quite logically related to Erhard's positions on civilian industrial production and consumerism concerned his views on cartels and syndicates and the forms which they assumed in the Third Reich. To understand this aspect of his thought it is important to remember that no other major industrial country had so refined the organisation and regimentation of the market by the producers to the detriment of the consumers as had inter-war Germany. Cartelisation reached its peak then, and there existed literally thousands of legally binding cartel agreements in all branches of industry with corresponding associations which regulated production quotas, fixed prices and looked after the selling of products. What all this amounted to was that the principle of competition had been virtually eradicated from German capitalism before 1933.[22] When the Nazis came in, they merely formalised this system by decreeing compulsory cartels. Although after 1945 all manufacturers deplored this compulsion, most of them did not really have to be forced into the system at the time.[23] On the contrary, they had become so conditioned by the earlier cartel practices that they were quite happy about their official recognition and institutionalisation in the Third Reich.

It is not quite certain what Erhard's position was towards the German cartel system in the early years of Nazism. Arno Sölter, as head of the cartel department of the West German Bundesverband der Deutschen Industrie, one of his main antagonists in the struggle for an anti-cartel law in the 1950s, quoted with some relish from an article which Erhard was said to have published in Deutsche Handelswarte in February 1936 and in which he confessed never to have hidden his 'positive attitude' towards cartels.[24] Nevertheless, there must be some question as to the depth of his convictions on this score, given his veneration for Franz Oppenheimer who, in his search for new forms of economic organisation, had seen the fight against the power of economic monopolies as a prerequisite of a more balanced socio-economic equilibrium between all social classes. It appears therefore that Erhard was first confronted with the whole and extensive German debate on cartels and monopolies during his time at Frankfurt University. His subsequent work at the Nuremberg Institut für Wirtschaftsforschung der deutschen Fertigware involved him quite deeply in problems of market research and hence in the contradictions of a capitalist system in which the basic mechanisms of the market had been put out of action. In short, even if he did write the above-mentioned statement, his training and earlier experiences as well as his work within a situation which made market research in the ordinary sense at least very difficult, if not impossible, must have made a change of heart for him much easier and less agonising than it later turned out to be for those who had been steeped in cartel practice and for whom it had become part of their managerial personality. As Alfred Müller-Armack, Erhard's post-war adviser and collaborator, phrased it:[25] 'The period of the central direction of the economy by the Nazis led him to occupy himself with a critical analysis of the weaknesses [of this system], as was true of many other German economists. It was, if nothing else, his deep-seated rejection of the political system, which was behind it, which sharpened his eyes for the decomposition of competition [in the Third Reich] and caused him to engage in a critical debate with those overpowerful tendencies which regarded the end of a free economy as irrevocable and thought liberal economic theory to be out of date.' Further close scrutiny of his writings is likely to reveal a more open-ended position which accepted as given the emergence of concentrations of economic power and recognised the distorting effects of such concentrations on competition; but rather than subscribing to the idea of a return to economic liberalism, he was not averse to seizing this opportunity for a rationalisation of markets while at the same time deploying the legislative power of the state to create a legal framework within which stifling cartels would be prevented from emerging, though not oligopolies. There is hence a certain dirigiste element in Erhard's thinking which, though mitigated by his insistence on consumer choice and advertising, may have been stronger before 1945 than later, at the time of the anti-cartel debate of the late 1940s and 1950s when he stressed the framework-setting task of the political authorities while opposing extensive positive controls of the market.

It is probably also safe to assume that Erhard's involvement with the consumers' industries facilitated this rethinking process - industries, in other words, which during the period of Nazi austerity imposed by rapid rearmament and subsequent war, had been forced to live a shadow-existence during the Third Reich. He believed he knew about the potentialities of civilian mass consumption in industrial societies and appreciated what military preparations and conflict were doing to the country's economic structure and to the resources of non-military industries. Moreover, as an economist, he was also conscious of the tremendous reservoir of suppressed demand that was building up as a result of Nazi economic policies and war effort. All this implies that by the mid-1940s, if not before, Erhard had arrived at certain principles and positions concerning the organisation of a capitalist economy which were not directly influenced by members of the circles which had constituted themselves in South-western and Western Germany by 1945.[26] As far as is known, only Wilhelm Röpke's Gesellschaftekris der Gegenwart, which was written in exile and reached Erhard through underground channels, appears to have impressed him in terms of its more general political argument and to have confirmed him in his conviction that German industry had to start from different ideological and structural premisses than the ones that had governed German capitalism during the Third Reich. It was not the abolition of a private enterprise system as such which he was looking towards, but the destruction of those elements and practices which were peculiar to the German model and of which he had had so much first-hand experience as a consultant and critical observer. That model had rejected the idea of a consumer goods society based on competitive industrial production. It had also rejected the economic internationalism and had attempted to block for good, through autarky and Grossraumwirtschaft, the restoration of the open multilateral trading system on a global scale which the United States leadership continued to call for throughout the 1940s. Cartels represented one of the key elements of the German type of capitalism; nationalist autarky and formal imperialism and expansionism another.[27]

It is against the background of such insights and considerations that Erhard's untiring post-war struggle for the establishment and safeguarding, in West Germany, of the competitive principle must be seen, preferably for him with a legal-constitutional anchorage because there was not enough time for the slow accumulation of a case law through the courts as had evolved in the United States over some 60 years of Anti-trust legislation. Erhard's bill was to see to it that competition could never again be easily abandoned in Germany - with what Erhard rightly considered to have been disastrous results.[28] It was also in line with these views that he emerged as an advocate of an 'Open Door' world economy untrammelled by protectionism and block thinking. This was in his opinion the framework within which it would be possible to unleash once more the productive potential of a dynamic capitalist economy. This economy had demonstrated, albeit for the 'wrong' purposes, its viability during the Second World War. If this effort could be harnessed to civilian production rather than to a destructive military machine, the age of prosperity and peaceful mass consumption was expected to be within reach. Implicit in this programme was also a solution of what might be called the Social Question of the early post-war period: the millions of unemployed, the refugees and uprooted people who vegetated in Occupied Germany. Erhard did not agree with those who saw economic planning, redistribution and welfare statism as the major instruments for tackling these problems. Nor was he a 19th-century laissez-faire liberal. On the contrary, he accepted that, given the destitution and abject poverty of large parts of the European population, a considerable dose of Sozialpolitik was necessary and inevitable, just as there was generally more of a 'planner' in him than some people have made out.[29] However, he was also convinced that in the long run the best Sozialpolitik was to achieve the highest possible degree of productivity for civilian consumption within the framework of an American-style competitive capitalism which explicitly contained quite large enterprises as motors of cheap mass production.

T.W. Hutchinson, in a recent article on the 'German Social Market Economy',[30] raise the question of the 'effects of ideas on policy' before inclining towards the more traditional position which has emphasized the close links between Soziale Marktwirtschaft and the economic ideas of the 'Freiburg School'. At the same time he quotes J.S. Mill's dictum of 1845 to the effect that 'ideas, unless outward circumstances conspire with them, have in general no very rapid or immediate efficacy in human affairs'. He then goes on to examine the 'outward conditions' which he feels favoured the establishment of a Social Market Economy in post-war Western Germany. Yet, in trying to show 'how recent economic and political experiences, and the currents and climates of opinion, and of expectations which they create, are of crucial significance with regard to what kinds of policies are politically feasible for governments, or easier to implement in a particular country at a particular time', it emerges that he subscribes to rather a special definition of 'outward conditions'; for these conditions are interpreted as a negative force, i.e. the widespread rejection of planning in early post-war Germany, not only because it was associated with dictatorship and defeat, but also with inefficiency. Given the support which the economic recipes of the Social Democrats and the 'Christian Socialists' enjoyed among the German population, this hypothesis concerning the nature of the 'outward conditions' may well be questioned. Nor did 'outward conditions' in a broader sense conspire in favour of Erhard's Soziale Marktwirtschaft. The chaotic state of the German economy seemed to make an elaborate planning of scarcity wellnigh unavoidable. In short, seen within a German or even European framework, circumstances were hardly of the kind which seemed to lend plausibility to an adoption of the ideas which Erhard, though not he alone, adhered to. His programme and the risk-happy optimism with which it was put into practice make sense only if related to the ideas and perceptions of the world held by the dominant faction in the Office of the U.S. Military Governor and their backers among the political and economic elites across the Atlantic. It is to these that we must now turn.[31]

The American elites had in their majority come out of the crisis of the 1930s with the firm conviction that the re-establishment of an 'Open Door' world economy and a multilateral trading system was not only vital for the reconstitution of the community of nations, but also fundamental to American national interest. Seen from the perspective of the international economy, this is in fact what the Second World War had been about in the eyes of the American business elites. The year 1945 saw both the destruction of the closed, autarkic and violently expansionist system of the fascist powers and the emergence of the United States as the dominant economic factor in the world. The opportunity to create a 'One World' based on open multilateral trading and prosperity appeared to have arisen. But this idea was soon thwarted when, with the onset of the Cold War, the Soviet Union and its satellites refused to be part of an American-led world economy. Yet it would be wrong to assume that Washington was discouraged by this development and retreated into an isolationist shell. On the contrary, from 1946/47 the American political leadership set out to implement its ideas of a new international economic order within the 'half-world' (M. Balfour) that was left, with Europe and occupied Germany becoming the focal point of these post-war efforts and the confrontation with Stalinist Russia providing additional ideological ammunition for why action was imperative.

It is not surprising that the details of this 'grand design' would run into many obstacles which would diminish its initial thrust and deflect from some of its objectives. Two such stumbling-blocs were Britain and France who were by no means in full agreement with American plans in Europe in general and in Germany, where they had their own zones of occupation, in particular.[32] These Western zones of occupation thus became the ground on which the struggle over divergent conceptions of the post-war European order was fought out. In the long run, Washington, using its superior economic and political weight, was able to assert itself against Paris and London. What complicated the picture further was that the American political and economic elites themselves did not speak with one voice. There was at least one faction which, while broadly agreeing with the idea of an 'Open Door' internationalism, stood for a different treatment of postwar Germany, just as they promoted an alternative programme for the handling of the domestic economy. At home they inclined towards Keynesian demand management and interventionism as well as an 'anti-trust' position characteristic of the 'trust-busters' of the New Deal era.[33] As regards Germany, they aimed not merely at the abolition of those structural elements of German capitalism under Hitler which were symbolised by cartels and the abolition of competition; rather they also did not wish to revive the latent potential of German large-scale industry which, on the basis of its past record, they deemed to be inherently aggressive and violently expansionist.[34]

This group, which had one of its strongholds in the U.S. Treasury Department and also had its protagonists in the American Military Government in Germany, found itself, by the end of the war, locked in a serious conflict over strategy with those who, on the whole, reflected the views of American Big Business. As to domestic economic policy, the latter, while agreeing that full employment had to be achieved after the war, preferred to demand management a policy designed to unleash the no doubt impressive energies of private industry, unfettered by government controls, for civilian production and a new period of prosperity.[35] This is how they expected to satisfy pent-up demand for goods which wartime austerity had suppressed. The means to be applied towards this end can only be called conventional: a reform of the tax system to provide larger disposable incomes and to stimulate private investment. Furthermore government expenditure, including defence, was to be scaled back and the public debt to be held down. The first proposals of this kind were mooted in the early 1940s. But at that time the number of sceptics who, pointing to the 1930s, believed that such a programme would not work was still quite large. They advocated a more interventionist policy instead. Only when victory over Germany came into sight did optimism rise among the leaders of the National Association of Manufacturers (NAM) and other industrial organisations that the shift towards peacetime production could be achieved without recession and government controls. This growing self-confidence in the strength and viability of American business also coloured the views of industry and finance about Europe and Germany in particular.

Its spokesmen were less haunted by Germany's latent industrial potential and industrial concentration. Although they were not opposed to the splitting-up of giants like I. G. Farben and Vereinigte Stahlwerke, they aimed at decartelisation in the narrow sense, i.e. at a destruction of those organisational features of German capitalism which were dysfunctional to a revived and competitive world economy based on free enterprise and, of course, dominated by the United States. In other words, bigness was much less of a problem to this group and their allies in the Pentagon and the State Department, but it took some time to assert itself. Thus the Directive JCS 1067 which tried to formulate the principles to be implemented by the American occupation authorities in Germany still reflected some of the hardline positions on the issue of the future size of German industry. The wording of the Potsdam Agreement of August 1945 was much more ambiguous:[36] 'At the earliest practicable date, the German economy shall be decentralized for the purpose of eliminating the present excessive concentration of economic power as exemplified in particular by cartels, syndicates, trusts and other monopolistic arrangements.' When subsequent negotiations to give specific meaning to these resolutions on a four-power basis failed, the United States, in February 1947, decreed its own decartelisation and deconcentration law No. 56 for the American Zone. For General William Draper, one of the key figures in the U.S. Military Government in the early post-war years and a man with many connections with American industry and finance, there was never much doubt that decartelisation meant the destruction of those German cartels and syndicates.

General Lucius D. Clay, who had been in close touch with Treasury

Secretary Henry Morgenthau during the war on matters of war production and who became General Dwight D. Eisenhower's deputy for the U.S. Military Government in Germany, began to change his mind once he had taken over his new assignment. As he put the general problems in April 1945 to John McCloy, later his successor and another man with many links in business:[37] 'I think that Washington must revise its thinking relative to the destruction of Germany's war potential as an immediate problem. The progress of the war has accomplished that and it is my view now (based on general impressions, I must admit) that the industry which remains, with few exceptions, even when restored will suffice barely for a very low minimum living standard in Germany.' By August 1946 Clay was writing to Major-General Oliver Echols, who had become Assistant Secretary of State for Occupied Areas at Washington five months earlier, that 'I can see no fear of economic concentration in a program to be completed under Allied supervision'.[38] But while Clay and Draper kept on explaining their positions to their superiors across the Atlantic, other members of the U.S. Military Government in Germany were fighting for the implementation of a tougher line on economic deconcentration.[39] It is against the background of these differences of opinion that the 'level of industry' debate within the American administration must be seen, which was ultimately won by Draper and Clay and their supporters in Washington. German industry was not only to be allowed to operate at levels which would enable the population to maintain itself without having to rely permanently on American aid; it was also to be strong enough to become the engine of the projected revival of the European economy. In view of this, the abolition of the German cartel tradition remained on the agenda of American industrial policy towards Germany; the break-up of large firms, on the other hand, was pursued with less and less vigour and ultimately implemented in a very mild form.

Erhard was practically from the start close enough to American policy-making to recognise the changing emphasis on decartelisation and deconcentration which accorded very much with his own views. After the Americans had made him Minister of Economics in his home-state of Bavaria in 1946, he moved on to become director of the Sonderstelle 'Geld und Kredit' when an Anglo-American Bizonal administration was established in the following year. Finally in March 1948 he was nominated director of the Verwaltung für Wirtschaft at Frankfurt. And like his American supervisors he favoured the abolition of cartels as a means of 'political decontamination of the German economy', but was strongly opposed to a deconcentration policy which would merely weaken its dormant strength.[40] The long-term practical and 'educational' consequences of this were the drafting and eventual ratification of a Law for the Securing Competition which bore many of the hallmarks of U.S. Anti-trust legislation.[41] It has been examined elsewhere why it took Erhard until 1957 to get parliamentary approval for his anti-cartel bill.[42] This is the place to come back to some of the broader questions which this article has been trying to raise with reference to his economic programme during the late 1940s and early 1950s.

After looking at some of the central ideas underlying this programme, it should be clear that the influence of the 'Freiburg School' must not be overemphasised. Many of these ideas were formulated earlier in his career or were conclusions drawn from experiences with the Nazi economic system. In particular Erhard was no more an advocate of a petty capitalism than his sponsors in the U.S. Military Government. He was not averse to large-scale enterprise and in fact saw it as a necessary prerequisite if the country's economic recovery was to succeed. These views on the inter-related topics of competition, high productivity and company size greatly facilitated the meeting of minds which not even the Korean War was able to shake. It would thus seem worthwhile to look more closely at the 'American Connection' in Erhard's policies of which he and other contemporaries were conscious. He himself is on record as having called himself an 'American invention',[43] just as his Americanism provoked a good deal of opposition and resentment among those whom he tried to convince that Germany's return to the world market could not be brought about without painful adjustments and structural changes to fit industry into an American-dominated trading system. Given the nationalism and anti-Occupation feelings which were rampant among German industrialists well into the 1950s, it was obviously unwise to publicise the similarities in approach. But this may also be precisely the reason why the points which this article has raised have passed into oblivion.

Finally, as far as Mill's dictum is concerned, it seems that Erhard's economic ideas had a 'very rapid or immediate efficacy' because of the 'outward circumstances' which conspired with them.[44] But unless these 'circumstances' are to be defined in very broad terms of suppressed wartime demand which was bound to lead to a post-war boom, it would appear to be more sensible to see them as programmes and convictions held by the dominant factions in the American business community and the U.S. Military Government in Germany. These factions had the necessary power and leverage to assert their views in Occupied Germany. But what helped them in their course of action was their firm conviction that their economic programme, simple as it may be in retrospect, could move mountains in a world exhausted by the Second World War.

Notes

1. See, inter alia, R. Blum, Soziale Marktwirtschaft, Tübingen 1969; C. Blumenberg-Lampe, Das wirtschaftspolitische Programm der 'Freiburger Kreise', Berlin 1973; E. E. Nawroth, Die Sozial- und Wirtschafts-philosophie des Neoliberalismus, Heidelberg 1961; C. Watrin, 'The Principles of the Social Market Economy - Its Origins and Early History' in: Zeitschrift für die gesamte Staatswissenschaft, September 1979, 405-25; M. Wulff, Die neoliberale Wirtschaftsordnung, Tübingen 1976.
2. A. Hunold, 'Sir Robert Peel and Ludwig Erhard' in: E. von Beckerath et al., eds., Wirtschaftsfragen der freien Welt, Frankfurt (1957), 59.
3. See, e.g., H. Biedenkopf, 'Die Anspruchsgesellschaft bedroht "seine" Soziale Marktwirtschaft' in: Die Zeit, 4.2.1977, 18; H.-H. Götz, 'Die geistigen Väter der sozialen Marktwirtschaft' in: J. Eick, ed., So nutzt man den Wirtschaftsteil einer Tageszeitung, Frankfurt 1971, 57-61.

4. See the titles listed above Note 1. See also the article by A.J. Nicholls, above, pp.164-77.
5. E.E. Nawroth, op.cit., 425.
6. H. Mey, 'Marktwirtschaft und Demokratie' in: Vierteljahreshefte für Zeitgeschichte, 2/1971, 160-86.
7. Ibid., 168.
8. Presse-und Informationsamt der Bundesregierung, ed., Die Formierte Gesellschaft, (Bonn 1966), 7-14.
9. See the articles from newspapers and journals reprinted ibid.
10. See, e.g., R. Opitz, 'Der grosse Plan der CDU: Die "Formierte Gesellschaft"' in: Blätter für deutsche und internationale Politik, 9/1965, 75-77.
11. A closer analysis of these developments and also of the influence of people like Alfred Müller-Armack and Rüdiger Altmann on Erhard will be undertaken by K. Hildebrand in his forthcoming history of the Federal Republic in the 1960s.
12. See also R. Roberts, Konzentrationspolitik in der Bundesrepublik, Berlin 1976, 116; W. Abelshauser, 'Probleme des Wiederaufbaus der westdeutschen Wirtschaft, 1945-1953' in: H.A. Winkler, ed., Politische Weichenstellungen im Nachkriegsdeutschland, Göttingen 1979, 253.
13. See R. Blum, op.cit., 66, 73ff.; C. Blumenberg-Lampe, op.cit., 65, 69, 92ff.
14. R. Altmann and J. Gross, 'Gespräch über Erhard' in: G. Schröder et al., eds., Ludwig Erhard, Frankfurt 1972, 23.
15. Der Spiegel, 5.2.1949.
16. L. Erhard, 'Herrn Schachts "Grundsätze"' in: Das Tagebuch, 20.8.1932, 1300-6, also for the following.
17. R. Risse, 'Alltag mit Erhard' in: G. Schröder et al., eds., op.cit., 591.
18. Rohrer was a member of the board of Osram; Blessing was a member of the Reichsbank Direktorium just before the war and joined the board of the Margarine Union in 1939. After the war he became President of the West German Bundesbank.
19. Th. Eschenburg, 'Die Denkschrift' in: G. Schröder et al., eds., op.cit., 529. Eschenburg himself worked for a number of industrial associations before 1945. He became one of the most influential Professors of Political Science in West Germany.
20. The personal links forged with the Reichsgruppe personnel lasted beyond 1945. See R. Lahr, Zeuge von Fall und Aufstieg, Hamburg 1981, 168f.
21. L. Erhard, Kriegsfinanzierung und Schuldenkonsolidierung (1943/4), Frankfurt 1977; L. Herbst, 'Krisenüberwindung und Wirtschaftsordnung' in: Vierteljahreshefte für Zeitgeschichte, 3/1977, 307-40.
22. M.J. Bonn, Das Schicksal des deutschen Kapitalismus, Berlin 1930.
23. See, e.g., A. Barkai, Das Wirtschaftssystem des Nationalsozialismus, Cologne 1977; A. Schweitzer, Big Business in the Third Reich, Bloomington 1964; R. Lahr, op.cit., 44.
24. A. Sölter, Kartelliaden, Munich 1977, 92. See also L. Erhard, 'Einfluss der Preisbildung und Preisbindung auf die Qualität und Quantität des Angebots und der Nachfrage' (1939), quoted in: Der Spiegel, 19.11.1952, where he argues that free prices do not, as a matter of principle, mean fairer prices. 'On the contrary, in some individual

cases a free price can even amount to profiteering, whereas a fixed price may be dictated by the highest sense of moral responsibility.' This was not exactly an overenthusiastic affirmation of price-fixing. See also the discussion in L. Herbst, op.cit., p.314ff., and C. Heusgen, Ludwig Erhards Lehre von der Sozialen Marktwirtschaft, Berne 1981, pp.91ff.

25. A. Müller-Armack, 'Wirtschaftspolitik zwischen Wissenschaft und Politik' in: G. Schröder et al., eds., op.cit., 474. On Müller-Armack's ideas see, e.g., his Wirtschaftsordnung und Wirtschaftspolitik, Freiburg 1966.

26. On these circles see C. Blumenberg-Lampe, op.cit., passim. Rolf Lahr (op.cit., 171) who was able to observe Erhard at close range also describes him as a man who held his own ideas. In 1945, Erhard did for a while belong to a study circle constituted at Munich by Professor Adolf Weber. For a somewhat different interpretation see above A.J. Nicholls's article, pp.164-74.

27. See A. Bay, Der nationalsozialistische Gedanke der Grossraumwirtschaft und seine ideologischen Grundlagen, Cologne 1962; C. Bettelheim, L'économie allemande sous le nazisme, 2 vols., Paris 1971; J.S. Greer, Der Markt der geschlossenen Nachfrage, Berlin 1961; G. Hallgarten and J. Radkau, Deutsche Industrie und Politik, Frankfurt 1974; D. Petzina, Autarkiepolitik im Dritten Reich, Stuttgart 1968; H.-E. Volkmann, 'Autarkie, Grossraumwirtschaft und Aggression' in: Militärgeschichtliche Mitteilungen, 19/1976, 51-76; W. Schumann et al., Konzept für die 'Neuordnung' der Welt, Berlin (East) 1977; L. Zumpe, Wirtschaft und Staat in Deutschland, 1933-1945, Berlin (East) 1981.

28. See R. Robert, op.cit., 102ff.; V. von Bethusy-Huc, Demokratie und Interessenpolitik, Wiesbaden 1962; V.R. Berghahn, 'Westdeutsche Unternehmer, Weltmarkt und Wirtschaftsordnung' in: L. Albertin and W. Link, eds., Politische Parteien auf dem Weg zur parlamentarischen Demokratie in Deutschland, Düsseldorf 1981, 301-24.

29. See R. Robert, op.cit., 107ff. See also above Note 25 on Müller-Armack's ideas. He was particularly close to Erhard in those years.

30. T.W. Hutchinson, 'Notes on the Effects of Economic Ideas on Policy' in: Zeitschrift für die gesamte Staatswissenschaft, 3/1979, 426-41.

31. For the following see, inter alia, L.S. Kaplan, 'Western Europe in "The American Century": a Retrospective View' in: Diplomatic History, Spring 1982, 111-23: W. Knapp, ed., Die deutsch-amerikanischen Beziehungen nach 1945, Frankfurt 1975; W. Link, Deutsche und amerikanische Gewerkschaften und Geschäftsleute, Düsseldorf 1978; B. Martin, 'Amerikas Durchbruch zur politischen Weltmacht' in: Militärgeschichtliche Mitteilungen, 2/1981; C.A. MacDonald, The United States, Britain and Appeasement, London 1980; W.S. Hill, 'The Business Community and National Defense', unpubl. PhD. thesis (on Michigan Univ. Microfilm) 1980.

32. Neatly reflected in: J.E. Smith, ed., The Papers of General Lucius D. Clay, 2 vols., Bloomington 1974, passim.

33. However, there remains some question as to whether those who supervised the Anti-trust laws saw bigness as the main problem. Certainly Thurmond W. Arnold, one of the most prominent 'anti-trusters', went out of his way to emphasise that it 'is not the evils of size, but the evils of industries which are not efficient or do not pass efficiency on to

the consumers' which worried him: 'If the anti-trust laws are simply an expression of a religion which condemns largeness as economic sin, they will be regarded as an anachronism in a machine age. If, however, they are directed at making distribution more efficient, they will begin to make sense and, incidentally, they will also solve the problem of bigness wherever bigness is blocking the channels of trade.' T.W. Arnold, 'The Bottlenecks of Business, New York 1940, 3f. Clearly this was not the dream of a petty capitalism either.

34. See, e.g., J.S. Martin, All Honorable Men, Boston 1950.
35. See W.S. Hill, op.cit., passim.
36. Potsdam Agreement of 2 August 1945, Section B 12.
37. Quoted in J.E. Smith, ed., op.cit., Vol.1, 8.
38. Ibid., 246.
39. For details see ibid., passim, and J.S. Martin, op.cit.
40. Thus Erhard in his 'Gutachten zum Gesetz über Verhinderung wirtschaftlicher Machtzusammenballungen' of 4 December 1946, quoted in R. Robert, op.cit., 100.
41. The 're-educational' aspects of German anti-cartel legislation were frequently emphasised both by the Americans and by Erhard.
42. See the studies in Note 28 above.
43. R. Blum, op. cit., 262f.
44. See above, 172-4.

AN IDEA ENTERS DIPLOMACY: THE SCHUMAN PLAN, MAY 1950

Roger Bullen

On 9th May 1950 Robert Schuman, the French Foreign Minister, announced his plan 'to place all Franco-German coal and steel production under a common authority'.[1] The French government believed that its proposals, which became known as the Schuman Plan, were revolutionary. If they were implemented 'the situation', declared Schuman, 'will be completely transformed'.[2] Even less optimistic observers were prepared to admit that the plan marked 'a new phase in the affairs of the West'.[3] The French government claimed it was necessary to look beyond the sovereign state and old style treaties of defensive alliance and instead consider the pooling of key industries under the authority of a new supra-national institution.[4] With Schuman's dramatic announcement a new idea was thrust into the centre of western politics and diplomacy.

Western diplomats and statesmen were perplexed by the suddenness of the French initiative. Some believed that it was merely an attempt to play the beau rôle in public before French diplomats resumed their traditional obstructive tactics at the tripartite talks on German affairs which were due to begin in London the day following Schuman's announcement. Others conceded the sincerity of the initiative but feared that once subjected to the ordinary processes of negotiation it was doomed to wither and die. The fact was that western diplomats, politicians and journalists were disconcerted by their complete lack of any prior knowledge of the plan. They assumed that a major shift in French foreign policy would be preceded by timely and delicate leaks. This was how the Quai d'Orsay was accustomed to conduct its affairs. There was a general agreement that Schuman had broken the rules of diplomacy, a view shared by some of his own diplomats, for example Massigli, the French ambassador in London.[5] Both Schuman and Jean Monnet, the Head of the French Planning Commission, who was responsible for the secret preparation of the plan, prided themselves on the unorthodox entry of their ideas into French politics and western diplomacy; they deliberately bypassed the French Foreign Ministry, which was therefore unable to leak the proposal, and they consciously dispensed with the usual diplomatic soundings in the major western capitals. 'Experience has shown', stated Schuman, 'that the most hopeful initiatives die away when before seeing the light they linger too long amidst preliminary consultations'.[6] Both men were convinced that the ideas and methods of conventional diplomacy had been tried and found wanting. They turned instead to 'the force of a new idea and counted upon the impulse of the hope it roused'.[7] In the spring of 1950 Monnet saw an idea waiting its moment; he gave concrete form to the hopes and aspirations of frustrated federalists. Schuman became its sponsor; he was above all anxious to break the deadlock on Franco-German relations and to provide France with security against the dangers of a revived Germany. Moreover, by changing both the scope and the pace of European integration, he was presented with the opportunity of seizing the leadership in western Europe from Great Britain.

The Schuman Plan was presented as a momentous step towards the realisation of the ideal of a new integrated western Europe. 'The urge to have done with our violent past,' declared Monnet, 'has left us no choice but to advance towards a common goal'.[8] It was for this reason that the French proposal was a statement of intent and of principle. It was not a detailed plan in which the precise implications of the proposal for the coal and steel industries of western Europe were carefully worked out. Indeed, when Monnet came to London to discuss the plan with British ministers and civil servants they could hardly credit the vagueness of the proposal and the complete absence of detailed planning which had preceded its announcement.[9] It was this, as much as the unorthodox entry of the proposal into western diplomacy, which initially irritated many British politicians and officials. Throughout the preliminary discussions of May and June 1950 the French emphasised that 'the Plan should not be judged from the economic angle only but from the wider political consequences which should flow from its successful implementation'.[10] What then were these wider political consequences? Why did the French government put forward this far-reaching proposal?

The Schuman Plan was designed to rescue French policy towards Germany from further setbacks and humiliations. Its origin lay in the French realisation of the collapse of their efforts either to prevent or successfully to delay the recovery of Germany. Although Germany was still occupied and divided, it was evident that the three western zones of occupation were, largely as a result of American pressure, gradually being freed from controls. One of the main purposes of the tripartite talks in London in May 1950 was to decide how quickly this process could be taken to the logical conclusion of removing all controls and granting statehood to the western zones. French concern centred on the failure to prevent the re-emergence of Germany as the industrial giant of western and central Europe. It was from this position of strength that Germany had three times invaded France and occupied French territory.

Since 1945 the French had concentrated their attempts to weaken Germany on the Ruhr: this was the heartland of German industrial power and Germany without the Ruhr would lack the power to menace France. At first the French had tried to detach the Ruhr from Germany. When this failed they sought Anglo-American consent for extra-territorial status for the Ruhr. This too failed, and once again the French were forced to narrow their objectives. At the London Conference of April 1948, in return for their agreement to the establishment of a West German government, the French insisted upon the creation of the International Authority of the Ruhr (I.A.R.) which they hoped would effectively control the heavy industry of the region. The agreement of December 1948 which gave life to the I.A.R. was extremely imprecise in the definition of its functions. By the summer of 1950 it was apparent to the French that the I.A.R. had no real future and certainly would be no substitute for the economic controls exercised by the High Commission of the three occupying powers.[11] The Germans bitterly resented its existence and neither the Americans nor the British were prepared to work with France to transform the nebulous agreement of December 1948 into an effective instrument of control.[12] The French feared that in the near future they would face the prospect of an independent Germany capable of rapid industrial expansion. In the light of that prospect French policy towards Germany was in ruins. Her government could either cling to its remnants and particularly to the tactic of delay or it could abandon it and search for a new policy. The latter seemed beyond the resources of French diplomacy. French diplomats were dismayed by their record of failure and they had nothing to offer as an alternative. This was why Monnet who was not bound by the conventions of diplomacy was able to present Schuman with an alternative cast in what seemed a narrow and specific form and yet wide-ranging in its implications.

The Schuman Plan reshaped French policy towards Germany. It started from the premiss that France must accept the logic of what she could not prevent. As she could not persuade her allies to keep Germany weak she would propose that the new Germany should be held fast to and confined within a partnership in the west. The German economy would be integrated with those of her western neighbours or at least with that of France. As the economic controls of the High Commission disappeared they would be replaced by the controls of a new supra-national institution. In return for political independence West Germany must subject her economy to voluntary supervision: integration would follow occupation. It was clear that in French thinking about Germany the High Commission of the occupying powers was the model for the High Authority of the Schuman Plan. It was adapted and modified but most of all it was transformed from a symbol of defeat into the ideal of co-operation. This was why in the first instance the French proposal was addressed to Germany.

In their presentation of the Plan in May 1950, the French government stressed that its long-term purpose was to 'bind Germany economically and politically into the structure of Western Europe'.[14] In other words the Schuman Plan was the French quest for security cast in a new form. Germany tied to the west would have neither the opportunity nor the need to seek a rapprochement with the Soviet Union nor to seek markets for her expanding industrial capacity in Eastern Europe.[15] The French were determined to deny Adenauer the advantages which Stresemann had so successfully exploited in the 1920s. The French realised that only the offer of equality and co-operation on a permanent basis and in a new form would accomplish this. At this level the Schuman Plan was a historic reversal of policy; a diplomatic revolution was concealed behind a public preoccupation with coal prices and the levels of steel production. Instead of seeking allies to ensure German good conduct, the French now proposed that Germany should participate in her own containment. Moreover in the short term the Plan offered an end to the dismal legacy of bitterness and conflict which had characterised Franco-German relations since the formation of the West German government. Of the many disputes that existed, the future status of the Saar and the ownership of its mines was the most divisive.

The High Authority, once established, would provide a new forum for the discussion of these problems and, it was hoped, a new atmosphere of confidence. A fresh start on the problems of the Saar was a pressing need; in January 1950 the French and Germans publicly admitted a deadlock on the matter. The Schuman Plan was in part an attempt to break this deadlock.[16]

For the French the vital diplomatic element in the Plan was that Germany should accept her offer of a new partnership and would, as a consequence of her participation in the creation and operation of the new High Authority, be released from the remaining controls of the High Commission. This was less of a gamble than it appeared; the German good faith it assumed had already been offered. In celebrated interviews with an American journalist Adenauer, the German Chancellor, had stressed the need for a fresh start in Franco-German relations and his willingness to meet France half-way.[17] He realised that Germany could not become fully independent until France was satisfied that Germany had ceased to threaten her. Despite the immediately hostile French reaction to Adenauer's offer[18] of a Franco-German confederation in the spring of 1950 it was an essential preliminary step to the French suggestion of the pooling of coal and steel resources. In his preparation of the Plan Monnet counted upon German willingness to accept it. He assumed that Adenauer sought an exclusively western orientation for an independent Germany. He counted upon the conservative, Catholic and western attitude of the German government. The main gamble for the French was whether the German government would accept the substitution of one form of control for another. In short, would political or economic factors determine the response of the German government? For Monnet this was a vital question. He trusted that political considerations would predominate but equally he hoped that German industrialists would regard the Plan as the easiest and quickest route to rapid industrial expansion.

In their explanation of the Schuman proposals the French government emphasised that it had chosen the coal and steel industries because they were the key industries of the French and German economies and that further economic integration could naturally follow from this first step.[19] This was perhaps the least sincere part of the French statement elaborating their proposals. It was at best a half truth. The British were convinced that the French, having failed to secure specific economic objectives within the High Commission, were now pursuing them by other means. The Plan offered a solution to a number of specific disputes both between the three western occupying powers and between them and the German government. First, the Americans were pressing for an increase in the permitted levels of German steel production, which was fixed below the maximum output of which West German industry was capable.[20] Hitherto France had either resisted such proposals or combined her agreement with a refusal to contemplate the abandonment of the control itself.[21] Under the new plan this control could be transferred from the High Commission to the High Authority. Secondly, after the failure of the French appeal on the preamble to High Commission Law 27 (formerly Law 75), they were faced with the possibility that the German government might nationalise either or both the coal and steel industries and thus create a concentration of economic power dangerous to France.[22] Within the new High Authority France could continue to protect her interests on this vital question. Thirdly, the French government believed that the new Authority could deal with the problem with which Monnet was particularly pre-occupied: the imminent prospect of the over-production of steel in Europe.[23] By the summer of 1950 there were widespread fears that the steel producers would seek to recreate the cartels of the inter-war years.[24] In his elaboration of the Plan Monnet took great pains to refute the notion that it was essentially cartelist.[25] British officials remained unconvinced by his protestations and assumed 'that there will be at least considerable pressure to shape the Schuman proposals into some international cartel arrangement'.[26] Lastly, the French hoped that within the new High Authority they could more effectively challenge German price differentials for coal and steel than they had done in the High Commission. They were anxious, if possible, completely to abolish the differential between the domestic and export prices of German coal[27] and to prevent the revival of the old Ruhr vertical combines which would enable the steel companies to obtain their own coal at less than the normal commercial rates. At least under the new arrangements France and Germany would negotiate as equals, whereas the French believed that on many issues the British and American High Commissioners protected German at the expense of French interests. Schuman and Monnet were aware of all these coal and steel issues, of their interaction and of their importance for the future of France as well as Germany. It was on the particular problems of coal and steel that the continuity of French policy towards Germany was apparent. France was obviously not willing to abandon her attempt to secure some control over the future of the Ruhr and its industries. On these issues the Schuman Plan was not an abandonment of French objectives in Germany but basically an attempt to provide new means with which to pursue them. Schumacher, the German Social Democratic leader who opposed the plan, said it was 'putting the economic strength of Germany ... in the service of French diplomacy'.[28]

The binding of Germany to the west also bound France to the west. With Germany politically, economically and perhaps militarily integrated into the western alliance France could finally abandon the need to keep open the traditional option of a Franco-Russian rapprochement to contain a powerful and independent Germany. The successful implementation of the Schuman Plan would be a decisive rebuff to the Soviet Union. It would seriously undermine Soviet attempts to play on French fears of a revived Germany in order to separate her from her Atlantic allies. This was well appreciated by the American government and was in part responsible for its enthusiastic reception of the Plan and for the pressure it exerted to secure support for it amongst the other west European states. For the government of Bidault and Schuman the anti-Russian aspect of the Plan had obvious domestic advantages. By ending the historic enmity of France and Germany it would enable the government to emphasise Soviet expansion as the real danger to France. The need to substitute 'fear of Russia' for 'fear of Germany' in French public opinion was a task to which the French government and its British and American allies accorded a high priority.[29] If, as was expected, the French Communist party opposed the Plan as capitalist, cartelist and designed to serve American interests and if, as hoped, leading non-communist politicians and journalists enthusiastically welcomed it, then the government would reap the advantages of putting forward a new and decisively western initiative.[30] In short, the domestic purpose of the Plan was further to isolate the Communist Party and, at the same time, undermine neutralist and 'third force' opinion within France. With Germany safely westernised France need no longer look eastward. With Germany as her ally and major trading partner, France could firmly range herself with those opposed to Soviet expansion. This was not just a problem of diplomacy, it was central to the deep cleavages of French political life. In the immediate aftermath of the announcement of the Plan both Schuman and Monnet carefully monitored its impact on French public opinion. They were above all concerned to prevent any wasting of what they called its 'psychological impact'.[31]

The British government was quick to appreciate that the French Plan, with its aims of creating new relationships in western Europe and of strengthening the western states, was potentially anti-American. In a conversation with Stikker, the Dutch Foreign Minister, after the acceptance by the six states of the Schuman proposal Bevin bluntly stated 'that we had to try and convince the French that European unity was not possible on a purely European basis but that it was possible on an Atlantic basis and only on an Atlantic basis'.[32] The British government feared that twin pillars for the western alliance, one European and one Atlantic, would be a source of weakness rather than strength. Moreover it saw such a development as posing an impossible dilemma for itself of having to choose where to place its own emphasis. The French by contrast were convinced of the need to create a strong western Europe. They believed that Europe had a separate heritage and an identity which must be cultivated otherwise western Europe would become merely a pawn in the struggle between the two superpowers.[33] Monnet was anxious in the summer of 1950 to direct attention away from excessive preoccupation with the Cold War and its dangers.[34] Only a new and bold stroke could hope to have such an impact. On this level the Plan was a rejection both of American perceptions of east-west relations and of American priorities for the western alliance. The British government feared that the French thought that as the Plan would remove the German threat to France it would then 'reduce French and indeed West Europe's need to strengthen defences'.[35] In its view the Plan strengthened French and European neutralist sentiment.

British determination to highlight these dangers was resented in Paris. Schuman and Monnet were anxious to secure American support for their proposals and they presented them with a careful eye to an enthusiastic American reception. They emphasised that the Plan was pre-eminently based on the notion of self-help, an American virtue par excellence. By 1952 American aid to western Europe under the Marshall Plan would come to an end. Europe must demonstrate that it could provide a prosperous and secure future by the rational use of its own resources. This could be best achieved by the creation of a new large market, similar in size and organisation to that which existed in the

United States of America. Moreover by ending the Franco-German antagonism and binding Germany to the west, the French opened up the distinct possibility which the Americans immediately recognised of providing a 'framework within which German production could contribute to N.A.T.O. ... without raising the difficulties that separate German activity would entail'.[36] In Washington security for France and a western orientation for Germany were regarded as essential bulwarks of the western alliance. The American government was prepared to make some sacrifices to achieve them. It was at least willing to support France in her bid for the leadership in western Europe. The Americans frankly informed the British that they approved of the French 'readiness to take a more positive attitude, to put forward policies of their own instead of leaving it to the United States and the United Kingdom to take the lead'.[37]

The Schuman Plan was a decisive rejection of the British view that European integration could only proceed slowly, on the basis of inter-governmental co-operation over which each state must retain a veto and only in the wider context of what Bevin called the Atlantic community.[38] Moreover the British were determined to ensure that European economic integration did not impair the independence of the sterling area or call into question the tariff principles of Imperial preference. On this basis the British would lead and since 1948 the British had exercised leadership in western Europe. By offering integration on a different basis, with the central principle of an independent High Authority, and at a faster pace, the French seized the initiative from Great Britain. This was a difficult step to take; the French had to abandon their sometimes grudging but nevertheless conscious deference to British leadership. Above all, the French had to consider the possibility of making a new Europe without Great Britain. In short, they had to put forward a proposal for European integration which could work without British participation. The British would be offered the chance of participating on French terms or remaining outside. In 1950 only France, with American backing, could have made such a decision. In his memoirs Massigli suggests that it was Monnet rather than the officials of the Quai d'Orsay who took this decision.[39] Once again the Quai d'Orsay was reluctant to abandon the tradition of compromise with Great Britain. French diplomats were alarmed by Monnet's search for victory; in their view it was incompatible with the character of alliance diplomacy.

It was the Anglo-French dispute over the future of the Plan which came to dominate the negotiations in late May and early June. It was the French who set the fast pace. They wanted the earliest possible start to the negotiations to implement the Plan. They feared that prolonged delay would have undesirable consequences; public interest and enthusiasm would fade and other governments would be better placed to question the principles of the Plan and concert opposition to them. Moreover, having secured American support for their new initiative, the French felt they had to demonstrate that the trust placed in them was not destroyed by tactical blunders. Their confidence was on trial. All this meant that the French were determined firstly to secure early and unqualified German acceptance of the proposal and secondly either firm

British acceptance or an equally firm rejection. What Monnet in particular was determined to avoid was a half-hearted British assent whereby they agreed to participate in the negotiations without fully endorsing the central principle of supra-national authority. The effect of such a proposal would merely be to give Germany freedom to exploit her strength.

The view in London was that the French proposal had decided political advantages. The Foreign Office welcomed the prospect of providing security for France combined with a decisive western orientation for Germany. These were objectives which Bevin had long sought to achieve. On the purely economic level the British government had no objection to a west European coal and steel community. The cabinet instructed a committee of officials to consider the possible effects of the creation of such a community on the British coal and steel industries, on British exports, on defence policy and Commonwealth relations.[40] The British assumed that the strength and size of their own coal and steel industries would ensure for them a leading role in such a community. There was therefore no determination in London to wreck the French proposal. British misgivings were concentrated on the question of how the new international authority would be organised and how it would operate. Attlee and his ministers as well as Foreign Office and Treasury officials were opposed to the idea of a supra-national authority. They were not prepared to relinquish the sovereign authority of Parliament to a body not subject to ministerial control.[41] The French proposal for a supra-national authority was in the British view an attempt to ensure the triumph of the federalist over the inter-governmental view of European integration. The British saw no reason to abandon their anti-federalist predilections as a consequence of a sudden French initiative of which they had had no warning and the future of which was, to say the least, uncertain. Moreover Bevin was certainly displeased by the French bid for the leadership in western Europe and by the fact that it evidently had strong American backing. During the crucial negotiations in late May Bevin was in hospital and Kenneth Younger, the Minister of State at the Foreign Office, was in charge in London although Bevin was kept in touch and consulted throughout.[42] He was however disconcerted by the tactics adopted by the French. On a purely diplomatic level Bevin's fears were fourfold. If the negotiations were successful, then the western alliance would be divided into two communities, one European and one Atlantic. Secondly, if western Europe took a decisive step towards federalism, then Great Britain would have to remain apart and as a consequence she would lose the leadership. Thirdly, the British were by no means convinced that if this new federal Europe emerged the French could retain the leadership; indeed they feared that in their absence West Germany would inevitably become the leading member. Lastly, if the negotiations failed, and Bevin and his officials did not regard this as an unlikely possibility, then the French would only have succeeded in exacerbating their own fears and accentuating the divisions within the western alliance.[43] The British response to the Schuman Plan in late May 1950 was organised around the attempt to avert all these dangers.

The essence of the difference between the two governments was that the French sought to secure unreserved commitment to the creation of the High Authority and the British sought to arrange a preliminary ministerial meeting to discuss the principles on which the subsequent negotiations should proceed. The British tactic seemed a good one: most of the other European states had expressed some private misgivings about the nature and power of the proposed High Authority and it was well known in London that the French government was also divided on this question.[44] The British thought that they were in the position of being able to defend their own interests and at the same time to act as a possible mediator between conflicting views. After the tripartite talks in London were over Bevin and his advisers quickly sought the middle ground of welcoming the French proposal and attempting to reconcile the differences which it had aroused. There were many indications in London and Paris that French and British diplomats were anxious to find a solution acceptable to both Bevin and Schuman.[45] The fact was however that Schuman was subject to conflicting advice; his diplomats urged compromise, Monnet insisted on no concessions. The outcome of the Anglo-French negotiations was in effect dependent upon a struggle in Paris over which the British had no control. Nor were they aware until towards the end of the negotiations that such a struggle was going on.[46] When Schuman finally opted for Monnet's advice, the possibility of compromise was ruled out.

It seems clear that when Monnet put forward his proposal he envisaged it operating on three different bases. First and foremost the new community must be Franco-German. Beyond this France and Germany could carry with them the other four western states, Italy and the Benelux group. It was assumed that they would follow a Franco-German lead rather than remain outside the community which could seriously affect their own heavy industries. Lastly the British could join the six on French terms and thus create a full western federation. After his talks in London in mid-May with Sir Edwin Plowden, Monnet assumed that the British would probably reject the principle of the High Authority.[47] In his view British support for a modified proposal was only useful to the French if the Germans rejected the principle of the High Authority. In a less tightly organised community France would need British support as a makeweight against German strength. When on the 24th May the Germans gave unqualified acceptance to the French draft communiqué which meant negotiating to create the High Authority Monnet knew he had secured the essential Franco-German base. The assent of the other four to the French communiqué quickly followed although the Dutch soon unofficially leaked their misgivings about the High Authority.[48] At this stage the French realised there was no longer any need to hold in reserve the possibility of consenting to a British compromise proposal and Monnet persuaded Schuman to bring negotiations with the British to a quick conclusion by insisting that they must accept the French draft communiqué as a condition of participating in the negotiations.[49] This the British Cabinet refused to do.[50]

On the purely diplomatic level Bevin and his advisers were displeased by the way the French had conducted the negotiations; they argued that the French had forced them to play the game according to

French rules and that the rules had been framed to ensure that France could not lose. In his post-mortem on the failure of the negotiations Harvey rightly attributed these tactics to Monnet.[51] In June 1950, although he could explain what had happened, it was less easy for him to explain why it had happened. As a result of a later conversation with Monnet he was able to do so. In June 1950 France, declared Monnet, could not afford a compromise because 'the recreation of a German national state would ultimately be fatal to us all because it would inevitably sooner or later be drawn into the Eastern orbit. The French objective in starting the Schuman Plan had therefore been to begin the process of assimilating the Germans into another unit, a process which could not end with the Schuman Plan ... But Monnet could see no alternative for France, since the Germans as a free national unit would be even more dangerous for her.'[52]

Notes

1. For the text of the French communiqué see The Times, 10 May 1950.
2. Ibid.
3. The Economist, 20 May 1950.
4. Konrad Adenauer, Memoirs 1945-53 (English translation London 1966), p.363. The age of mutually hostile complexes of sovereignty in Europe must be speedily terminated if our continent was not to fall prey to barbarism.
5. Sir William Strang, Permanent Under-Secretary at the Foreign Office, recorded a conversation with Massigli on 11 May 1950: 'He made no attempt to excuse the manner in which the French government had burst their proposal on the world.' F.O. 371/85841.
6. Acheson, the American Secretary of State, who was visiting Paris, was informed on the evening of 8 May and Adenauer was informed by a special French emissary on the morning of 9 May. The phrase quoted in the text was used by Schuman at the opening of the negotiations of the six powers in Paris quoted in Harvey to Bevin, 20 Jun 1950. F.O. 371/85851.
7. Ibid.
8. Jean Monnet, Mémoires (Paris 1967), p.521.
9. See Cab. 130/60 1950.
10. Harvey to Bevin quoting Parodi of the Quai d'Orsay. F.O. 371/85843.
11. 'The failure of their policy with respect to the International Authority of the Ruhr was apparent to the French almost from the beginning of their talks with the British and American officials on the subject in May.' See minute by Duncan Wilson, 6 Jun 1950, F.O. 371/8584.
12. Ibid.
13. An extremely useful article on the preparation of the French Plan by Pierre Gerbet, 'La Genèse du Plan Schuman. Dès origines à la déclaration du 9 Mai 1950'. Revue Française de Science Politique, July/September 1956, p.525-553, discusses Monnet's role in the making of the Plan.

14. Harvey to Bevin, 19 May 1950, F.O. 371/85842.
15. Ibid.
16. Foreign Relations of the United States (hereafter F.R.U.S.) Western Europe, 1950, p.696.
17. These interviews were with the American journalist Kingsbury Smith. For a British analysis of their significance see Robertson to Kirkpatrick, 22 March 1950. F.O. 371/85147. For Adenauer's own account see his Memoirs, pp.244-7.
18. Gerbet, op. cit., p.533.
19. 'Monnet said that the Schuman Plan as it stood was an anomaly, a supra-national body in a community organised on predominantly national lines. If it came into being it could not remain static but must either perish or infect the whole of the rest of the community. The French intention was of course that it should do the latter.' Harvey to Bevin, 1 March 1951. F.O. 371/93827.
20. 'The economic case for an early increase in the permitted level of steel production seems strong and is likely to grow stronger.' Draft Brief for the U.K. Delegation to Foreign Ministers' Meeting, 1 May 1950. F.O. 371/86033.
21. 'It will be most difficult to induce the French to agree to an increase', ibid.
22. Economic Implications of the Franco-German Steel and Coal Authority. 11 May 1950. Cab. 130/60.
23. The Economist, 20 May 1950.
24. The Economist, 22 July 1950.
25. Cab. 130/60.
26. Ibid.
27. Minute by Duncan Wilson, 6 June 1950. F.O. 371/85848.
28. Adenauer, Memoirs, p.375.
29. Harvey to Bevin, 22 May 1950. F.O. 371/96051.
30. Harvey to Bevin, 19 May 1950. F.O. 371/85842.
31. In the third tripartite talks in London on 12 May Schuman declared, 'The proposal could only have been made by France. A proposal from any other government could scarcely have been accepted by French opinion and would not have produced the requisite change in the psychological atmosphere'. F.O. 371/85317.
32. Bevin Papers F.O. 800/483.
33. 'The French thought first and foremost in terms of Europe which represented for them great historical and cultural values and a high civilization. They were anxious lest these values should be submerged and lost in any wider association which would be dominated by the U.S. and other overseas powers'. Harvey to Bevin, 18 May 1950. F.O. 371/85841.
34. Monnet, Mémoires, p.290-91.
35. F.R.U.S., Western Europe, 1950, pp.744-46.
36. Ibid., p.696.
37. Franks to Bevin, 31 May 1950. F.O. 371/85845.
38. Franco-German Coal and Steel Community Political Implications, 11 May 1950. Cab. 130/60.
39. René Massigli, Une Comédie des erreurs 1943-1951 (Paris 1978), pp.202-209.

40. Cab. 130/60.
41. Memorandum by Ivone Kirkpatrick. F.O. 371/85841. Minute by R.L. Hall, Cab. 21/3229.
42. F.O. 371/85846. Record of a conversation between Lord President of the Council, the Minister of State at the Foreign Office and the Secretary of State, 1 June 1950.
43. For a useful summary of the position adopted by the British government see Makins to Franks, 17 July 1950. F.O. 371/85859.
44. Harvey to Bevin, F.O. 371/85842.
45. Minute by Sir W. Strang, 1 June 1950. F.O. 371/85846.
46. Harvey to Bevin, 6 June 1950. F.O. 371/85487.
47. Monnet, Mémoires, pp.362-364.
48. Sir P. Nichols to Bevin, 5 June 1950. F.O. 371/85846.
49. Harvey to Bevin, 3 June 1950. F.O. 371/85846.
50. Cabinet Meeting, 2 June 1950. Cab. 128/17.
51. Harvey to Bevin, 16 June 1950. F.O. 371/85850.
52. Harvey to Bevin, 1 March 1951. F.O. 371/93827.

A BIBLIOGRAPHY OF THE WRITINGS OF JAMES JOLL

BOOKS

Britain and Europe. Pitt to Churchill 1793-1940. (Adam and Charles Black. First published 1950, reprinted 1961)

The Second International 1889-1914 (Weidenfeld and Nicolson. First published 1955, reprinted 1968)

Three Intellectuals in Politics (Weidenfeld and Nicolson, 1960)

The Anarchists (Eyre and Spottiswoode. First published 1964, reprinted by Methuen in association with Eyre and Spottiswoode 1969)

Europe since 1870 (Weidenfeld and Nicolson. First published 1973, reprinted Pelican Books 1976)

Antonio Gramsci (Fontana Modern Masters 1977)

ARTICLES ETC. (excluding book reviews)

'Georges Sorel: the Unorthodox Marxist', The Listener, 3 January 1952

'Treitschke and the Prussian Legend', History Today, Vol.II No.3 March 1952

'Arabs and Jews: the Onlooker's Dilemma', The Listener, 5 June 1952

'The Course of German History', History Today, Vol.III 1953 Reprinted in Robert F. Hopwood (ed.) Germany: People and Politics, (Edinburgh 1968)

'Laburismo e Democrazia Sociale Europea', Occidente (Turin) Anno VIII no. 6 (Nov-Dec 1952)

'La Tradition et la Politique étrangère Britannique', La Politique étrangère et ses Fondements, (Cahier 55 de la Fondation Nationale des Sciences Politiques. Paris 1954)

'Intellectuals and German Politics', Occidente Anno X no. 1. (Jan-Feb 1954)

'On being an Intellectual', Twentieth Century, June 1955

'A historian in Mexico', The Listener, 9 April 1959

'The Making of the Popular Front', in J. Joll (ed). The Decline of the Republic (St. Antony's Papers No. V London 1959)

'Das "Mythos" der Collaboration', Das Dritte Reich und Europa (Veröffentlichungen des Institut für Zeitgeschichte, Munich 1960)

'Germany and the Spanish Civil War', M. Beloff (ed.) On the Track of Tyranny (Essays presented to Leonard G. Montefiore, London 1960)

'Englands Weltstellung in der Sicht Englischer Historiker', Historische Zeitschrift 190.2 1960

'Prussia and the German Problem 1830-1866', The New Cambridge Modern History Vol. X: The Zenith of European Power (Cambridge 1960)

'The Historian and the Contemporary World', Geschichte und Gegenwartsbewusstsein: (Festschrift für Hans Rothfels zum 70 Geburtstag. Göttingen 1963)

A Bibliography of the Writings of James Joll

'Japan - Asian State or Western Society?', The Listener, 31 December 1964

'Rathenau and Harden: a footnote to the history of Wilhelmine Germany', M. Gilbert (ed.) A Century of Conflict 1850-1950 (Essays for A.J.P. Taylor, London 1966)

'The Front Populaire after thirty years', Journal of Contemporary History, Vol.I no. 2, 1966

Introduction to F. Fischer, Germany's Aims in the First World War (London 1967).

'Authority and Protest: Patterns of Change from 1848 to 1900', Asa Briggs (ed.) The Nineteenth Century: The Contradictions of Progress (London 1970)

'Europe Supreme', J.M. Roberts (ed.) Europe in the 20th Century Vol. 1 1900-1914 (Readings in 20th Century History. London 1970)

'Anarchism - a living tradition', Government and Opposition, vol. 5 no 4 1970, reprinted in David Apter and James Joll (eds) Anarchism Today

'Anarchism between Communism and Individualism', Anarchici e Anarchia nel Mondo Contemporaneo (Fondazione Einaudi 'Studi' 2 Turin 1971)

'The Decline of Europe 1920-1970', International Affairs, (Special Anniversary Issue 1970)

'The 1914 Debate continues: Fritz Fischer and his Critics', Past and Present no. 34 1966, reprinted in H.W. Koch (ed.), The Origins of the First World War (London 1972)

'1914: the Unspoken Assumptions'. An Inaugural Lecture. (London 1968) reprinted in H.W. Koch The Origins of the First World War (London 1972)

'Europe: a historian's view', The 27th Montagu Burton Lecture on International Relations (Leeds 1969) reprinted in History of European Ideas vol.I 1980.

'The English, Friedrich Nietzsche and the First World War', J. Geiss and B.J. Wendt (eds) Deutschland in der Weltpolitik des 19 and 20 Jahrhunderts (Festschrift für Fritz Fischer Düsseldorf 1973)

'War guilt 1914: a continuing controversy', B. Kluke (ed.) Aspekte der deutsch-britischen Beziehungen im Laufe der Jahrhunderte (Veröffentlichungen des Deutschen Historischen Instituts London Band 4. Stugart 1978

'Das Bild eines Zukünftigen Krieges 1919-1939', Heinz Löwe (ed.) Geschichte und Zukunft (Berlin 1978)

'Politics and the Revolt of the Masses: Representation and Political Parties in Modern Europe', Bösl and K. Möckl (eds) Der moderne Parlamentariamus und seine Grundlagen in der ständische Repräsentation (Berlin 1977)

'Politicians and the Freedom to Choose: the case of 1914', Alan Ryan (ed) The Idea of Freedom (Essays in Honour of Isaiah Berlin Oxford 1979)

'Walther Rathenau - Intellectual or Industrialist?', Volker R. Berghahn and Martin Kitchen (eds) Germany in the Age of Total War: Essays in Honour of Francis Carsten (London 1981)

'Socialism between Peace, War and Revolution', S. Bertelli (ed) Per Frederico Chabod (1901-1960): II. Equilibrio Europeo ed Espansione

Coloniale (Annali della Facoltà di Scienze Politiche, Università di Perugia 1980-81), also in Opinion Politique et Politique Extérieure 1870-1915, Colloque organisé par l'Ecole Française de Rome ... Feb 1980 (Rome 1981)

'The Ideal and the Real: Changing Concepts of the International System 1815-1982". The 30th Stevenson Memorial Lecture (International Affairs Vol. 58. Spring 1982)

CONTRIBUTORS

Volker Berghahn	Professor of History, University of Warwick
Roger Bullen	Lecturer in International History, LSE
Modris Eksteins	Professor of History, University of Toronto
Roderick Kedward	Reader in History, University of Sussex
Paul Kennedy	Professor of History, Yale University
Robin Lenman	Lecturer in History, University of Warwick
Charles S. Maier	Professor of History, Harvard University
Tim Mason	Fellow of St. Peter's College, Oxford
David Morgan	Professor of History, Wesleyan University
Anthony Nicholls	Fellow of St. Antony's College, Oxford
Jeremy Noakes	Reader in Modern European History, University of Exeter
Hartmut Pogge von Strandmann	Fellow of University College, Oxford
Antony Polonsky	Reader in International History, LSE
David Schoenbaum	Professor of History, University of Iowa
Zara Steiner	Fellow of Newnham College, Cambridge

INDEX

(Prepared by Felicity Strong)

Index